The Big Book of Essential Knowledge

I Used to Know That

Spilling the Beans on the Cat's Pajamas

$E=MC^2$

A READER'S DIGEST BOOK

ISBN: 978-1-60652-353-7

PROJECT STAFF
I Used to Know That
Consulting Editor: Sandra Kear
Canadian Project Editor: Pamela Johnson
Canadian Consulting Editor: J. D. Gravenor

Spilling the Beans on the Cat's Pajamas
Project Editor: Siobhan Sullivan
Canadian Project Editor: Pamela Johnson
Canadian Consulting Editor: Jesse Corbeil
Project Production Coordinator: Nick Anderson

E=MC²
Project Editor: Siobhan Sullivan
Copy Editor: Barbara McIntosh Webb
Canadian Project Editor: Pamela Johnson
Canadian Consulting Editor: Jesse Corbeil
Project Production Coordinator: Nick Anderson

READER'S DIGEST TRADE PUBLISHING
U.S. Project Editor: Kim Casey
Copy Editor: Barbara Booth
Project Designer: Jennifer Tokarski
Project Production Coordinator: Wayne Morrison
Senior Art Director: George McKeon
Executive Editor, Trade Publishing: Dolores York
Associate Publisher, Trade Publishing: Rosanne McManus
President and Publisher, Trade Publishing: Harold Clarke

We are committed to both the quality of our products and the service we provide to our customers. We value your comments, so please feel free to contact us.

The Reader's Digest Association, Inc.
Adult Trade Publishing
44 S. Broadway
White Plains, NY 10601

For more Reader's Digest products and information, visit our website, www.rd.com (in the United States)

Printed in China

1 3 5 7 9 10 8 6 4 2

Contents

I Used to Know That
Stuff You Forgot from School

Spilling the Beans on the Cat's Pajamas
Popular Expressions—
What They Mean and How We Got Them

$E=MC^2$
Why Balloons Rise, Apples Fall, and Golf Balls Go Awry

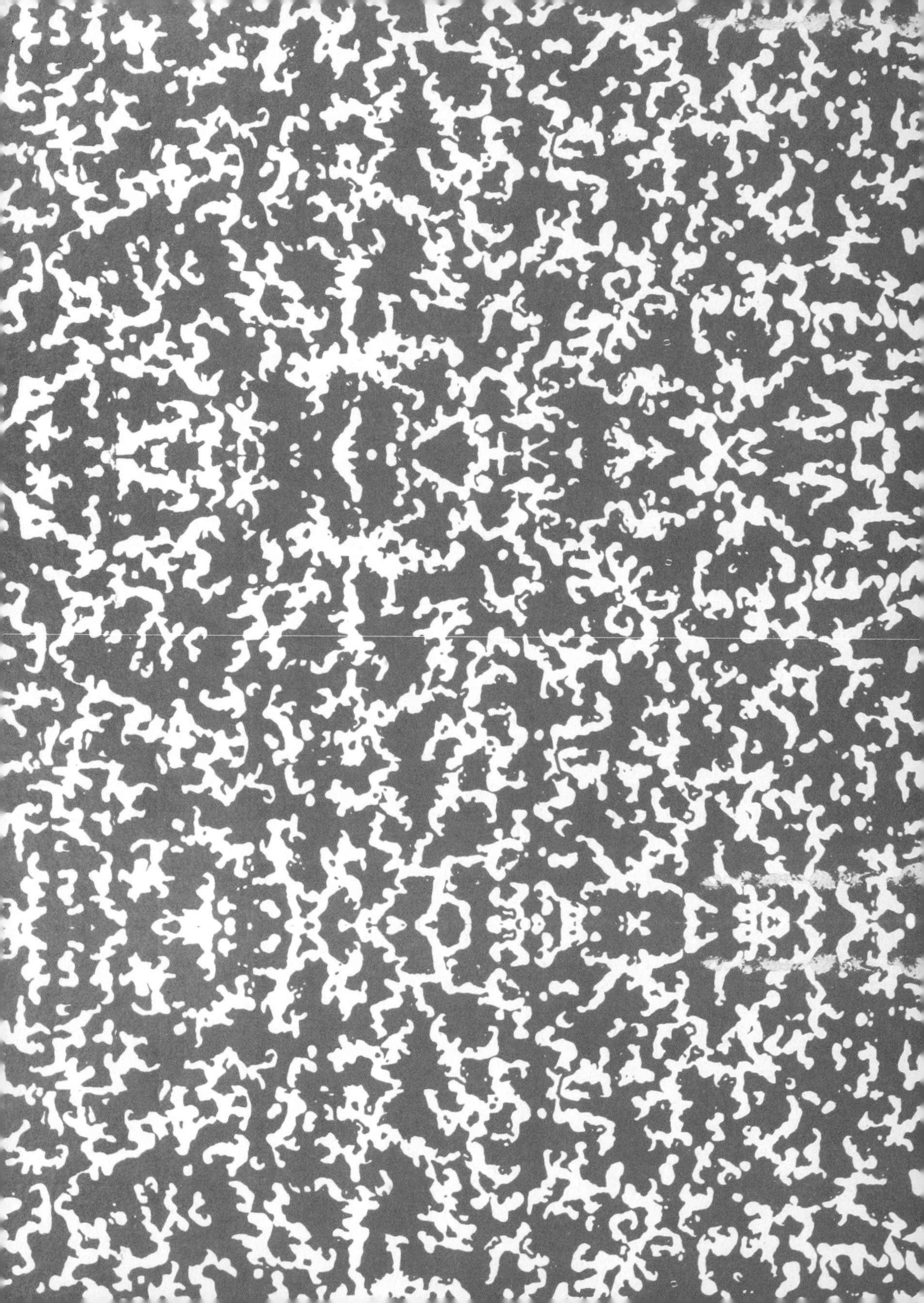

I Used to Know That

stuff you forgot from school

CAROLINE TAGGART

Introduction

When I started to write this book, I realized that I did remember lots of different things, but I didn't always remember those facts completely, or necessarily accurately. I knew, for example, that "The Assyrian came down like a wolf on the fold" was a perfect example of—what—a dactyl or an anapest? I had to look it up. I remembered a bit about sines and cosines but had no idea why they were important. I used to know most of the principal bones in the body. How did that song go? "The head bone's connected to the neck bone, the neck bone's connected to the..." Hmmm. And after years of study, I could not seem to name the dates of important wars or, for that matter, why they were fought (I'm still having some trouble with that).

Geography was especially challenging—just when I thought I knew the capital of Burma, they change everything. Myanmar is tragically all over the news, and I'm left scratching my head in bewilderment as to where it is exactly. There's also a wealth of general information that I thought I knew, like Roman numerals and the Roman equivalent to the Greek gods.

Sometimes I hear a symphony and all I can remember is that it was composed by a man whose last name starts with V…or was it B?

In the course of talking to other people about what I should include in this book, I discovered two things: one, that everybody I spoke to had been to school, and two, that that was pretty much all they had in common. They had all forgotten completely different things. So with every conversation the book seemed to grow longer. One chat with an editor friend sent me rushing to add the active and passive voices to the English chapter. Another friend could recite British poetry verbatim but could not remember if the poem she so eloquently performed was by Keats or Shelley. Yet another friend confessed that she had completely forgotten what a square root was (though I have no idea why she suddenly wanted to know). In the end I had to stop discussing it, or this book would have surpassed the size of *War and Peace*. I also found in the course of researching the things I used to know that I learned more than a few things that I didn't.

All of which is a roundabout way of saying that I hope you, too, will learn something new or find things here that strike a chord, however faintly. Things that make you say, "Oh, yes, I used to know that." Because by the time you read this, I will almost certainly have forgotten most of them again.

ENGLISH

Learning to read and write was just the beginning. After you had mastered that, you had to study how the language worked and, when you started to write your own stories, how to stay focused, develop content, organize material, maintain a consistent voice and style, *and* use proper grammar. If (perish the thought) you had to write poetry as well, there was a whole new set of conventions....

Parts of Speech

This is a way of categorizing words according to the function they perform in a sentence, and there are nine of them:

adjective: a describing word. Some examples include *tall, short, brown,* and *blue.* With one possible exception—*blond/blonde*—adjectives in English (unlike most European languages) are invariable; that is, they don't change according to the number and gender of the thing they are describing.

adverb: a word that describes a verb, an adjective, or another adverb. Adverbs answer such questions as how, when, or where: *She walked aimlessly; light brown hair* (where *light* is an adverb describing the adjective *brown*); *they lived fairly frugally* (where *fairly* is an adverb describing the adverb *frugally*). Most, but by no means all, adverbs in English are formed by adding *-ly* to the adjective.

article: *Merriam-Webster* defines an article as "any small words or affixes...used with nouns to limit or give definiteness to the application." That's not very helpful, is it? It may be easier just to remember that the definite article is *the* and the indefinite articles are *a* and *an*.

conjunction: a joining word. Examples include *and, but, though,* and so on. Conjunctions link two words, phrases, or clauses together: Pride **and** Prejudice *is Jane Austen's most popular book,* ***but*** *I also love* Sense **and** Sensibility, ***though*** *Marianne can be really annoying.*

interjection: a word to express emotion. For example, *Aha!* or *Alas!*

noun: a naming word. There are three categories:

- <u>Collective nouns</u> describe a group of things. However, they are funny things. There are some genuinely useful ones to describe animals that live in groups—you wouldn't talk about a gaggle of elephants, for example, or a flock of lions. But at some stage in history, someone thought it was useful to give collective names to almost a hundred birds where you might have thought that *group, colony,* or *a whole bunch* would serve the purpose. And there are many variations. If you are talking about a group of ducks, for example, you could say a *badelynge, brace, bunch, dopping, flock, paddling, plump, raft, safe, skein, sord, string,* or *team. A charm of goldfinches, an exaltation of larks,* and *a parliament of owls* are often quoted but rarely used in real life—but once you start Googling for this sort of thing, you also come across *a dopping of goosanders.* (Goosanders? Some people have too much time on their hands.)

- Proper nouns name a person, place, or thing that requires a capital letter, such as *Caroline, Paris,* or the *Smithsonian Institution.*
- Common nouns cover general terms, such as *street, book,* and *photograph.*

preposition: a word that links nouns, pronouns, and phrases and indicates their relationship to the object in a sentence. Prepositions include words such as *beside, through, over, during, at, in, to, on: The boy stood* on *the burning deck; it was Greek* to *me.*

pronoun: a word that stands in the place of a noun. For instance, *Caroline has forgotten a lot of stuff. That is why* she *is writing this book*—where the pronoun *she* in the second sentence takes the place of the proper noun *Caroline* in the first. Other examples include *it, he, her, his, me,* and *they.*

verb: a doing word. A verb indicates the occurrence or performance of an action, or the existence of a state or condition, such as *to be, to do, to run, to happen.* This form of a verb (normally containing the word *to*) is called the **infinitive.** Verbs change their form according to tense, person, and number: *I am, I was, you were, he is, they are.* Verbs can also be in the **active** or **passive voice**—*I bake the bread* is active; *the bread is baked* is passive. English also has three verb moods: the **indicative** makes a simple statement—*I bake the bread*; the **subjunctive** indicates something that is wished or possible—*If I were you, I would bake the bread*; and the **imperative** gives a command—*Bake that bread!*

Phrases and Clauses

Now it is time to take a look at the building blocks of sentences: phrases and clauses. Each depends on the other to express a complete thought, but knowing the difference between them can be quite confusing. Generally, you can rely on the following definitions:

- A **phrase** is a group of words (in a sentence) that does not contain a subject or predicate—or either one: *In the afternoon,* we went to the store.
- A **clause** does contain a subject and a verb and may stand alone as a sentence or as part of a sentence. However, in the sentence *He loves dogs but doesn't have one,* the clause *but doesn't have one* is the subordinate clause.

Sentences—and each clause of a sentence—can be divided into a **subject** and a **predicate**.

- The **subject** is the noun or noun phrase that the sentence is about, the thing that does the action expressed in the verb.
- The **predicate** is everything else. In sentences involving the verb *to be*, what follows the verb is known as the **complement**, as in *Silence is golden,* where *golden* is the subjective complement of the verb.
- A verb may be **transitive** or **intransitive,** which means it may or may not need a direct object in order to make sense. The **object** is the thing on which the subject performs the action of the verb. In the sentence *He hit the ball*, the object is *ball.*

To see some examples of all this, consider a line from *A Midsummer Night's Dream:*

I know a bank whereon the wild thyme blows.

The main statement or principal clause is *I know a bank.* Not very interesting, but it stands alone as a sentence. *I* is the subject, *know a bank* is the predicate and can be subdivided into the verb *know,* and the object (answering the question What do I know?), is *bank. Know* in this sentence is a transitive verb—it doesn't make much sense without the object.

The subordinate clause is *whereon the wild thyme blows.* The clause has a verb (*blows*) with a subject (*the wild thyme,* which is a noun phrase), but it isn't a sentence. Note, however, that *blows* makes sense on its own—it doesn't need an object, so it is intransitive.

Blow is one of many verbs that can be either transitive or intransitive, depending on context: The wind blows intransitively, but you can blow a horn or blow glass in a transitive way.

Taking a sentence apart to analyze its components is called **parsing**. You may remember drawing a parse tree or **sentence diagram** in elementary school.

Synonyms, Antonyms, and the Like

The suffix *-nym* derives from the Greek for *name*, but in fact, these words are currently used to refer to meaning. So a **synonym** is a word that has the same or similar meaning as another, while an **antonym** has the opposite meaning.

Here are some examples:

- *Spooky, scary, frightening,* and *eerie* are **synonyms,** as are *pale, wan,* and *ashen.*
- *Mean* is an **antonym** of *generous.*

Illogically, a **homonym** is a word that has the same spelling as another, but a different meaning. A **homophone** sounds like another word but doesn't have the same spelling. Confused?

English abounds in homonyms and homophones, which are often completely unrelated in the etymological sense.

- *Eerie* (spooky) is a homophone of *eyrie* (an eagle's nest).
- *Pale* (light in color) is a homonym of *pale* (a fence, as in *beyond the pale*) and a homophone of *pail* (a bucket).
- *Mean* (miserly) is a homonym of *mean* (intend) and a homophone of *mien* (appearance).

All those silly mistakes that spell-checkers fail to detect, such as *there* and *their,* are homophones.

Diphthongs

Diphthongs are complicated things. What most people think of as a diphthong is actually a digraph or ligature, and true diphthongs are often written as a single letter, which makes them less obvious to readers.

Huh?

OK. *Merriam-Webster* defines a diphthong as "a gliding monosyllabic speech sound that starts at or near the articulatory position of one vowel and moves to or toward the position of another."

Try it for yourself and feel the difference when you say *late* and *bat* or *loud* and *catch.* Listen for the glides (*y* or *w*) at the end of the vowel sound.

Diphthongs may be written as a single letter (the *i* in *white* and the *o* in *no*, for example) or as two (*ui* in *fruit*, *ea* in *heat*). Any combination of two letters, whether vowels or consonants that produces a single sound is known as a *digraph,* so that includes not only the *ui* in *fruit* and the *ea* in *heat* but also the *ph* in *photograph* and the *dg* in bridge.

Many North American words that are spelled with a single letter are represented by two letters in their British counterparts. The *ae* written together in the British spelling of *encyclopaedia* or *mediaeval* is, strictly speaking, a ligature, which means that the two letters are joined together as one. This has its origins with medieval scribes who were simply trying to save time and space by combining the two letters on the same block when it was transferred to hot metal type. Modern typesetting doesn't recognize ligatures, so the tendency since the 1950s has been to write the two letters separately or, increasingly, to drop one of them altogether—with the result that, in British English, *encyclopaedia* and *mediaeval* look rather old-fashioned, while in American English *encyclopedia* and *medieval* have become the standard.

Figures of Speech (and other devices for spicing up your writing)

A figure of speech is technically an expression used in a nonliteral (that is, a figurative) way, such as when you say *My lips are sealed.* Obviously, this is not possible unless you have put glue over them. When most people learn ways to expand their writing style, they are often directed to utilize such techniques as **alliteration** and **onomatopoeia**, which poets also use for effect. Here is a basic list that you may (or may not) remember:

alliteration: when a number of words in quick succession begin with the same letter or the same letter is repeated. For example, *Full fathom five thy father lies*, as Ariel sings in *The Tempest*.

assonance: similar to alliteration, but now with the repetition of vowel sounds. For example, *And so, all the night-tide, I lie down by the side/ Of my darling—my darling—my life and my bride,/ In the sepulchre there by the sea,/ In her tomb by the sounding sea.* (Edgar Allan Poe, *Annabel Lee*)

euphemism: replacing an unpleasant word or concept with something less offensive, as in substituting the term *Grim Reaper* for *death*. Some are also intended to be funny, as when morticians refer to *corpses* as *clients*.

hyperbole: Pronounced hy-PER-bo-lee. Not HY-per-bowl. Exaggeration for effect, as in *I've told you a hundred times*. This is the opposite of...

litotes: understatement for effect, as when *not bad* means *completely wonderful*. Litotes can be interpreted differently, depending on culture and verbal emphasis.

metaphor: an expression in which a word is used in a nonliteral sense, saying that *x is y* rather than *x is like y*, which would be a simile. For example, Macbeth's *Life's but a walking shadow, a poor player, That struts and frets his hour upon the stage.*

metonymy: *Merriam-Webster* defines this as "a figure of speech consisting of the name of one thing for that of another of which it is an attribute or with which it is associated." For example, the term *press*, which originally was used for printing press, now connotates the news media. Easily confused with synecdoche.

onomatopoeia: a word or phrase that sounds (a bit) like the sound it is meant to convey: *buzz, purr,* or Tennyson's *the murmuring of innumerable bees.*

oxymoron: an apparent contradiction for effect, the classic example being *jumbo shrimp.*

personification: giving human qualities, such as emotions, desires, and sensations to an inanimate object or an abstract idea. Emily Dickinson's *The Railway Train* is often cited as an example of personification:

I like to see it lap the miles,
And lick the valleys up,
And stop to feed itself at tanks;
And then, prodigious step
Around a pile of mountains...

simile: a comparison that—unlike a metaphor—expresses itself as a comparison, usually with the words *as* or *like.* Examples include *dead as a dodo* or *like a bat out of hell.*

synecdoche: a form of metonymy, but in this instance specifically "a whole for the part or a part for the whole." For example, *a set of wheels* used to denote the term *automobile,* or the command *All hands on deck* to summon a crew of sailors.

Prosody

Confusingly, prosody has nothing to do with prose—it is defined by *Merriam-Webster* as "the study of versification; especially: the systematic study of metrical structure."

The basic unit of a line of poetry—normally comprising two or three syllables—is called a **foot**, and the most common feet are:

iamb (adj. **iambic**)**:** a short syllable followed by a long one. The most widely used foot in English poetry. Much of Shakespeare's verse is written in *iambic pentameter,* which means that a line consists of five iambic feet, or ten syllables in all:

Shall I / compare/ thee to/ a sum/ mer's day?
(*Sonnet 43*)

If mu/ sic be/ the food/ of love,/ play on
(*Twelfth Night*)

trochee: a long syllable followed by a short one, although the final syllable is often missing:

Tiger!/ Tiger!/ burning/ bright
In the/ forest / of the/ night
(Blake, *The Tiger*)

dactyl: a long syllable followed by two short ones (again, the final syllable is often dropped). It produces a gentle, flowing rhythm:

This is the/ forest prim/ eval. The/ murmuring/ pines and the/ hemlocks

(Longfellow, *Evangeline*)

anapest: two short syllables followed by a long one. In contrast to a dactyl, this conveys pace and action. It is often used in comic verses such as the nonsense poem by Lewis Caroll, *The Hunting of the Snark:*

In the midst of the word he was trying to say/ In the midst of his laughter and glee/ He had softly and suddenly vanished away/ For the Snark was Boojum, you see.

spondee: two long syllables, giving a heavy, rhythmical effect. The following example combines spondee and trochee so that you can almost hear the soldiers marching along:

We're / foot—slog/ —slog—slog/
—sloggin'/ over/ Africa—

Foot—foot/—foot—foot/—sloggin'/ over/ Africa—

(Boots—boots/—boots—boots/—movin'/ up and/ down a/ gain!)

(Kipling, *Boots*)

LITERATURE

Oh, those dreadful textbooks and anthologies. Who could ever forget the detailed chapter on tying knots in *Moby Dick?* Perhaps *Julius Caesar* was your particular nemesis. On the other hand, *Macbeth, Frankenstein,* and just about any of Poe's dark stories could deliciously disturb your evenings for nights on end. After all, as a teenager, it was sometimes hard to immerse yourself in the literature of serious life-and-death situations. So here's your second chance.

British Authors and Playwrights

There are some authors who embody the definition of "classic" literature. We all recognize the names: Austen, the Brontë sisters, Dickens, and Shakespeare. However, could you pass a pop quiz on their greatest works? Here's a brief rundown to review—just in case.

☞ JANE AUSTEN (1775–1817)

Jane Austen completed only six novels, which makes it easy to do a rundown of her complete works. In no particular order:

Emma: Emma Woodhouse is the most important young lady in her village, living alone with her aging father (the one who thinks that the sooner any party breaks up the better). Clever and pleased with herself, she amuses herself with matchmaking.

Despite the disapproval of her friend and neighbor, Mr. Knightley, she persuades her protégée, Harriet Smith, not to marry a respectable farmer, Robert Martin, thinking that Harriet (despite being poor, ignorant, and illegitimate) should set her sights on the new vicar, Mr. Elton. Mr. Elton, however, has set his sights on Emma and is deeply offended when she rejects him. He promptly marries someone else entirely, and Harriet, recovering from her disappointment, falls in love with Mr. Knightley instead. Emma's eyes are suddenly opened to the fact that no one should marry Mr. Knightley but herself. Fortunately, this turns out to be what he has always wanted.

Mansfield Park: Jane Austen's least appealing heroine is the virtuous but dull Fanny Price, who is sent to live at Mansfield Park with her aunt, Lady Bertram, and promptly falls in love with her cousin Edmund, another deeply virtuous person. The arrival of the worldly Crawfords, brother and sister Henry and Mary, upsets the calm of the neighborhood, with Edmund becoming smitten with Mary despite his disapproval of her character, and Henry attracting the attention of both Bertram sisters, Maria and Julia, despite the fact that both have admirers of their own. Henry, however, falls in love with Fanny, who is almost persuaded that her good influence can redeem his character, but then he elopes with Maria, now Mrs. Rushworth. Amid all the scandal and disappointment, Edmund finally recognizes Fanny's worth.

Northanger Abbey: Catherine Morland's head is full of ghoulish Gothic novels, so when she is invited to Northanger Abbey by her friend Elinor Tilney (with whose brother, Henry, she is already in love), she thinks she has discovered a horrific mystery: Elinor's father, the general, has murdered his wife. It turns out to be nonsense, of course, and she is deeply embarrassed that Henry should know of her silly suspicions. General Tilney now discovers that Catherine is not, as he has been led to believe, an heiress, and turns her out of the house. She is back at home thinking gloomy thoughts about her future when Henry appears and...

Persuasion: Eight years before the novel starts, Anne Elliot was persuaded by her proud father, Sir Walter, and her well-meaning friend Lady Russell to break off her engagement to Captain Frederick Wentworth. Now twenty-six, she has never met anyone else she can care for (and indeed has turned down a proposal from a neighbor, Charles Musgrove, who subsequently marries her sister, Mary). Chance brings Captain Wentworth, now wealthy, back into the neighborhood, but throws him together with Charles Musgrove's sisters, Henrietta and Louisa. Anne is forced to watch in silence as he apparently becomes involved with Louisa, whose steadfastness of character seems to appeal to him more than the weakness he has not forgiven in Anne. An outing to Lyme Regis ends with Louisa insisting on jumping off the Cobb, falling and causing herself serious injury. Just as Captain Wentworth's feelings toward Anne are reawakening, he finds that all his friends believe he is committed to Louisa, and he cannot honorably renege on this perceived promise. But Louisa, in the course of her convalescence, conveniently falls in love with Captain Wentworth's friend Captain Benwick, and Wentworth is free again.

Pride and Prejudice: Spirited but poor Elizabeth Bennet (Lizzy) takes a stand against the proud but extremely wealthy Mr. Darcy, particularly when he destroys the chances of her sister Jane marrying his friend Mr. Bingley. Darcy falls in love with Lizzy much against his better judgment and is tactless enough to tell her so. Scandal hits the Bennet family when the youngest daughter, Lydia, elopes with the charming but feckless Wickham, but Darcy saves the day. An unlikely scenario for bringing lovers together, but it does, as many readers predict, and the two "deserving" daughters make the happy marriages at the end of the novel. After all, "a single man in possession of good fortune must be in want of a wife."

Other characters include two more Bennet sisters, plain and studious Mary and silly Kitty; their parents, the empty-headed Mrs. Bennet and introverted, sarcastic Mr. Bennet; Mr. Bennet's cousin and heir, the bumbling clergyman Mr. Collins; and his haughty patroness Lady Catherine de Bourgh, who also happens to be Darcy's aunt.

Sense and Sensibility: The Dashwood sisters, Elinor and Marianne, are completely different in temperament, and, when Marianne falls in love with the dashing Willoughby, the whole world knows it. Elinor, on the other hand, suffers her disappointment over Edward Ferrars in silence. Willoughby is summoned to London just as he appears to be on the brink of proposing to Marianne and instead becomes engaged to a wealthy woman. Marianne's heartbreak is eventually healed by the less dashing Colonel Brandon, and Elinor gets Edward in the end.

Jane Austen also wrote fragments of two other novels, *The Watsons* and *Sanditon,* which have been published in their incomplete forms and variously completed by other authors.

☞ THE BRONTËS

There were three sisters who wrote novels—Anne (1820–49), Charlotte (1816–55), and Emily (1818–48). All, especially

Emily, were also poets of some distinction. Charlotte wrote *Shirley, Villette,* and *The Professor,* but her most famous novel is *Jane Eyre:*

***Jane Eyre* by Charlotte Brontë:** A poor orphan girl secures a job as governess to the ward of Mr. Rochester at Thornfield Manor, a place where strange noises tend to emanate from the attic. Jane and Rochester fall in love, but their wedding is stopped by the intervention of Mr. Mason, who announces that Rochester is, in fact, married to his sister, Bertha. And indeed he is, but she is mad and confined to the attic and watched over by the fearsome Grace Poole. Jane runs away and seeks refuge with her cousins, the Rivers; on the point of accepting a proposal of marriage from St. John Rivers, she thinks she hears Rochester calling her and insists on returning to Thornfield. There she finds that Bertha has broken out of her attic, set fire to the house, perished in the flames, and left Rochester blind, disfigured, and dependent. "Reader," as she famously says, "I married him."

***The Tenant of Wildfell Hall* by Anne Brontë:** Although Anne wrote *Agnes Gray,* a story about the horrors of being a governess in Victorian England, *The Tenant of Wildfell Hall* is slightly better known, perhaps for its public-television BBC series. This work could exemplify one of the first feminist novels, since it illustrates the inequities sometimes evident between men and women in marriage. The story involves the arrival of a mysterious new tenant, Helen Huntingdon, who with her young son moves to a small village in Yorkshire. A farmer falls in love with her, only to learn that she is still married to a wealthy man back in London. The husband becomes ill, inevitably from his life of debauchery, and eventually dies, leaving Helen free. You can likely guess what happens next.

***Wuthering Heights* by Emily Brontë:** This *extremely* dark tale of unrequited, misguided love and revenge oftentimes reaks with an uncomfortable intensity. Heathcliff is a wild orphan brought home to Wuthering Heights by kindly Mr. Earnshaw, Cathy's father. The two fall passionately in love, but Cathy refuses to marry a nobody and instead marries their drippy neighbor, Edgar Linton. Heathcliff, in revenge, marries Edgar's sister, Isabella, and cruelly mistreats her. Cathy dies in childbirth. Heathcliff goes a bit bonkers and ends up pretty much killing himself so as to be reunited with Cathy in death.

☞ CHARLES DICKENS (1812–70)

Love him or hate him, Dickens inspired many great films, and everyone knows what *Dickensian* means.

A Christmas Carol: The miserly Ebenezer Scrooge tries to ignore Christmas and is haunted by the ghost of his former partner, Marley, and by the ghosts of Christmases Past, Present, and Yet to Come, who show him the error of his ways.

David Copperfield: Dickens's favorite—the life story of a boy who is sent to boarding school by his evil stepfather, runs away to his eccentric aunt, becomes a lawyer, and then a writer. Sounds pretty dull, but really it is about growing up, learning from experience, and coming to terms with life. It's full of colorful characters such as Mr. Micawber, always hoping that something will turn up; the ever so 'umble Uriah Heep; Aunt Betsy Trotwood; and her mad companion, Mr. Dick, who is obsessed with the execution of Charles I; not to mention the Peggotty family, the deeply drippy Dora, and the saintly Agnes.

Oliver Twist: About the boy from the workhouse who is kicked out after he "wants some more" food and finds his way into a gang of pickpockets led by Fagin. The novel contains considerably more misery and rather less singing and dancing than the musical version.

If you don't remember much about Dickens, chances are most of the characters you do recall are from the ones previously mentioned from *David Copperfield;* the Artful Dodger, Nancy, the evil Bill Sikes, and Mr. Bumble the beadle from *Oliver Twist;* and Bob Cratchit and Tiny Tim from *A Christmas Carol.* But here are a few more stories that may ring bells:

The plot of *Bleak House* centers around the ongoing case of Jarndyce vs. Jarndyce, which eventually eats up all the money that is being disputed; the Circumlocution Office, Dickens's savage attack on civil service bureaucracy, appears in *Little Dorrit;* and *Barnaby Rudge* is set against the background of the Gordon Riots (anti-Catholic riots in London in 1780).

☞ SHAKESPEARE (1564–1616)

William Shakespeare wrote 37 plays, 154 sonnets, and a number of much longer poems. There isn't room in this book to summarize all the plays, so here are—arguably—the 10 best known.

Hamlet, Prince of Denmark: Another one where everyone dies. Hamlet's father, also Hamlet, has died in suspicious circumstances, and his widow, Gertrude, has married—with indecent haste—Hamlet senior's brother, Claudius. The ghost of King Hamlet tells his son that he has been murdered by

Claudius. Prince Hamlet then spends much of the play worrying about what to do and talking to himself—hence all the famous soliloquies. He has previously been attached to Ophelia, daughter of Polonius, the lord chamberlain, but he now rejects her ("Get thee to a nunnery"). Talking to his mother in her room, Hamlet realizes that someone is eavesdropping behind a wall hanging, and Hamlet stabs the individual, believing it to be Claudius. It is, in fact, Polonius. Ophelia goes mad and drowns herself. Her brother, Laertes, is determined to avenge his family, so Claudius arranges a fencing match in which Laertes will have a poisoned sword. Laertes wounds Hamlet; then there is a scuffle in which the two exchange swords and Hamlet wounds Laertes. Knowing that he is dying, Laertes confesses, Hamlet stabs Claudius, and Gertrude drinks poisoned wine that Claudius had prepared as a fallback for outing Hamlet. "Good night, sweet prince," says his friend Horatio as he prepares to clear up the mess.

Hamlet contains more quotations than the other plays. For example, Polonius's paternal advice to his son Laertes:

Neither a borrower nor a lender be:
For loan oft loses both itself and friend;
And borrowing dulls the edge of husbandry.
This above all—to thine own self be true;
And it must follow, as the night the day,
Thou canst not then be false to any man.

And a bit of Hamlet's most famous soliloquy…

To be, or not to be; that is the question:
Whether 'tis nobler in the mind to suffer
The slings and arrows of outrageous fortune,

Or to take arms against a sea of troubles,
And by opposing end them? To die, to sleep;
No more; and by a sleep to say we end
The heart-ache and the thousand natural shocks
That flesh is heir to,—'tis a consummation
Devoutly to be wish'd. To die, to sleep;
To sleep! Perchance to dream: ay, there's the rub;
For in that sleep of death what dreams may come,
When we have shuffled off this mortal coil,
Must give us pause.

Julius Caesar: A number of Roman citizens, notably Caesar's close friend Marcus Brutus and his brother, Cassius, are worried that Caesar is becoming too powerful, so they kill him ("*Et tu, Brute?* Then fall Caesar"). But that happens in Act III Scene I, only halfway through the play. The rest is about the fallout from the assassination: the vengeance wrought on the conspirators by Caesar's supporters, led by Mark Antony; the conflict between Brutus and Cassius (the one who has "a lean and hungry look—he thinks too much; such men are dangerous."); the effect on them and their feelings of guilt; and their eventual defeat and suicide. And speaking of rabble-rousing, Antony's funeral oration, which works the crowd up into a frenzy so that they will avenge the murder, runs fairly close to *Henry V:*

Friends, Romans, countrymen; lend me your ears;
I come to bury Caesar, not to praise him...
He was my friend, faithful and just to me:
But Brutus says he was ambitious;
And Brutus is an honorable man...

and so on and so forth, until the mob is fairly baying for Brutus's blood.

King Lear: Lear is "the foolish, fond old man" who decides to retire and divide his kingdom among his three daughters, Goneril, Regan, and Cordelia. The two eldest make fancy speeches about loving their father above all else; Cordelia refuses to play this game and is promptly exiled. Lear plans to spend half his time with Goneril and half with Regan, but these two wicked sisters have other ideas and soon kick him out. He wanders around in the rain, goes mad, meets up with Cordelia again, and then everyone dies. There is a subplot concerning the Earl of Gloucester's bastard son Edmund, who plots against everyone and becomes betrothed to both Goneril and Regan (despite the fact that they are both married). They all die, too.

Macbeth: The Scottish play. Three witches prophesy that Macbeth will become Thane of Cawdor and subsequently king. When he is proclaimed Thane of Cawdor, he starts wondering about hurrying the second prophecy along. Egged on by his wife, he murders King Duncan and is proclaimed king in his place. And it's all downhill from there. One murder leads to another, he is haunted by guilt (personified by the ghost of his friend Banquo, who appears at a banquet), Lady Macbeth goes mad and dies (after the famous "Out damned spot" hand-washing/sleepwalking scene), and Macbeth is finally killed in battle. Ultimately, Duncan's son Malcolm is restored to the throne.

The Merchant of Venice: Shylock the Jewish moneylender hates Antonio the Christian merchant. When Antonio needs to borrow money from him to help out his friend Bassanio, Shylock makes him sign a bond promising that he will pay

Shylock one pound of his own flesh should he fail to repay the loan. Bassanio takes the money and successfully courts the wealthy Portia. Antonio's ships are lost at sea, and he is unable to pay Shylock, who claims his pound of flesh. Portia disguises herself as a lawyer and rescues Antonio by pointing out that, contractually, Shylock is entitled to take a pound of flesh but no blood—a logistical impossibility. Her speech beginning "The quality of mercy is not strained" comes from this scene. A happy ending—unless you are Shylock.

A Midsummer Night's Dream: The one about the fairies. Three plots interwoven: In a wood outside Athens, two pairs of young lovers brush up against the squabbling king and queen of the fairies, Oberon and Titania, and Oberon's servant Puck. In the same wood a group of workmen, including Bottom the Weaver, are rehearsing the play *Pyramus and Thisbe* to perform at the forthcoming wedding of the Duke of Athens. Oberon has a magic potion that, when squeezed on the eyelids of someone who is asleep, makes that person fall in love with the first object he or she sees upon awakening. As a result, Titania falls in love with Bottom, whom Puck has given an ass's head, and Puck confuses the young lovers so that they keep falling in and out of love with the wrong partners. But in the end "all is mended."

Othello, the Moor of Venice: Othello is a successful general, but the problem is that he is black and has secretly married a white girl, Desdemona. The other problem is that Iago hates him, partly because Othello has promoted a young lieutenant, Cassio, over Iago's head. Iago persuades Othello that Cassio is having an affair with Desdemona. Mad with jealousy ("the green-eyed monster"), Othello smothers Desdemona in her bed. Iago also tries to have Cassio murdered, but the plot fails, and letters proving Iago's guilt and Cassio's innocence are discovered. Othello realizes that he has murdered Desdemona for no reason and kills himself. Othello was the man who loved "not wisely but too well," and it was Iago who said, "Who steals my purse steals trash." (But he was lying, of course.)

This section ends with words from one famous sonnet—number 18—whose first four lines have provided titles for at least two novels:

Shall I compare thee to a summer's day?
Thou art more lovely and more temperate;
Rough winds do shake the darling buds of May,
And summer's lease hath all too short a date.

Romeo and Juliet: The original star-crossed lovers. Romeo is a Montague, Juliet a Capulet, and the two families hate each other. Romeo and Juliet secretly marry. However, Juliet has already been commissioned to marry her cousin, Paris. To get out of this, Juliet comes up with one of those clever schemes that you just know will go wrong: She takes a potion that puts her into a coma for a couple of days so that everyone thinks she is dead. The message telling Romeo about this goes astray (of course), and he arrives at her tomb believing that she is dead. He poisons himself just before she wakes up, so Juliet, discovering him dead, stabs herself with his dagger.

The balcony scene is full of famous lines. For example, when Romeo lurks in the garden, Juliet appears on the balcony above and, talking to herself, says:

O Romeo, Romeo! Wherefore art thou Romeo?...
What's in a name? That which we call a rose,
By any other name would smell as sweet.

And at the end of the scene, she says:

Good-night, good-night! Parting is such sweet sorrow
That I shall say good-night till it be morrow.

The Taming of the Shrew: Katharina is too bad-tempered to secure a husband, but her father will not allow her younger (and better behaved) sister, Bianca, to accept any of her many suitors until Katharina is married. Petruchio comes along and accepts the challenge, more or less beating Kate into submission. Twenty-first-century feminists do not care for this play, although Cole Porter's musical version, *Kiss Me Kate,* is wonderful.

Twelfth Night: Twins Viola and Sebastian become separated in a storm, and each believes the other dead. Viola disguises herself as a boy, Cesario, and enters the service of Duke Orsino, with whom she falls in love. Orsino, however, is in love with Olivia and uses Cesario as a messenger to woo her. Olivia—you guessed it—falls in love with Cesario, and it takes the reappearance of Sebastian to make everyone live happily ever after. The subplot concerns Olivia's pompous steward, Malvolio, who is conned by Olivia's uncle and his friends into believing that Olivia is in love with him and that she wishes to see him wearing yellow stockings and cross garters. The well-known saying "Some are born great, some achieve greatness, and some have greatness thrust upon them" appears in the letter that Malvolio believes Olivia has written to him.

Other Notable British Authors

Name	Major Works	Notes
William Blake (1757–1827) poet and artist	*Songs of Innocence*	Painter, and a bit of a religious upstart.
The Brownings, Elizabeth Barrett (1806–1861) and **Robert** (1812–1889) poets	"How Do I Love Thee" from *Sonnets for the Portuguese*, and "Grow Old Along with Me" from *Rabbi Ben Ezra*	Secretly married in 1846. He loved her despite her frail health. In 1861 she died in her husband's arms.
Sir Arthur Conan Doyle (1859–1930)	Sherlock Holmes stories, *The Lost World*	Started writing when his medical practice slowed.
George Eliot (1819–1880) pen name	*Middlemarch, Silas Marner*	Real name was Mary Ann Evans, but she changed it so her work would be taken more seriously; also because of her relationship with a married man.
E. M. Forster (1879–1970)	*A Room with a View, Howards End, Where Angels Fear to Tread, A Passage to India, The Longest Journey, Maurice*	Recent PBS series, *A Room with a View,* contained an alternative ending. Most of his novels were adapted for film.
John Galsworthy (1867–1933)	*The Forsyte Saga* and its sequels	Pulitzer Prize for Literature, 1932. People skipped church to see the BBC adaptation of *The Forsyte Saga* in the 1960s!
William Golding (1911–1993)	*Lord of the Flies, Pincher Martin, Darkness Visible, To the Ends of the Earth*	Was in D-Day invasion in Normandy. Won Booker Prize and Nobel Prize. Knighted by Queen Elizabeth II.
Ted Hughes (1930–1998) poet	*Crow, Tales from Ovid, Birthday Letters*	Poet Laureate. Married to Sylvia Plath. Great poet but merciless philanderer.

Name	Major Works	Notes
D. H. Lawrence (1885–1930)	*Sons and Lovers, The Rainbow, Women in Love, Lady Chatterley's Lover*	His work, considered scandalous for its time, was burned and banned.
C. S. Lewis (1898–1963) Irish-born	*The Chronicles of Narnia, A Grief Observed, Mere Christianity, The Allegory of Love*	*The Lion, the Witch, and the Wardrobe* and *Prince Caspian* recently adapted for film.
Christopher Marlowe (1564–1593) playwright, poet	*Edward II, Doctor Faustus, The Passionate Shepherd to His Love* ("Come live with me and be my love and we will all the pleasures prove")	Killed in Deptford tavern; some speculate that he spied for Elizabeth I. Freethinker and contemporary to Shakespeare.
Somerset Maugham (1874–1965)	*Of Human Bondage, The Razor's Edge, The Moon and Sixpence*	WWI spy; *Ashenden* influenced Ian Fleming's Bond series.
George Orwell, (1903–1950) pen name	*Animal Farm, 1984*	Real name was Eric Arthur Blair; died of tuberculosis at 46.
Alexander Pope (1688-1744) poet	"A Little Learning is a dangerous thing." *Essay on Man, The Rape of the Lock*	Also from *Essay on Man;* "To err is human, to forgive, divine."
Robert Louis Stevenson (1850–1894) Scottish	*Treasure Island, A Child's Garden of Verses*	Loved to travel despite poor health. Died at 44.
Jonathan Swift (1667–1745) Anglo-Irish	*Gulliver's Travels*	Wrote his own obituary.
J. R. R. Tolkien (1892–1973)	*The Hobbit, The Lord of the Rings*	"All that is gold does not glitter; not all those that wander are lost."
Virginia Woolf (1882–1941)	*A Room of One's Own, Mrs. Dalloway, To the Lighthouse, Orlando*	Filled her pockets with stones and drowned herself in the River Ouse.

North American Authors

There is a countless number of American writers who have earned their rightful place in literary history. While it is tricky to capture all of them in one relatively brief chapter, here are some that many students have come to know very well.

☞ **PEARL BUCK** (1892–1973)
Winner of both the Nobel Prize in Literature and the Pulitzer Prize, Buck wrote more than 100 titles, as well as short stories, plays, a book of verse, children's books, biographies, and a cookbook—much while sitting in her office at her Bucks County, Pennsylvania farmhouse watching her eight children play outside her window. Brought to China from Virginia as a young girl, Buck lived among the missionaries and based much of her work on her travels to Asia. In addition to the best-selling The *Good Earth,* a few other works by Buck include *Dragon Seed, East Wind: West Wind,* and the *House of Earth* trilogy. She also founded the charitable organization Pearl S. Buck International, which helps children around the world who have been marginalized due to mixed heredity, disease, hunger, poverty, or other tragic circumstances.

☞ **STEPHEN CRANE** (1871–1900)
Writer and journalist, Crane died at 28 years old and will forever be remembered for the required-reading novel, the *Red Badge of Courage,* which details the horrors of war experienced by a young soldier. This classic is based on memoirs and interviews with Civil War veterans.

☞ **RALPH WALDO EMERSON** (1803–82)

Essayist, philosopher, abolitionist, and poet, Emerson greatly influenced the transcendentalist movement of the mid-1800s. His associations include Henry David Thoreau (Walden Pond was on his property) and Nathaniel Hawthorne and his neighbor Louisa May Alcott. His collected essays included "Self-Reliance," which warned people to avoid conformity and to follow their own ideas and instincts. "Nature," "Circles," and "The Poet" are a few of his other most successful pieces.

☞ **WILLIAM FAULKNER** (1897–1962)

Known for his stream of consciousness, Faulkner's literary technique depicts what is going on in the speaker's head rather than simply relating the person's dialogue with others. In his novel *As I Lay Dying,* Faulkner presents 15 different points of view. Other well-known novels include *The Sound and the Fury; Light in August; Absalom, Absalom;* and *The Unvanquished.*

☞ **F. SCOTT FITZGERALD** (1896–1940)

Francis Scott Key Fitzgerald was the namesake and second cousin three times removed of the author of the United States' National Anthem. His six finished novels, including *Tender Is the Night* and *This Side of Paradise* and many short stories evoke the Jazz Age and his tumultuous relationship with his wife, Zelda Sayre. Like a fine wine, his masterpiece *The Great Gatsby* is about the futility and moral decay of the wealthy that gets even better with age. Fitzgerald died at 44, considering himself a failed writer. However, *Gatsby* continues as a best seller and is often required reading for many high school and college students.

☞ **NATHANIEL HAWTHORNE** (1804–1864)
Who could forget the *Scarlet Letter*'s all-too-human Hester Prynne, who—after being separated from her cool-hearted husband (Chillingworth)—has a passionate affair with her charismatic minister. The Puritans chide her and force her to wear a scarlet "A" upon her breast, advertising her sin. Hester dutifully (and wisely) protects Pastor Dimmesdale from public scorn, but his conscience catches up to him. The story warns of the scourge of sin and that people can be downright self-righteous. A few other examples from his published works include *The House of the Seven Gables;* a short-story collection, *Twice-Told Tales,* and the short stories "The Birthmark" and "Young Goodman Brown."

☞ **JOSEPH HELLER** (1923–1999)
Although he is often regarded as one of the best post-World War II satirists, Heller's career included stints as a blacksmith's apprentice, a B-25 bombardier, and an advertising copywriter. However, his novel *Catch-22* is one of the few whose title has created an idiom rather than employing an existing quotation. The plot centers on a group of American fighter pilots in Italy during World War II and their efforts to avoid flying suicidal missions. The problem is that the only way they can get out of flying missions is if they are crazy—but the moment they ask to be grounded because flying the missions is crazy, they are deemed to be entirely sane, and therefore fit to fly.

☞ **ERNEST HEMINGWAY** (1899–1961)
Remember the determined Santiago, the aging Cuban fisherman who struggles with a marlin in the Gulf Stream? *The Old Man and the Sea* won the Nobel Prize in Literature in 1954 and has been heavily analyzed in classrooms for its symbolism ever since. Hemingway, however, is posthumously quoted in a 1999 issue of *Time* ("An American Storyteller") as saying, "No good book has ever been written that has in it symbols arrived at beforehand and stuck in.... I tried to make a real old man, a real boy, a real sea and a real fish and real sharks. But if I made them good and true enough, they would mean many things." Hemingway was frank and wickedly tough, evident in some of his other great works: *The Sun Also Rises, A Farewell to Arms,* and *For Whom the Bell Tolls.*

☞ **ZORA NEALE HURSTON** (1891–1960)
Once criticized for her cultural depictions and political views, Hurston's work, *Their Eyes Were Watching God,* has grown into a seminal work for African-American and feminist writers, and it is a darn good read. The story relates the struggles of Janie Sparks, who in the end says, "Two things everybody got tuh do fuh theyselves. They got tuh go tuh God, and they got tuh find out about livin' fuh theyselves." Hurston's work grew from the Harlem Renaissance and was revived in the 1970s after an article in *Ms.* by *Color Purple* author Alice Walker.

☞ **WASHINGTON IRVING** (1783–1859)
Known for the *Legend of Sleepy Hollow,* which tells of the unfortunate disappearance of Ichabod Crane one autumn

night after being pursued by the infamous headless horseman (the ghost of a Hessian soldier who had his head blown off during the American Revolution). Irving also wrote the Grimm-influenced (some say stolen) *Rip Van Winkle,* where a henpecked husband who hates his honey-do list heads for the hills. He then takes the drink of some bowling ghosts and falls asleep for a mere 20 years, waking up to a changed geographical and political landscape, a foot-long beard, and a deceased wife. Rip, however, resumes his old walks and habits.

☞ **HENRY JAMES** (1843–1916)

Although born in New York City, James eventually settled in England, becoming a British subject shortly before his death. James often wrote books that crossed the continents. *The Portrait of a Lady* was adapted for film in 1996, directed by Jane Campion. The story involves a newly wealthy, young American woman who travels to Europe and becomes scammed into marriage by two U.S. expatriates. James's other admired works include *Washington Square, The Bostonians,* and his shorter pieces, "The Aspern Papers," and "The Turn of the Screw."

☞ **HARPER LEE** (1926–)

Born in Monroeville, Alabama, Lee was a childhood friend and next-door neighbor of novelist Truman Capote. In 1956 some close friends gave her a year's salary for Christmas so she could take the time to write. Within that time she wrote one book, *To Kill a Mockingbird,* which was published in 1960 and won the Pulitzer Prize for fiction in 1961. The novel depicts the story of a white lawyer in a Deep South town who defends a black man who is wrongly accused of raping a white girl.

☞ **HERMAN MELVILLE** (1819–91)
You either love him or hate him, but one thing is for sure: After you read *Moby Dick,* you will know how to tie several different knots. Melville's immense detail and multileveled symbolism combine to make what is often called the epitome of American Romanticism (of epic proportions). The first chapter opens with the famous line "Call me Ishmael." Then soon the reader is afloat on this vessel as it ventures forth, fighting to surmount both fate and nature. Melville wrote other works, such as *Pierre* and the unfinished *Billy Budd.*

☞ **LUCY MAUD MONTGOMERY** (1874–1942)
Her works would become a favorite of young women around the world, and whose famous protagonist Anne Shirley once said, "Marilla, isn't it nice to think that tomorrow is a new day with no mistakes in it yet?" Some other "Anne" books include: *Anne of Green Gables, Anne of Avonlea, Anne of the Island, Anne of Windy Poplars,* and *Anne's House of Dreams.* In 1985 a miniseries based on her first novel was among one of the highest-rated programs of any genre to air on Canadian television and won several awards. The films starred Megan Follows as Anne and Colleen Dewhurst as Marilla Cuthbert.

☞ **EDGAR ALLAN POE** (1809–1849)
Poe's major success, *The Raven,* was published two years before the death of his first wife (his 13-year-old first cousin). After this unfortunate event and scandalous allegations of amorous indiscretions, Poe became dejected and began drinking. Two years later he was scraped off the streets of Baltimore, sick and

delirious, and he died soon after. His wife's death influenced his writing, such as in *Annabel Lee.* Poe has a long list of bone-chilling stories, including *The Cask of Amontillado, The Fall of the House of Usher, The Masque of the Red Death,* and *The Pit and the Pendulum.* Many of his tales were adapted for film in the 1960s and starred horror legend Vincent Price.

☞ **J. D. SALINGER** (1919–2010)

The reclusive Salinger's biggest success is *The Catcher in the Rye,* the ultimate disaffected-teenager novel. It is told in the first person by sixteen-year-old Holden Caulfield, who loathes everything to do with his life and his parents' "phony" middle-class values. Although the novel was written in 1951, it remains popular and sells approximately 250,000 copies a year.

☞ **JOHN STEINBECK** (1920–68)

While growing up Steinbeck worked as a hired hand on nearby ranches, which fostered his impressions of the California countryside and its people. These thoughts contributed to the Pulitzer Prize-winning novel, *The Grapes of Wrath.* The book tells the story of the Joad family, who after the Oklahoma dust bowl disaster of the 1930s abandon their land and head for what they imagine is "Promised Land" in California, only to find that life is no easier there. His novels *Tortilla Flat* and *Cannery Row* also achieved critical acclaim.

☞ **HARRIET BEECHER STOWE** (1811–96)

Best known as the author of *Uncle Tom's Cabin,* a violent antislavery novel (published in 1852, when this was *the* political hot potato in America). According to legend, when Abraham Lincoln met Stowe in 1862 he said, "So you're the little woman who wrote the book that started this Great War!" Her writing career spanned 51 years, during which she published 30 books and countless shorter pieces as well as raising seven children. A year after she and her family moved into their Hartford, Connecticut house, Samuel Clemens, also known as Mark Twain, moved into a house just across the lawn.

☞ **HENRY DAVID THOREAU** (1817–62)
Sometimes called the father of environmentalism, he stated, "Thank God men cannot fly and lay waste the sky as well as the earth." He retreated to the woodland, isolating himself from society and wrote *Walden,* an account of simple living in natural surroundings. He also wrote an essay on Civil Disobedience after being arrested for not paying his taxes, which he did to protest slavery and the Mexican-American War.

☞ **MARK TWAIN** (1835–1910)
(Samuel Langhorne Clemens)
Drawing on his experience as a river pilot, this author's pen name comes from a riverboat term for two fathoms or 12 feet when the depth of water is sounded; "Mark twain" means that it is safe to navigate. Although Twain was also a popular humorist, satirist, and lecturer, he is best known as the author of *The Adventures of Tom Sawyer,* which drew on his childhood in the Mississippi River port of Hannibal, Missouri, and *The Adventures of Huckleberry Finn,* a much more serious book—sometimes called the Great American Novel—that had the issue of slavery at its heart.

☞ **BOOKER T. WASHINGTON** (1856–1915)

A former slave, freed after the Civil War, this author and educator worked tirelessly through school. He later became a noted educator and major proponent of education and rights for African Americans, working to establish vocational schools so they could learn trades, obtain jobs, and bolster their standing in society. The details of his life can be found in his compelling autobiography and best seller, *Up from Slavery.*

☞ **EDITH WHARTON** (1862–1937)

She became the first woman to win the Pulitzer Prize for Literature in 1921, for *The Age of Innocence,* which deals with upper-class society in New York City during the turn of the century, where marriage for connection was encouraged. Wharton could subtly poke fun at the upper classes, while displaying a warm, sympathetic tone. She had ample time and opportunity to observe her subjects, since her maiden name was Edith Newbold Jones, the wealthy family associated with the adage "Keeping up with the Joneses." Some of her other notable works include *The House of Mirth, Ethan Frome,* and her unfinished work (finished in 1993 by Marion Mainwaring) *The Buccaneers,* which was adapted for Masterpiece Theatre in 1995—a series that was soon forgotten.

British Poets

The myths, legends, and romance of the major British poets have sparked millions of imaginations. The following list mentions just a handful of the most familiar ones.

☞ **W(YSTAN) H(UGH) AUDEN** (1907–73, English)
Shot to renewed fame 20 years after his death, thanks to the film *Four Weddings and a Funeral. Stop all the clocks, cut off the telephone,* which is recited at the funeral, is taken from his "Twelve Songs."

☞ **ROBERT BURNS** (1759–96, determinedly Scottish)
His birthday was January 25, and for some reason many people still celebrate the event by eating haggis and reciting his poetry. In addition to the wonderfully bloodthirsty "Address to a Haggis," he also wrote "To a Mouse" (*Wee sleekit, cow'rin' tim'rous beastie* and *The best laid schemes o' mice an' men/ Gang aft a-gley*) and the words of *Auld Lang Syne.*

☞ **GEORGE GORDON BYRON, LORD BYRON**
(1788–1824, English/Scottish)
The one who *awoke one morning and found myself famous* after the publication of *Childe Harold's Pilgrimage.* He led a wild life, left England after one scandal too many, lived in Italy, where he was friendly with Shelley, then fought for Greek insurgents against the Turks. He died at Missolonghi, in Greece, of rheumatic fever.

☞ **GEOFFREY CHAUCER** (*c.*1340–1400, English)
Chaucer is credited as being one of the first great poets to write in English rather than in French or Latin. Although his language is pretty unfamiliar to the uninitiated, he is best known for *The Canterbury Tales,* in which a party of outrageous pilgrims travel from the Tabard Inn in Southwark, London, to Canterbury Cathedral, where they tell stories to pass the time. The prologue presents a vivid portrait of 14th-century life; among the best-known tellers of tales are the Knight, the Miller, the Man of Law, and the Wife of Bath.

☞ **SAMUEL TAYLOR COLERIDGE** (1772–1834, English)
He wrote only two famous poems—one of them unfinished—but what successes they were: "The Rime of the Ancient Mariner" (that's the one about the wedding guest and the albatross) and "Kubla Khan" *(In Xanadu did Kubla Khan/ A stately pleasure-dome decree).* His friend Wordsworth could have learned a useful lesson about quality versus quantity.

☞ **JOHN DONNE** (1572–1631, English)
The greatest of the metaphysical poets (a loose term for a group of 17th-century poets whose work investigated the world using intellect rather than intuition). His most famous line, *"No man is an Island, entire of itself,"* oft misquoted, is from a book of devotions rather than a poem.

☞ **T(HOMAS) S(TEARNS) ELIOT** (1888–1965, American-born, worked in England)
Author of "The Wasteland" *(April is the cruellest month)* and "The Love Song of J. Arthur Prufrock."

☞ **THOMAS GRAY** (1717–71, English)
Gets a mention here because we all have read his *Elegy Written in a Country Churchyard:*

> *The curfew tolls the knell of parting day,*
> *The lowing herd wind slowly o'er the lea,*
> *The plowman homeward plods his weary way,*
> *And leaves the world to darkness and to me.*

If you wrote only one poem in your life, you probably would have been quite happy to have written that one.*

☞ **JOHN KEATS** (1795–1821, English)
Another great Romantic, he's the one who died at the intimidatingly young age of 26 of consumption in Rome—you can visit his house, located near the Spanish Steps. "La Belle Dame Sans Merci" *(O what can ail thee, knight-at-arms/ Alone and palely loitering?)*, "Ode to a Nightingale" *(My heart aches, and a drowsy numbness pains/ My sense, as though of hemlock I had drunk)*, "On First Looking into Chapman's Homer" *(Much have I travelled in the realms of gold)* and "To Autumn" *(Season of mists and mellow fruitfulness).*

---

* There are four poems by Gray in the *Oxford Book of English Verse*, one of them the endearingly named *"On a Favourite Cat, Drowned in a Tub of Gold Fishes."*

☞ **RUDYARD KIPLING** (1865–1936, English)
Prolific chronicler of the soldier's lot in South Africa and India, but best known for "If:"

If you can keep your head while all about you
Are losing theirs and blaming it on you...
If you can meet with Triumph and Disaster
And treat those two impostors just the same...
Yours is the Earth and everything that's in it,
And—which is more—you'll be a Man, my son!

☞ **JOHN MILTON** (1608–74, English)
Best known for his epic poems, *Paradise Lost* and *Paradise Regained,* which were composed in his later years while blind; *Areopagitica,* Milton's treatise on censorship, also earned him recognition.

☞ **PERCY BYSSHE SHELLEY** (1792–1822, English)
One of the great Romantic poets, married to Mary, the author of Frankenstein. Lived mostly in Europe, latterly Italy, where he drowned in a boating accident. Author of "Ode to a Skylark" *(Hail to thee, blithe Spirit!),* "Ozymandias" *(Look on my works, ye Mighty, and despair!)* and *Adonais,* an elegy on the death of Keats.

☞ **EDMUND SPENSER** (*c.*1552–99, English)
Author of *The Faerie Queene,* an epic poem celebrating the Tudor dynasty and Elizabeth I, and known to his peers as "the prince of poets." His poem "Epithalamion" has 365 long lines,

representing the sum of 52 weeks, 12 months, and 4 seasons of the annual cycle, and 24 stanzas, corresponding to the diurnal and sidereal hours.

☞ **ALFRED LORD TENNYSON** (1809–92, English)
Another prolific one. His great work is "In Memoriam," written on the early death of his friend Arthur Hallam; but most people are probably more familiar with "Come into the Garden," "Maud," and "The Lady of Shalott":

Out flew the web and floated wide;
The mirror crack'd from side to side;
'The curse is come upon me!' cried
The Lady of Shalott

☞ **DYLAN THOMAS** (1914–53, Welsh)
Famous drunkard, but you forgive him most things for having written "Under Milkwood" and enabling Richard Burton to record it for posterity.

☞ **WILLIAM WORDSWORTH** (1770–1850, English)
The most important of the Lake Poets (the others were Coleridge and Robert Southey). I have to say, I think "prolix" rather than "prolific" is the *mot juste* for Wordsworth. He churned it out, and goodness he was dull. The often-quoted "Daffodils" (*I wander'd lonely as a cloud*) is one of his, as is the "Sonnet Written on Westminster Bridge" *(Earth hath not anything to show more fair).*

☞ **W(ILLIAM) B(UTLER) YEATS** (1865–1939, Irish)
Theosophist and Rosicrucian as well as poet and playwright; dedicated his early poems to Maud Gonne. Best known are "The Song of Wandering Aengus" and "The Lake Isle of Innisfree" *(I will arise and go now, and go to Innisfree).*

North American Poets

Although this is an extremely short list of extraordinary poets, the writers listed here captured the voice and history of their generations. Hopefully they will inspire you to seek out the many remarkable poets that followed in their footsteps.

☞ **ANNE BRADSTREET** (1612–72)
A puritan, she immigrated with her family in 1630 to the New World. Anne, who was used to an Earl's manor, had to adjust to near-primitive living conditions. She struggled to take care of her home and raise eight children but still found time to write and became the first female writer to publish work in colonial America. Some notable poems include "The Prologue" and "To My Dear and Loving Husband."

☞ **EMILY DICKINSON** (1830–1886)
Dickinson spent a large part of her 55 years writing about death and immortality. After all, her home overlooked the Amherst, Massachusetts, burial ground, and since Emily was a bit of a recluse and spent a large part of her adult life caring for her ailing mother, she had plenty of time to contemplate life and death through her window. Fewer than a dozen of

her poems were actually published during her lifetime. Some of her well-known poems include "Because I could not stop for Death," "Success is counted sweetest," and "A wounded deer"—leaps highest, which contains the line *Mirth is the mail of Anguish.*

☞ **ROBERT FROST** (1874–1963, American)
Probably second only to Whitman as "the great American poet," Frost won the Pulitzer Prize three times. His works include "Stopping by Woods on a Snowy Evening" *(And miles to go before I sleep)* and "The Road Not Taken" *(Two roads diverged in a wood, and I—/I took the one less traveled by).*

☞ **HENRY WADSWORTH LONGFELLOW** (1807–1882)
He is known for his lyric poetry—"Paul Revere's Ride," "Evangeline," and "The Song of Hiawatha" *(By the shore of Gitche Gumee,* which, incidentally, is Lake Superior). Hiawatha may be the most mocked and parodied poem of all time, receiving reconstruction from agents such as Lewis Carroll ("Hiawatha's Photographing") and the producers of *Saturday Night Live.*

☞ **WALT WHITMAN** (1819–92, American)
The great American poet of the 19th century. His masterwork is *Leaves of Grass,* a massive collection of short poems, including "O Captain! My Captain!" and "When Lilacs Last in the Dooryard Bloom'd," both from the section "Memories of President Lincoln," inspired by the president's assassination.

International Authors

Most of us had teachers of English or general studies who encouraged us to broaden our horizons by reading some of the foreign "greats" in translation. Keeping this to a Top 10 has meant cheating a bit on the Greek tragedians and leaving out Horace, Ovid, Rabelais, Molière, Schiller, Balzac, Zola... and that's before I really hit the 20th century. But I think these are the ones you are most likely to have read without knowing the original language.

☞ **DANTE ALIGHIERI** (1265–1321, Italian)
Known for *The Divine Comedy,* Dante divided his epic into three parts: *Inferno* (Hell), *Purgatoria,* and *Paradiso.* It narrates Dante's journey through these three worlds, the first two guided by Virgil, the final by Beatrice, a woman with whom he had been madly in love since he was nine, although it seems they met only twice. Hell is depicted as having various circles, indicating degrees of suffering, depending on how bad you had been in life: the ninth and worst contained the poets.

☞ **MIGUEL DE CERVANTES** (1547–1616, Spanish)
One of the most influential works of Spanish literature is Cervantes's *Don Quixote.* The novel is about a man who becomes obsessed with books on chivalry and decides to go out into the world to do noble deeds. Toward this end, he imagines that a local village girl is the glamorous lady in whose name these deeds will be carried out, and he christens her Dulcinea del Toboso. His steed is actually a broken-down old horse called Rosinante, which means "previously a

broken-down old horse." Along with other foolish whims, he adopts Sancho Panza as his squire and goes around attacking windmills because he thinks they are giants.

☞ **FYODOR DOSTOEVSKY** (1821–81, Russian)

Often credited as a founder of 20th-century existentialism, Dostoevsky graduated as a military engineer. However, he soon resigned that career, began writing, and joined a group of utopian socialists. He was arrested and sentenced to death, but the punishment was commuted and he spent eight years in hard labor and as a soldier. His best-known works include *Crime and Punishment,* an account of an individual's fall and redemption, *The Brothers Karamazov,* a tale of four brothers involved in their father's brutal murder.

☞ **GUSTAV FLAUBERT** (1821–80, French)

One of the most important novels of the 19th century, *Madame Bovary* was attacked for its obscenity when it was published more than 150 years ago. The novel focuses on Madame Bovary—Emma—who is married to a worthy but dull provincial doctor, Charles. She longs for glamour and passion and has adulterous affairs, rebelling against the accepted ideas of the day. The novel served to inspire the beginnings of feminism.

☞ **JOHANN WOLFGANG VON GOETHE** (1749–1832, German)

Once called "Germany's greatest man of letters," Goethe is best known for his two-part drama *Faust,* the tragic play about a man who sells his soul to the devil—here called Mephistopheles—in return for worldly success. Surprisingly, he is saved by angels. Christopher Marlowe's play *Doctor Faustus* was the inspiration for Goethe's work. Goethe's influence spread, extending across Europe, becoming a major source of inspiration in music, drama, poetry, and philosophy.

☞ **HOMER** (*c.* 9th century B.C., Greek)
The great epics the *Iliad* and the *Odyssey* are the basis of pretty much everything we know about the Trojan War and about Odysseus (Ulysses)'s 10-year journey to get home to Ithaca. A quick rundown on the Trojan War: Paris, prince of Troy, abducted Helen, the beautiful wife of Menelaus, who was the King of Sparta (in Greece). Various Greek heroes—Odysseus, Achilles, Agamemnon—were pledged to fight to bring her back. They laid siege to Troy for 10 years before finally hitting on the idea of a wooden horse: Soldiers hid inside it, the Trojans were fooled into taking it within the city walls, the soldiers leaped out, and the Trojans were defeated. The Trojan hero was Paris's older brother, Hector. Their parents were Priam and Hecuba, and their sister Cassandra was the one who made prophecies that no one believed. Then Odysseus set off for home, encountering Circe, Calypso, and the Cyclops Polyphemus on the way. Back home his wife, Penelope, had promised her suitors that she would marry one of them when she had finished the piece of weaving she was doing, but she secretly unraveled the day's work every night.

☞ **VICTOR HUGO** (1802–85, French)

One of the most notable French Romantic writers, Hugo created his own version of the historical novel by combining historical fact with vivid, imaginative details. His great achievements were *Notre-Dame de Paris,* known to us as *The Hunchback of Notre-Dame,* and *Les Miserables.* The hunchback Quasimodo is the bell ringer at Notre-Dame, and the plot concerns his love for the Gypsy girl Esmeralda. *Les Miserables,* known to many because of its successful stage adaptations, is set in Paris in 1815, at the time of the Battle of Waterloo. The central character, Jean Valjean, is a reformed thief who is persecuted by the police agent Javert.

☞ **SOPHOCLES** (*c.* 496–406 B.C., Greek); **EURIPIDES** (*c.* 480–406 B.C.); **ARISTOPHANES** (*c.* 448–380 B.C.)

Oedipus Rex, also known as *Oedipus the King,* is the play about the man who accidentally married his mother. It is the first in Sophicles's *Oedipus* Trilogy, followed by *Oedipus at Colonus* and then *Antigone. Medea*, the play about the woman who murdered her children to avenge herself on their father is by **Euripides**, who lived around the same time. And while we're at it, there was the comic playwright **Aristophanes**, who wrote *Lysistrata,* about the women who put a stop to the Peloponnesian War by refusing to have sex with their husbands.

☞ **LEO TOLSTOY** (1828–1910, Russian)
Born into Russian nobility and widely regarded by fellow writers as one of the world's greatest novelists, Tolstoy is best known for his epic, *War and Peace*. A rich tale of early 19th century czarist Russia under Alexander I, it discusses the absurdity and shallowness of war and aristocratic society. Tolstoy's *Anna Karenina* is the book he considered to be his first novel. Considered a true example of realist fiction, it centers on adultery and self-discovery while social changes storm through Russia.

☞ **VIRGIL** (70–19 B.C., Roman)
His most famous work is *The Aeneid*, the story of the Trojan prince Aeneas, the ancestor of the Roman people (also an ancestor of Romulus and Remus, who actually founded the city). Some of *The Aeneid* was inspired by Homer and relates to the story of the fall of Troy. Escaping from Troy, Aeneas eventually reached Italy but stopped off en route in Carthage, where he had an affair with the queen, Dido, who burned herself alive when he left her. The first words of the *Aeneid* are "*Arma virumque cano*"—"*I sing of arms and the man*"—which is where the title of George Bernard Shaw's play comes from.

MATH

Remember when you used to harangue your parents about why you needed to know "this stuff"? It was only later that you found out why as you wrestled with the challenges of chemistry, engineering, physics, architecture or more ordinary kinds of problems such as figuring your income tax and balancing your checkbook. That math you found so useless as a child is not so useless after all, is it? But perhaps over the years you have found yourself floundering for some of those rules and answers you might have known if you hadn't been doodling on your notebook during class. Well, flounder no more....

Arithmetic

Arithmetic is all about sums—adding, subtracting, multiplying, and dividing—each with its own vocabulary:

- If you add two or more numbers together, their total is a **sum**. So 7 is the sum of 4 + 3.
- With subtraction you find the **difference** between two numbers. The difference between 9 and 7 is the smaller number subtracted from the larger: 9 – 7, and the difference is 2.
- If you multiply two or more numbers together, the answer is a **product**. So 30 is the product of 6 x 5.
- With division you divide a **divisor** into a **dividend** and the answer is a **quotient**. If there is anything left over, it is called a **remainder**. So 15 divided by 2 gives a quotient of 7 with a remainder of 1.

☞ LONG MULTIPLICATION

If you are old enough to have taken math exams without the aid of a calculator, you will have learned the times tables. The easiest one is the 11 times table because it goes 11, 22, 33, 44, and so on—but it all goes a bit wrong after 99. Many people learn by rote up to 12 x 12 = 144; beyond that a person really needs to understand what they are doing. For example:

$$\begin{array}{r} 147 \\ \times\ 63. \\ \hline \end{array}$$

After the number 9, you have to use two digits. The right-hand digit in any whole number represents the units; to the left are the tens and then the hundreds and so on. So 63 is made up of 6 tens, or 60, plus 3 units. And in this problem, you need to multiply 147 by each of those elements separately.

Start from the right: 3 x 7 = 21, so you write down the 1 and "carry" the 2 to the next column;

3 x 4 = 12, plus the 2 you have carried = 14. Write down the 4 and carry the 1;

3 x 1 = 3, plus the 1 you carried = 4.

So 3 x 147 = 441.

To multiply 147 by 60, put a 0 in the right-hand column and multiply by 6 (because any number multiplied by 10 or a multiple of 10 ends in 0);

6 x 7 = 42, so write down the 2 and carry 4;

6 x 4 = 24, plus the 4 you have carried = 28. Write down the 8 and carry 2;

6 x 1 = 6, plus the 2 you have carried = 8.

So 60 x 147 = 8,820;

63 x 147 is therefore the sum of 60 x 147 (8,820) and 3 x 147 (441), which equals 9,261.

Or

```
  147
 x 63
 ----
  441
 8820
 ----
 9261.
```

Songwriter and mathematician Tom Lehrer plays a tune about New Math, in which he does his problem in base 8. If you do a search on Youtube.com for Lehrer's New Math, you'll see why this section avoids that technique.

☞ LONG DIVISION

Division is multiplication in reverse, so start with 9,261 and divide it by 63.

If you have a divisor of 12 or less, the times tables does or did the work for you: You *know* or knew that 72 divided by 8 was 9, without having to work it out. But with a number larger than 12, you need to be more scientific:

```
63) 9261.
```

With division you work through the number from left to right.

You can't divide 63 into 9, for the simple reason that 63 is larger than 9. So look at the next column. You *can* divide 63 into 92—once—so you write a 1 at the top of the sum. But it doesn't go into 92 once exactly—there is a remainder, which is the difference between 92 and 63; in other words, 92 minus 63, which is 29.

Carry 29 forward into the next column and put it in front of the 6 to give you 296. Does 63 go into 296? Yes, it must, because 296 is bigger than 63, but how many times? Well, look at the left-hand figures of the two numbers and you'll see something that you can solve using the times table: 6 into 29. That's easy: Four 6s are 24, so 6 goes into 29 four times, with a bit left over. So it's likely that 63 will go into 296 four times with a bit left over. Indeed 4 x 63 = 252, and the bit left over is 296 minus 252, which equals 44.

Write 4 at the top of the sum, next to the 1, and carry 44 forward into the next column to make 441. How many times does 63 go into 441? Well, 6 goes into 44 seven times (6 x 7 = 42), so let's try that. And, conveniently, 63 x 7 = 441. Which means that 63 goes into 441 exactly seven times, with nothing left over, and that answers the problem: 147.

Fractions, Decimals, and Percentages

☞ PROPER FRACTIONS

A **fraction** is technically any form of number that is not a whole number; what most people think of as fractions—numbers such as ½, ⅔, ¾, and so on—are properly called vulgar, simple, or common fractions (as opposed to decimal fractions; see page 60).

The top number in these fractions is called the **numerator**, the bottom one the **denominator** (remember, **d**enominator **d**own).

In fact, the examples given above are all **proper** fractions, with the numerator smaller than the denominator (the fraction represents less than 1). In an **improper** fraction the reverse is true, as in $\frac{22}{7}$ (an approximation for pi, see page 73), which can also be written as $3\frac{1}{7}$, because 7 goes into 22 three times, with a remainder of 1.

If you want to solve problems that involve fractions, it is important to know that if you divide or multiply both the numerator and denominator by the same number, you produce a fraction that is the same value as the original fraction. Take $\frac{1}{2}$. Multiply both numerator and denominator by 2 and you get $\frac{2}{4}$. Which is still a half, because 2 is half of 4. Or multiply $\frac{1}{2}$ by 3 and you get $\frac{3}{6}$. Which again is still a half, because 3 is half of 6.

The same principle applies to division: If you start with $\frac{3}{6}$ and divide top and bottom by 3, you reduce your fraction down to $\frac{1}{2}$ again. This process is called canceling. When you can't cancel anymore, the fraction is in its lowest terms.

With addition and subtraction, however, you can only add and subtract fractions that have the same denominator. You can add $\frac{1}{2} + \frac{1}{2}$ and get $\frac{2}{2}$, which equals 1, because two halves make a whole. But what you have done is add the two numerators together. The denominator stays the same, because you are adding like to like. (It's no different from adding 1 apple to 1 apple to get 2 apples.)

Now say you want to add ½ + ⅓. It's easy to do, but first you must convert them so they have the same denominator. The lowest common denominator of 2 and 3 (the smallest number into which both will divide) is 6. To turn ½ into sixths, you need to multiply both parts of the fraction by 3:

$$\frac{1 \times 3}{2 \times 3} = \frac{3}{6}.$$

So ½ is the same thing as 3⁄6.

To convert ⅓ into sixths, you need to multiply both parts by 2:

$$\frac{1 \times 2}{3 \times 2} = \frac{2}{6}.$$

So ⅓ is the same thing as 2⁄6.

Now you have something that you can add, on the same principle of adding the numerators together:

$$\frac{3}{6} + \frac{2}{6} = \frac{5}{6}.$$

The same applies to subtraction:

$$\frac{7}{10} - \frac{3}{10} = \frac{4}{10}.$$

But both 4 and 10 can be divided by 2, to give the simpler fraction ⅖.

☞ DECIMAL FRACTIONS

The word decimal refers to anything *with the number 10,* and the English system is based on multiples of 10. As previously mentioned in the multiplication section, a single-digit number—say, 6—means that you have six units of whatever it is. When you have more than nine, you have to use two digits, with one digit representing the tens on the left and one digit representing the units on the right.

Decimal fractions work on the same principle, except that they go from right to left. The fraction is separated from the whole number by a dot called a **decimal point.** The figure immediately to the right of it represents tenths, to the right of that is hundredths, and so on. So 1.1 (pronounced one point one) = 1 plus one tenth of 1; 1.2 = 1 + $^2/_{10}$ (or $^1/_5$); 1.25 (pronounced one point two five) = 1 + $^2/_{10}$ + $^5/_{100}$, or 1 + $^{25}/_{100}$.

An interesting example is 1.25, because it is the same as 1¼. How do we know that? Well, return to the idea of dividing numerators and denominators by the same thing. For example, $^{25}/_{100}$ can be divided by 5 to give $^5/_{20}$. But 5 and 20 are both also divisible by 5, giving ¼. (Once you've got your numerator down to 1, you know that you have simplified the fraction as far as it will go.) So 1.25 is exactly the same as 1¼.

Decimal fractions that are less than 1 can be written either 0.25 or just .25—it's the same thing.

☞ RECURRING DECIMALS

Not everything divides neatly into tens, so sometimes a decimal fraction can be no more than an approximation. For example, ⅓ is 0.333 recurring—no matter how many threes you add, you will never get a decimal that is exactly equal to one third.

If a decimal recurs, you can be certain that it's the same as some common fraction. For example, 0.222 recurring is $^2/_9$;

0.142857142857142857 recurring is $\frac{1}{7}$. A recurring decimal is sometimes indicated with a dot above the last digit, which is sort of the equivalent of ellipses (…) or "etc., etc., etc."

Pi is different (see page 73). Its decimal expansion goes on forever but without recurring, because it isn't the same as any common fraction. Pi is called a **transcendental** number, and it's probably the only one you'll ever meet.

☞ PERCENTAGES

Percent means *by a hundred*, so anything expressed as a percentage is a fraction (or part, if you prefer) of 100. So 25 percent is twenty-five parts of 100, or $\frac{25}{100}$ or 0.25. If you've been paying attention, you'll know that this is the same as $\frac{1}{4}$.

Similarly, 50 percent is $\frac{50}{100}$, which can be canceled down to $\frac{25}{50}$, which is $\frac{5}{10}$, which is $\frac{1}{2}$.

Mean, Median, and Mode

In arithmetical terms, **mean** is simply a fancy word for **average**. You calculate a mean by adding a group of numbers together and dividing by the number of numbers. (Strictly speaking, this is the **arithmetic mean**—there are other sorts of mean, too, but of interest only to mathematicians.) So the mean of 4, 8, 12, and 16 is the total of the four numbers, divided by 4:

4 + 8 + 12 + 16 = 40 divided by 4 = 10.

And it works for any number of numbers. For example, if a class of 11 children gets the following marks on an exam—55, 57, 57, 65, 66, 69, 70, 72, 75, 79, and 83—the total of the marks is 748. Divide that by 11, and you get a mean of 68.

The **median** of a set of values is literally the middle one. In the set of grades above, it is 69. There are five marks lower than 69 and five marks higher than 69—never mind their actual values. The median of an even number of values is the average of the middle two. For example, the median of 1, 4, 9, 16, 25, and 36 is 12.5—halfway between 9 and 16.

The **mode** of a set of values is the most common value. The mode of our set of marks is 57, because it is the only one that occurs more than once.

Measurements

Metric units and imperial (or what we will refer to as American) units are two different ways to measure the same things. Just as Fahrenheit and Celsius both measure temperature but in different ways (see page 94), so the metric system and system of American units quantify length, weight, and all sorts of other things, using different units. Metric units are also sometimes called SI units, which stands for Système Internationale.

The metric system calculates in tens or multiples of tens. The system of American units doesn't, and to the uninitiated it can seem pretty random. (American units used to mean something sensible, such as the foot was the length of a man's foot and the yard was the distance from his nose to the tip of his outstretched arm.)

☞ LENGTH

In American units length is measured in inches, feet, yards, and miles, and occasionally also in chains and furlongs. There are 12 inches in a foot, 3 feet (36 inches) in a yard, 22 yards in a chain, 10 chains in a furlong, and 8 furlongs (1,760 yards, 5,280 feet) in a mile. Other units are still in use for some special purposes, such as the fathom (6 feet) for measuring the depth of the sea, and the hand (4 inches) for measuring the height of a horse.

The basic unit of length in the metric system is the meter, with subdivisions and multiples for measuring little things and big things. Most commonly used are the millimeter (a thousandth of a meter), the centimeter (a hundredth of a meter, or ten millimeters), and the kilometer (a thousand meters).

To convert between the two:

- 1 inch = 2.54 centimeters, so to convert inches to centimeters, multiply by 2.54. To convert centimeters to inches, divide by 2.54. Remember that a centimeter is shorter than an inch, so you should have a larger number of centimeters.
- 1 yard = 0.91 meters; 1 meter = 1.09 yards, or 3.3 feet. Yards and feet are shorter than meters, so you will have a larger number of them.
- 1 mile = 1.6 kilometers; 1 kilometer = 0.625 (⅝) of a mile. This time the metric unit is smaller, so you have more kilometers than miles.
- A nautical mile is about 1.15 miles, or *exactly* 1,852 meters.

☞ WEIGHT

In American units weight is measured in ounces, pounds, a hundredweight (short), and tons: 16 ounces (oz.) = 1 pound (lb., from *libra,* Latin for pound); 100 pounds = 1 hundredweight (short); 200 hundredweight (2,000 lb.) = 1 ton. This is sometimes called a short ton, because the imperial system in the U.K. uses a long ton of 2,240 lb. And they also use a measurement of stones (14 pounds = 1 stone).

In the metric system weight is measured in grams or kilograms. (You can have milligrams and centigrams, but a gram is already pretty small, so unless you're a pharmacist or something of that sort, you don't often need them.) A kilogram is 1,000 grams.

- 1 gram (or g) = about 0.0353 ounce, so to convert grams to ounces, multiply the number of grams by .0353. To convert ounces to grams, divide by .0353.
- 1 kilogram (or kilo or kg) is about 2.2 pounds, so multiply kilograms by 2.2, divide pounds by 2.2.
- A metric ton is 1,000 kilograms, or 2,205 pounds, just a bit more than an American ton.

☞ VOLUME

In the American system volume is measured in fluid ounces, pints, quarts, and gallons; in the metric system it is measured in liters. This becomes even more complicated because the value of the units in the United States differs from the imperial system in the U.K.

In the United States 16 fluid ounces make a pint. But the U.S. pint and gallon are smaller than the U.K. ones. To convert U.S. pints to liters, divide by 2.1.

In the U.K. 20 imperial fluid ounces make 1 imperial pint, 2 imperial pints make 1 imperial quart, and there are 4 quarts (8 pints) in an imperial gallon. A liter is about 1.75 pints, so to convert imperial pints to liters, divide by 1.75; to convert liters to imperial pints, multiply by 1.75 (pints are smaller, so you will have more of them).

Algebra and Equations

Algebra is the branch of math that uses symbols (normally letters of the alphabet) to represent unknown numbers, along the lines of $a + b = 5$. If you assign a value to a, you can calculate b: If $a = 2$, then $b = 3$. This is known as an **algebraic equation**.

The main thing to remember when solving equations is that one side of the = sign is equal to the other side, so anything that you do to one side, you need to do to the other.*

For example, to solve the equation

$$3a + 1 = 16 - 2a,$$

you first add $2a$ to each side, giving:

$$5a + 1 = 16.$$

Then subtract 1 from each side, giving

$$5a = 15.$$

Now you can divide both sides by 5 and announce proudly that $a = 3$.

☞ SIMULTANEOUS EQUATIONS

A simultaneous equation is a more complicated form of

*You're allowed to do almost anything to an equation, as long as you do the same thing to both sides. You are not allowed, however, to a) take square roots; or b) divide by 0. You wouldn't normally divide anything by 0 anyway, but if you were to divide something by, say, a–3 and it turned out that a equaled 3, you would get some very odd answers. More on square roots later in this section.

algebraic equation, in which you have two or more unknowns. The general rule is that you must have exactly the same number of equations as you have unknowns in order to find the value of each. If you have fewer equations, there will be lots of solutions and no way to choose between them. If you have too many equations, there will be no solution at all.

This assumes that the equations are all different and don't contradict each other. For example:

$$a + b = 6,$$
$$2a + 2b = 12$$

are no good as a pair of simultaneous equations, because they both say exactly the same thing, while:

$$a + b = 6,$$
$$a + b = 7$$

will not work either, because there's no way both of them can be true at the same time.

Here's a look at a better-behaved set of simultaneous equations:

$$a+b = 6,$$
$$a-b = 2.$$

A way of solving these is to add the two equations together, so

$$a + a + b - b = 6+2$$

or, more simply, $2a = 8$ (because the $+b$ and $-b$ cancel each other out).

From there you can calculate that $a = 4$ and, because $a + b = 6$, b must equal 2. Which is verified by the second equation, $4 - 2 = 2$.

The principle remains the same regardless of how many unknowns you have:

$$a + b + c = 24,$$
$$a + b - c = 16,$$
$$2a + b = 32.$$

Add the first two equations together and you get $2a + 2b = 40$ (because this time the c's cancel each other out).

Now look at the third equation. It's very similar to the sum of the first two. Subtract one from the other:

$$(2a + 2b) - (2a - b) = 40 - 32.$$

The a's cancel each other out, so $2b - b$ (in other words, b) $= 8$.

Go back to the third equation, which contains only a's and b's, and substitute 8 for b:

$$2a + 8 = 32.$$

Deduct 8 from each side of the equation to give

$$2a = 32 - 8 = 24,$$

which means that $a = 12$.

Now go back to the first equation and substitute both a and b:

$$12 + 8 + c = 24,$$
$$20 + c = 24,$$
$$c = 24 - 20 = 4.$$

Verify this by going to the second equation:

$$12[a] + 8[b] - 4[c] = 16,$$

which is true.

☞ QUADRATIC EQUATIONS

These are more complex again, because they involve a square—that is, a number multiplied by itself and written with a raised ^{2} after it—so 16 is 4^2, and 36 is 6^2. Thus, 4 is the square root of 16, and 6 is the square root of 36. The symbol for a **square root** is √. Actually, $(-4)^2$ is also 16, so 16 has two square roots: +4 and –4. Any positive number has two square roots. A negative number doesn't have any square roots at all, because if you multiply a negative by a negative, you get a positive.

An algebraic expression can also be a square: the square of $a + 4$ is $(a + 4) \text{ x } (a + 4)$. You do this by multiplying each of the elements in the first bracket by each of the elements in the second:

$$(a x a) + (a x 4) + (4 x a) + (4 x 4)$$
$$= a^2 + 8a + 16.$$

To solve a quadratic equation, you need to turn both sides of it into a perfect square, which is easier to explain if we look at an example:

$$a^2 + 8a = 48.$$

The rule for "completing the square" in order to solve a quadratic equation is, "Take the number before the *a*, square it, and divide by 4." For example, 8 squared (64) divided by 4 is 16, so we add that to both sides; reassuringly, we already know that adding 16 to this equation will create a perfect square, because we just did it in the previous equation:

$$a^2 + 8a + 16 = 48 + 16 = 64.$$

Taking the square root of each side gives:

$$a + 4 = 8 \text{ (because 8 is the square root of 64).}$$

Again, we know that $a + 4$ is the square root of $a^2 + 8a + 16$, because it was part of the sum we did on the previous page. Anyway, we now have a simple sum to establish that $a = 4$.

Wait a minute, though. Taking the square root of both sides of an equation is not allowed. Why is this? Because a positive number like 64 has *two* square roots, +8 and –8. So the truth of the matter is that actually

$$a + 4 = +8 \text{ or } -8,$$

so a equals either +4 or –12.

Although this example is an easy one, the beauty of algebra is that the same principle applies whatever the numbers involved. So, to repeat: The rule for "completing the square" in order to solve a quadratic equation is, Take the number before the a, square it, and divide by 4.)

So if your equation is

$$a^2 + 12a + 14 = 33,$$

you first simplify the equation by getting rid of the 14. Subtract it from both sides to leave:

$$a^2 + 12a = 33 - 14 = 19.$$

Square the 12 to give 144, divide by 4 to give 36, and—as always—add that to both sides:

$$a^2 + 12a + 36 = 19 + 36 = 55.$$

The square root of that gives you

$$a + 6 = 55 = \text{(approximately) } 7.4\text{, or, of course, } -7.4.$$

Deduct 6 from each side to leave the simple statement $a = 1.4$ or -13.4.

You can check that this is right by going back to the original equation and putting in $a = 1.4$:

$$a^2 + 12a + 14 = 33$$

becomes

$$(1.4 \times 1.4) + (12 \times 1.4) + 14 = 1.96 + 16.8 + 14$$

(near enough for the purposes of this exercise)

$$= 2 + 17 + 14 = 33.$$

QED, as they say in math (or essentially, problem solved). You'll find it also works out with $a = -13.4$.

Geometry

Geometry is about measuring lines and angles and assessing the relationship between them, so let's start with some ways of measuring.

- The **perimeter** of a two-dimensional object is the total length of all its sides. For example, if these sides are straight, it's a matter of simple addition: A rectangle measuring 4 inches by 5 inches has two sides 4 inches long and two sides 5 inches long, so its perimeter is 4 + 5 + 4 + 5 = 18 inches.
- The **area** of a four-sided figure is calculated by multiplying the length by the width: In the above example 4 x 5 = 20 square inches ($in.^2$).
- **Volume** is calculated in the same way, by multiplying the length by the width by the height (or, if you prefer, the area by the height). For instance, a box that is 6 inches high, whose base measures 4 inches by 5 inches, has a volume of 4 x 5 x 6 = 120 cubed inches (in^3).

The volume of a pyramid is the area of the base multiplied by the height, divided by 3:

$$\frac{h \times b}{3}.$$

It's when you get to circles that it all becomes more complicated, because then you have to start dealing with…

☞ PI

Pi (π) is the Greek equivalent of the Roman *p* and is used in math to represent the ratio of the circumference of a circle to its diameter. Depending on how sophisticated you are as a mathematician, you can say that π = 3.142, 3.14159, or 3.14159265358979323846264338327950, but even then it is not 100 percent exact. Expressed as a fraction, pi is roughly $3\frac{1}{7}$, or $\frac{22}{7}$.

Before we go on, three more quick definitions:

- The **circumference** of a circle is its perimeter, the distance around the outside.
- The **diameter** is the length of a straight line through the middle, from one point on the circumference to another.
- The **radius** is half the diameter; that is, the distance from the center of the circle to the circumference.

So to calculate the circumference of a circle, you multiply the diameter by π: a circle that is, say, 7 inches in diameter has a circumference of 7 x $\frac{22}{7}$ = approximately 22 inches. The formula for this can be expressed as πd, but is usually given as $2(\pi r)$.

Area is πr^2—that is, π times the radius squared. So a circle of 6 inches radius has an area of $\frac{22}{7}$ x (6 x 6) = approximately 113 square inches.

The three-dimensional equivalent to a circle is a **sphere**, and its volume is calculated by the formula $\frac{4}{3}\pi r^3$—that is, four thirds (or one and one third) of the product of π and the radius cubed (multiplied by itself and then by itself again). So a sphere with a radius of 6 inches has a volume of $\frac{4}{3}$ x π x(6 x 6 x 6) = approximately 905 cubic inches.

A **cone** is effectively a pyramid with a circular base, so the pyramid formula applies: A cone with a base 6 inches in diameter and a height of 10 inches has a base area of π x (6 x 6) = approximately 113 square inches, and a volume of:

$$\frac{10 \times 113}{3}$$

or

$$\frac{1130}{3},$$

which equals approximately 377 cubic inches.

☞ TRIANGLES

The area of a triangle is calculated by:

$$\frac{\text{base} \times \text{height}}{2}.$$

There are three types of triangles, depending on the length of their sides:

- An **equilateral** triangle has three sides of equal length.
- An **isosceles** triangle has two sides of equal length.
- A **scalene** triangle has three sides that are all of different lengths.

The sum total of the angles of a triangle, whatever its shape, is 180°. A **right angle** is 90°; any angle smaller than 90° is called an **acute angle,** while anything above 90° but lower than 180° is **obtuse.** In a right-angled triangle the side opposite the right angle (also always the longest side) is called the **hypotenuse,** which brings us neatly to...

☞ THE PYTHAGOREAN THEOREM

This theorem states that the square on the hypotenuse is equal to the sum of the squares on the other two sides. The simplest example of this is what is called a 3:4:5 triangle, in which the hypotenuse is 5 inches (or centimeters or miles, it doesn't matter) and the other two sides are 3 inches and 4 inches.

The square on the side that is 3 inches long is 9 in.^{2} (3 x 3), the square on the 4-inch side is 16 in.^{2} (4 x 4), and when you add them together, you get 25 in.^{2}, which is the square of the hypotenuse (5 x 5).

This can also be remembered using the formula $a^2 + b^2 = c^2$, where c is the hypotenuse.

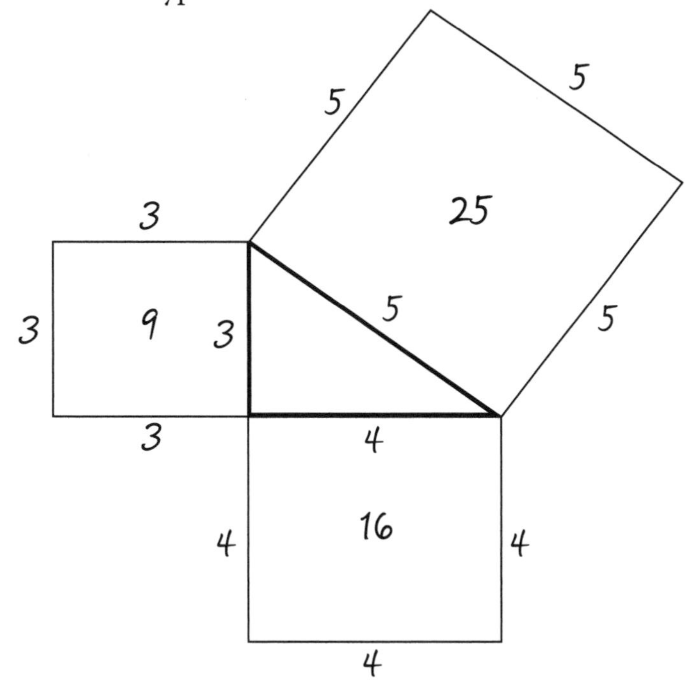

The burning question, of course, is, Why does it matter? Well, it *could* have had some practical value in the ancient world. It has been suggested, for example, that the Egyptians could have used ropes in the proportion 3:4:5 to produce right angles when building the pyramids. Unfortunately, there isn't the remotest scrap of evidence that they did any such thing. In fact, the Pythagorean theorem matters most to mathematicians because it is fundamental to our next topic.

Trigonometry

Trigonometry is "the branch of mathematics that deals with the relations between the sides and angles of a triangle," and a **trigonometric function** is "any function of an angle that is defined by the relationship between the sides and angles of a right-angled triangle."

There are six basic trigonometric functions: sine, cosine, tangent, cotangent, secant, and cosecant, and they are calculated as follows. In a right-angled triangle where the other two angles are valued at x and y degrees, the side opposite x is a, the side opposite y is b, and the hypotenuse is c:

$$\sin x = a/c$$
$$\cos x = b/c$$
$$\tan x = a/b$$
$$\cot x = b/a$$
$$\sec x = c/b$$
$$\text{cosec}\ x = c/a$$

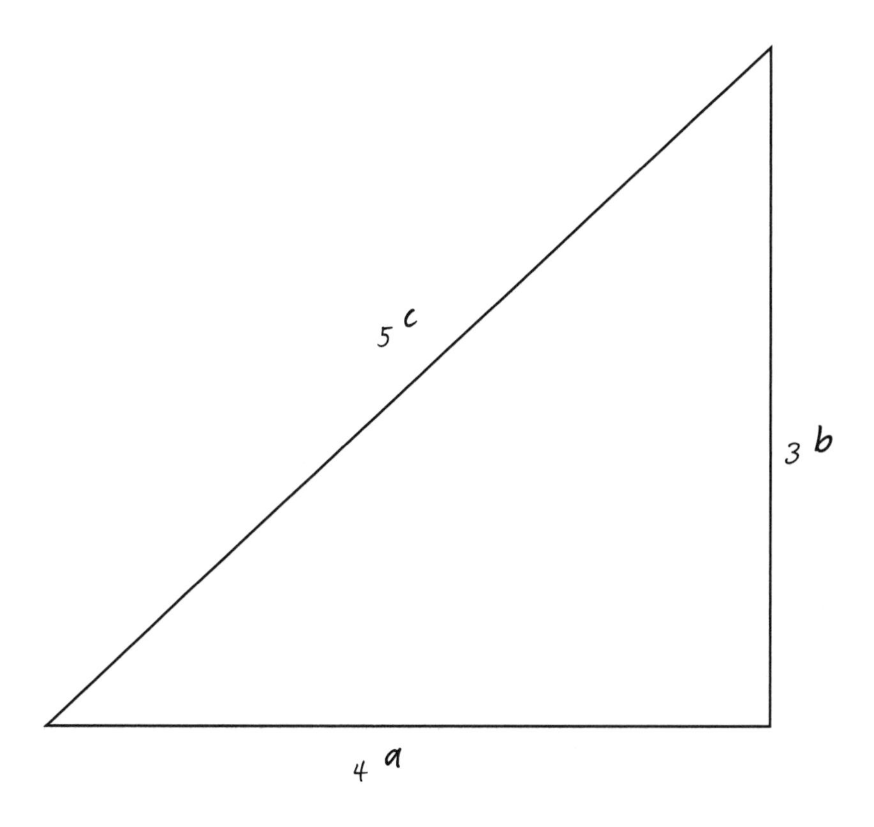

Why do we care? Well, the point is that the functions or ratios remain the same whatever the size of the triangle. So if you know the sine of a 90° angle in a triangle whose sides measure 3, 4, and 5 inches, you can extrapolate all sorts of measurements for a much larger triangle with the same proportions.

The trigonometric version of the Pythagorean theorem tells us that for any angle x,

$$\sin^2 x + \cos^2 x = 1,$$

where $\sin^2 x$ is a conventional way of writing $(\sin x)^2$ without the need for brackets. If you know the sine of an angle, you can use this formula to calculate all the rest of the trigonometric functions given above.

Trigonometry is vital to the study of higher mathematics and the sciences. At a more comprehensible and practical level, it is used in land surveying, mapmaking, engineering, astronomy, geography, satellite navigation systems, and so on.

SCIENCE

The world of science is so vast and expanding that to condense it into 30 pages seems like a futile experiment. Every school system teaches the topic differently, so what may seem familiar and commonplace to one person can remain a mystery to others. Consider this chapter the foundation on which you can build.

Biology

The term biology comes from the Greek, meaning *study of life;* therefore, this field of learning concerns plants and animals and how the human body works.

☞ PHOTOSYNTHESIS

This is the process by which plants convert carbon dioxide and water into the carbohydrates they need for growth, using energy that they absorb from light (hence, the photo element). Light is absorbed into the plant by the green pigment called chlorophyll, stored mainly in the leaves, which provides the green color of so many plants. In fact, plants need only the hydrogen element from water (H_2O), so photosynthesis releases oxygen back into the atmosphere, enabling the rest of us to breathe.

☞ THE STRUCTURE OF A PLANT

The **flower** contains the plant's reproductive organs. The stigma, style, and ovary make up the carpel, which contains the female cells; if a flower has more than one carpel, these combine to form the pistil. The male organ is called the stamen and consists of an anther that contains the pollen sacs and is supported on a filament. Most plants self-pollinate, but some, such as certain hollies and the kiwifruit, require a male and female plant of the same species in order to reproduce.

The **leaves** enable the plant to feed and breathe. They contain the chlorophyll that is essential to photosynthesis, which absorbs light. Leaves also contain pores (stoma), through which gases and water are absorbed and released back into the atmosphere. The shape of the leaf reflects the plant's needs: big, broad leaves are designed to absorb maximum light; the fleshy, succulent leaves of a cactus store water in case of drought.

The **stem** is the plant's support and the conduit between roots, leaves, and plants. It contains phloem, a tissue that transports food within the plant; and xylem, which principally transports water. It is the xylem that hardens to form the trunks of trees and shrubs.

The **roots** anchor the plant in the ground and absorb nutrients and water from the soil. A tap root system has a single main root; a fibrous system has—well, lots of fibers. In root vegetables, such as turnips and carrots, the vegetable part is, in fact, a swollen root. Adventitious roots are less common; the name means *coming from the outside,* and these roots grow in unusual places, such as from the stem.

☞ THE CARBON CYCLE

The process by which carbon (in the form of carbon dioxide) is absorbed from the atmosphere during photosynthesis and is then transferred from one organism to another and eventually released back into the atmosphere is known as the carbon cycle. For example, a plant takes in carbon dioxide; the plant

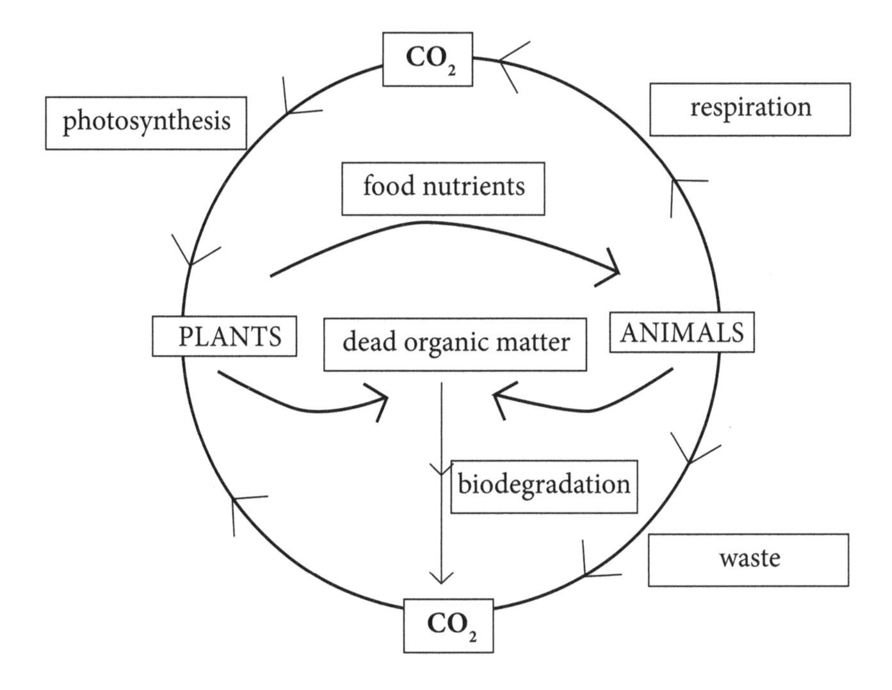

is eaten by a herbivorous animal, which is in turn eaten by a carnivore; when the animal dies, its rotting body releases carbon dioxide. Alternatively, the herbivorous animal excretes its waste, which also degrades to give off carbon dioxide.

This provides a smooth transition from plants to the human body.

☞ CHROMOSOMES

A normal human body has 46 chromosomes composed of 22 matched pairs and two sex chromosomes. Half of each pair, along with a single sex chromosome, is found in the sperm. The other half is in the egg. Fusion of the two creates the human embryo. Sex chromosomes are of two types, called X (female) and Y (male). The egg always contains an X chromosome, so the sex of the embryo is determined by whether a sperm is carrying an X or Y chromosome. Other chromosomes dictate other genetic factors, such as hair and eye color.

Chromosomes are made up of DNA, RNA, and protein.

DNA stands for deoxyribonucleic acid and is fundamental to the organization and functioning of living cells. It consists of the famous "double helix" (identified by the scientists Crick and Watson in 1953), with two strands coiled around each other. When the strands of a helix separate, each provides a template for the synthesis of an identical strand, containing the same genetic information. This enables normal growth, cell repair, and the production of cells that will turn into the next generation—which is why humans produce babies rather than tiger cubs, and why tigers produce tiger cubs rather than roses.

RNA stands for ribonucleic acid, which occurs as a single strand and contains different sugars and bases but is otherwise structurally similar to DNA. It's vital to the synthesis of...

Proteins, which fulfill many important roles in a living organism—they are involved in the makeup of tissue; the properties of muscles; and the functioning of hormones, the immune system, and the digestive system, to name a few. They are manufactured within cells using information conveyed by the DNA and RNA.

☞ THE SKELETAL SYSTEM

The human skeleton is made up of more than 200 bones, held together by fibrous tissue called **ligaments,** and linked at the **joints.** Joints allow varying degrees of movement from none (between the bones that make up the skull) through some (the hinge joints at the elbow and knee) to lots (the ball-and-socket joints at the hip and shoulder).

The principal bones of the body, starting at the top and working down, are:

- **cranium:** skull
- **spine:** made up of 26 smaller bones called vertebrae
- **clavicle:** collar bone
- **scapula:** shoulder blade
- **humerus:** upper arm
- **radius** and **ulna:** lower arm—the radius is the broader one on the thumb side, the ulna the narrower one on the little finger side
- **carpus:** a collective name for the bones of the wrist, individually known as carpals
- **metacarpus:** ditto for the five long bones of the hand
- **phalanges:** fingers
- **sacrum:** actually a fusion of five vertebrae attached to the
- **hip bone**
- **coccyx:** tail bone, a fusion of the lowest four vertebrae
- **femur:** thigh bone
- **patella:** knee cap
- **tibia** and **fibula:** lower leg—the tibia is the broader one that runs down toward the big toe; the fibula the narrower one that runs toward the little toe

- **tarsus:** a collective name for the bones of the ankle and heel, individually known as tarsals
- **metatarsus:** ditto for the five long bones of the foot
- **phalanges:** toes

☞ THE CIRCULATORY SYSTEM

Blood is the body's transportation system—everything from oxygen to hormones is transported around the body in the bloodstream, and its waste products, from carbon dioxide to urea, are carried away for disposal.

In order for blood to do its job, it needs to be pumped around, and that is the primary purpose of the **heart**. The heart is two pumps, each consisting of two chambers—an auricle and a ventricle—with a valve in between. The left side of the heart receives oxygen-rich blood from the lungs and forces it throughout the body; the right side receives the oxygen-depleted blood and returns it to the lungs to be re-oxygenated. (Oxygen, of course, comes into the lungs in the air that we breathe, and without it the cells in the body would die.)

All this requires a well-organized system of blood vessels. These are divided into **arteries,** which are strong and muscular and carry fast-flowing blood *away* from the heart, and **veins**, which are weaker and more sluggish and bring it back. The principal artery, the **aorta,** divides into smaller arteries and arterioles. Smaller veins are called venules, and really tiny blood vessels—whether veins or arteries—are called capillaries.

The exception to the useful mnemonia—*arteries go away*—is the pulmonary artery—the one that goes from the lung to the heart. The pulmonary vein runs from the heart to the lungs. Therefore, the truth is that the arteries simply carry the oxygen-rich blood.

Blood has four major components:

- **red blood cells,** which carry hemoglobin, made up of heme (an iron-containing pigment) and globin (a protein) (This combines with oxygen to form oxyhemoglobin, the means by which oxygen is transported throughout the body. Oxyhemoglobin also gives the blood its red color, which is why arterial blood is bright red; venous blood, having deposited oxygen in cells all over the body, has a bluish tinge.)
- **white blood cells,** or leukocytes, which fight infection
- **platelets,** which are necessary for the clotting process
- **plasma,** the liquid that makes the blood… well, liquid

☞ THE DIGESTIVE SYSTEM

The digestive process is divided into four parts:

- **ingestion:** eating food
- **digestion:** breaking the food down into constituent parts
- **absorption:** extracting nutrients from the food
- **elimination:** disposing of waste

Once you swallow food or drink, it enters the **esophagus,** or gullet, and passes (through a process of muscular contraction called **peristalsis**) into the stomach. From there it continues into the **small intestine** (comprising the duodenum, jejunum, and ileum), where digested food is absorbed into the bloodstream. The whole process is helped by the secretion of **enzymes**. One of the effects of the digestion of protein (which enters the body via meat, fish, eggs, etc.) is the release of **amino acids**, which are the building blocks of the protein the body needs for all sorts of different purposes.

Anything undigested after this stage passes into the **colon** (the beginning of the large intestine), where water is extracted from it. What remains are the feces, which pass through the rectum and out of the body via the anus.

Organs encountered along the way include:

- the **liver,** which in adult life often copes with our alcohol intake, but which has many more functions to do with digestion and keeping the blood healthy
- the **gall bladder,** which stores bile, needed in the digestion of fats
- the **pancreas,** which secretes various enzymes and the hormones insulin and glucagon, which regulate levels of blood sugar
- the **kidneys,** which control the amount of salt and water in the blood. (Excess fluid containing waste products is filtered through the kidneys down to the bladder and leaves the body in the form of urine.)

☞ THE RESPIRATORY SYSTEM

Air passes into the body through the **trachea** or windpipe via the mouth and nose. With the help of contractions from the **diaphragm,** which is a large muscle extending across the bottom of the rib cage, it is carried down into the lungs via two smaller tubes, called **bronchi,** which then split into even smaller bronchioles. Inside the lungs are lots of little air sacs, or **alveoli.** Within the alveoli oxygen is extracted from the air, absorbed into the bloodstream, and carried off to the heart via the pulmonary artery. The pulmonary vein brings "used" blood back to the alveoli, and the process is reversed as we breathe out air that now has a high carbon dioxide content.

☞ THE NERVOUS SYSTEM

The brain, spinal cord, and nerves make up perhaps the most

important and intricately complex system in the human body. The nervous system essentially controls all the other systems in your body. It is what allows you to remember things, or at least remember that you used to know something. It tells your muscles and organs what to do and how to do it. The three interconnected parts of the nervous system are:

- the **central nervous system,** composed of the brain and spinal cord, which sends nerve impulses and analyzes information from the sense organs (eyes, ears, nose, mouth, skin, etc.). These organs enable you to see, touch, taste, hear, and feel.
- the **peripheral nervous system,** which includes the craniospinal nerves, a vast network of nerves that extends from your brain and spinal cord to all parts of your body and carries signals back and forth. It carries nerve impulses from the central nervous system to the muscles and glands.
- the **autonomic nervous system (ANS),** which regulates involuntary actions, such as pulse rate and digestion. The ANS is broken into the sympathetic nervous system (fight or flight), the parasympathetic nervous system (rest so you can digest), and the enteric nervous system (the digestive system's personal messenger).

However, no discussion of the nervous system is complete without those trusty **neurons,** the nerve cells that send and carry the signals throughout your body. A neuron consists of a main cell body with a long nerve fiber, called an **axon,** branching from it. Electrical signals pass from axon to axon through small gaps called **synapses.** In order to do this, these electrical signals turn into chemical ones, called **neurotransmitters.** In fact, right now the neurons in the temporal lobe of your brain (which interprets language), your frontal lobe (which involves reasoning), and your occipital lobe (which controls sight) are firing away!

Chemistry

This is the study of elements and compounds and the reactions they undergo—which is a definition that surely cries out for a few more definitions.

atom: the smallest particle in an element that can take part in a chemical reaction, made up of a **nucleus,** which is containing positively charged **protons** and neutral **neutrons;** and a number of **electrons,** which are negatively charged particles that orbit the nucleus. Each atom normally has the same number of protons and electrons, leaving it with a neutral charge. The movement of electrons is responsible for most commonly observed chemical, electrical, or magnetic reactions. If an atom loses or gains an electron, it becomes either positively or negatively charged and is known as an **ion.**

element: a substance that cannot be decomposed into a simpler substance by a chemical process. Groups of elements come together to form a compound. So, for example, a combination of the element hydrogen (H) and the element oxygen (O) can form the compound water (H_2O).

mole: also known as Avogadro's number or Avogadro's constant, a mole contains the same number of particles as there are in 12 g of carbon-12 atoms—that is, 6.022×10^{23} particles.

Carbon has three naturally occurring isotopes (forms of the same substance with different numbers of neutrons), and one of these is carbon-12.

molecule: the smallest particle of a compound that can exist independently and retain its properties. So in the previous example, the smallest imaginable quantity of hydrogen and oxygen joined together in the right conditions and right proportions will still produce a molecule of water. Only when the hydrogen and oxygen are chemically separated again do they lose the properties that make them water and return to being atoms of hydrogen and oxygen.

☞ THE PERIODIC TABLE OF THE ELEMENTS

The periodic table was first devised in 1889 by the Russian chemist Dmitri Mendeleev. When putting the table together, Mendeleev realized there were gaps between some of the elements. Based on this, he predicted that some elements had yet to be discovered.

The table arranges the elements in ascending order of **atomic number** (the number of protons that each possesses) in such a way that the vertical columns contain groups or families with similar chemical properties. The horizontal rows represent periods, with the most electropositive (an alkali metal) on the left and the so-called inert gases on the right, and the whole thing proves that "the chemical properties of the elements are periodic functions of their atomic weights"—or, in other words, that similar properties in an element recur at regular intervals.

PERIODIC TABLE OF THE ELEMENTS

	2A	3B	4B	5B	6B	7B	8B		
1 **H** 1.00794 Hydrogen									
3 **Li** 6.341 Lithium	4 **Be** 9.012182 Beryllium								
11 **Na** 22.989769 Sodium	12 **Mg** 24.3050 Magnesium								
19 **K** 39.0983 Potassium	20 **Ca** 40.078 Calcium	21 **Sc** 44.955912 Scandium	22 **Ti** 47.867 Titanium	23 **V** 50.9415 Vanadium	24 **Cr** 51.9961 Chromium	25 **Mn** 54.938045 Manganese	26 **Fe** 55.845 Iron	27 **Co** 58.933195 Cobalt	28 **Ni** 58.6934 Nickel
37 **Rb** 85.4678 Rubidium	38 **Sr** 87.62 Strontium	39 **Y** 88.90585 Yttrium	40 **Zr** 91.224 Zirconium	41 **Nb** 92.90638 Niobium	42 **Mo** 95.96 Molybdenum	43 **Tc** [98] Technetium	44 **Ru** 101.07 Ruthenium	45 **Rh** 102.90550 Rhodium	46 **Pd** 106.42 Palladium
55 **Cs** 132.9054519 Cesium	56 **Ba** 137.327 Barium	57-71 *Lanthanides	72 **Hf** 178.49 Hafnium	73 **Ta** 180.94788 Tantalum	74 **W** 183.84 Tungsten	75 **Re** 186.207 Rhenium	76 **Os** 190.23 Osmium	77 **Ir** 192.217 Iridium	78 **Pt** 195.084 Platinum
87 **Fr** [223] Francium	88 **Ra** [226] Radium	89-103 **Actinides	104 **Rf** [267] Rutherfordium	105 **Db** [268] Dubnium	106 **Sg** [271] Seaborgium	107 **Bh** [272] Bohrium	108 **Hs** [270] Hassium	109 **Mt** [276] Meitnerium	110 **Ds** [281] Darmstadtium

*Lanthanides	57 **La** 138.90547 Lanthanum	58 **Ce** 140.116 Cerium	59 **Pr** 140.90765 Praseodymium	60 **Nd** 144.242 Neodymium	61 **Pm** [145] Promethium	62 **Sm** 150.36 Samarium	63 **Eu** 151.964 Europium
**Actinides	89 **Ac** [227] Actinium	90 **Th** 232.03806 Thorium	91 **Pa** 231.03588 Protactinium	92 **U** 238.02891 Uranium	93 **Np** [237] Neptunium	94 **Pu** [244] Plutonium	95 **Am** [243] Americium

The elements are traditionally designated by a one-, two-, or three-letter abbreviation, as you can see in the table, and there are 118 of them. The table above lists 103; listed below them are elements 104 through 118. From 93 upward the elements don't occur naturally but have been synthesized in particle accelerators. The last few are recent achievements, and they have temporary names based on their atomic numbers. Element 117, which will be called Ununseptium, hasn't been synthesized yet, but scientists are working on it. The lanthanides and actinides are usually separated from the rest of the table, as shown above, because—unlike the other rows—they have similar properties as you read across.

1B	2B	3A	4A	5A	6A	7A	
							2 **He** 4.002602 Helium
		5 **B** 10.811 Boron	6 **C** 12.0107 Carbon	7 **N** 14.0067 Nitrogen	8 **O** 15.9994 Oxygen	9 **F** 18.9984032 Fluorine	10 **Ne** 20.1797 Neon
		13 **Al** 26.9815386 Aluminum	14 **Si** 28.0855 Silicon	15 **P** 30.973762 Phosphorus	16 **S** 32.065 Sulfur	17 **Cl** 35.453 Chlorine	18 **Ar** 39.948 Argon
29 **Cu** 63.546 Copper	30 **Zn** 65.38 Zinc	31 **Ga** 69.723 Gallium	32 **Ge** 72.64 Germanium	33 **As** 74.92160 Arsenic	34 **Se** 78.96 Selenium	35 **Br** 79.904 Bromine	36 **Kr** 83.798 Krypton
47 **Ag** 107.8682 Silver	48 **Cd** 112.411 Cadmium	49 **In** 114.818 Indium	50 **Sn** 118.710 Tin	51 **Sb** 121.760 Antimony	52 **Te** 127.60 Tellurium	53 **I** 126.90447 Iodine	54 **Xe** 131.293 Xenon
79 **Au** 196.966569 Gold	80 **Hg** 200.59 Mercury	81 **Tl** 204.3833 Thallium	82 **Pb** 207.2 Lead	83 **Bi** 208.98040 Bismuth	84 **Po** [209] Polonium	85 **At** [210] Astatine	86 **Rn** [222] Radon
111 **Rg** [280] Roentgenium	112 **Uub** [285] Ununbium	113 **Uut** [284] Ununtrium	114 **Uuq** [289] Ununquadium	115 **Uup** [288] Ununpentium	116 **Uuh** [293] Ununhexium	117 **Uus** [294] Ununseptium	118 **Uuo** [294] Ununoctium

64 **Gd** 157.25 Gadolinium	65 **Tb** 158.92535 Terbium	66 **Dy** 162.500 Dysprosium	67 **Ho** 164.93032 Holmium	68 **Er** 167.259 Erbium	69 **Tm** 168.93421 Thulium	70 **Yb** 173.054 Ytterbium	71 **Lu** 174.9668 Lutetium
96 **Cm** [247] Curium	97 **Bk** [247] Berkelium	98 **Cf** [251] Californium	99 **Es** [252] Einsteinium	100 **Fm** [257] Fermium	101 **Md** [258] Mendelevium	102 **No** [259] Nobelium	103 **Lr** [262] Lawrencium

104	Rutherfordium	Rf
105	Dubnium	Db
106	Seaborgium	Sg
107	Bohrium	Bh
108	Hassium	Hs
109	Meitnerium	Mt
110	Darmstadtium	Ds
111	Roentgenium	Rg
112	Ununbium	Uun
113	Ununtrium	Uut
114	Ununquadium	Uuq
115	Ununpentium	Uup
116	Ununhexium	Uuh
117	Ununseptium	Uus
118	Ununoctium	Uuo

☞ ACIDS, BASES, AND SALTS

An **acid** is a substance (often sour and corrosive) that contains hydrogen atoms that, when dissolved in water, dissociate into ions and may be replaced by metals to form a salt.

A **base** is a compound that combines with an acid to form a salt plus water. Bases that are soluble in water are called **alkalis.** Many bases are oxides (so their formula ends in O, possibly with a little number after it) or hydroxides (OH).

A **salt** is a (usually crystalline) solid compound formed from the combination of an acid and a base by the replacement of hydrogen ions in the acid by positive ions in the base.

For example, combine sulphuric acid with the base cupric oxide in the right conditions and you have copper sulphate (that lovely bright blue stuff) and water:

$$H_2SO_4 + CuO \longrightarrow CuSO_4 + H_2O.$$

In a school lab you test whether a substance is an acid or a base with litmus paper. Acids turn litmus red; bases turn it blue. Serious scientists use the **pH**—potential of hydrogen—which is measured by sensors and electrodes and such. Pure water has a pH of 7, with anything less considered acidic and anything higher alkaline. Gardeners use this as a way of testing soil; you also sometimes see the pH listed on shampoo bottles.

Another term you might remember—and one worth mentioning here—is **valency,** which means the number of atoms of hydrogen that an atom or group displaces when forming a compound. Hydrogen has a valency of 1 and oxygen a valency of 2, which is why the formula for water is H_2O and not just

HO—because you need two atoms of hydrogen to "match" one of oxygen. Copper can have either of two valencies, which is why the one mentioned a moment ago is called cupric oxide, not just copper oxide. There's also cuprous oxide, CuO_2.

☞ OXIDATION

Oxidation is a commonly quoted chemical reaction, and the most common example of it is rust. In fact, anything that reacts when it comes into contact with oxygen is being subjected to oxidation: The green coating on an old copper coin is the result of oxidation; the browning of fruit is caused by oxygen burning away at the stuff that is released when you peel off the protective skin. Rust is, strictly speaking, the oxide that forms on iron or steel. Stainless steel doesn't rust, because it is protected by a layer of chromium, which doesn't react to oxygen in the same way.

☞ DIFFUSION AND OSMOSIS

Molecules are constantly in motion and tend to move from regions where they are in higher concentration to regions where they are less concentrated—a process known as **diffusion.** Diffusion can occur in gases, in liquids, or through solids.

Osmosis is a form of diffusion that is specific to the movement of water. Water moves through a selectively permeable membrane (that is, one that lets some types of molecules through but not others) from a place where there is a higher concentration of water to one where it is lower.

In any form of diffusion, when the molecules are evenly distributed throughout a space, they have reached **equilibrium.**

☞ BOILING AND FREEZING POINTS

If the temperature is low enough, every known substance except helium becomes a solid. The temperature at which this happens is called its **freezing point.** Above its freezing point a substance is a liquid. At the other end of the scale, if the temperature is high enough, it becomes a gas, and this is called the **boiling point.**

Solid is the only state in which a substance retains its shape; a liquid assumes the shape of its container but does not necessarily fill it; a gas expands to fill the space available.

Take water, for instance. In its solid state, it is ice and retains its shape—whether ice cube, icicle, or iceberg—until the temperature rises sufficiently for it to melt and become liquid (water). If you take a tray of melted ice cubes and pour the water into a pan, it will take the shape of the container—that is, spread out to cover the bottom—but it may only come a certain distance up the side. If, however, you then turn on the heat under the pan, put a lid on it, and boil the water, it will turn into gas (steam), fill the pan completely, and probably seep out under the lid as well.

Nonscientists commonly measure temperature according to one of two scales: Celsius and Fahrenheit, both named after the people who invented them. Celsius was also once called centigrade, from the Latin for *one hundred degrees.*

The freezing point of water is 0°C, and its boiling point is 100°C. The equivalent in Fahrenheit is 32°F and 212°F. This means that the difference between freezing and boiling is 100°C and 180°F (212 – 32).

To convert Celsius to Fahrenheit, you need to divide by 100 and multiply by 180, which can also be expressed as multiplying by 1.8, or 9⁄5. Then, because the freezing point of water is 32°F, not 0°F, you need to add 32:

$$15°C \times 1.8 = 27;\ 27 + 32 = 59°F.$$

To reverse the process, first deduct 32 from your Fahrenheit temperature, then divide by 9⁄5 (or multiply by 5⁄9; it's the same thing):

$$104°F - 32 = 72;\ 72 \times 5/9 = 40°C.$$

This works for any temperature above freezing.

There are two other scales used by scientists—the Réaumur and the Kelvin. According to René Antoine Ferchault de Réaumur, water freezes at 0° and boils at 80°. Kelvin is interesting because he invented the concept of absolute zero, a temperature at which particles cease to have any energy—so a scientific impossibility, although in the laboratory, scientists have achieved temperatures within a millionth of a degree of it. Absolute zero is 0°K, or –273.15°C, which is very, very cold. Imagine how much energy you would have at that temperature.

Physics

Physics deals with the properties and interactions of matter and energy, but its theories are constantly being redefined as physicists discover new things.

☞ OPTICS

Optics is all about light and there are several terms that may ring a bell.

Remember "The angle of incidence equals the angle of reflection"? You probably do. But do you remember what it means? Well, the **angle of incidence** is the angle at which light hits a surface; with **specular** (mirrorlike) reflection the light is reflected at the same angle. If the surface is rough, you get **diffuse** reflection, which means that the light bounces off in all directions.

Light may also pass through a medium—such as glass or water—and be **refracted** (change direction). This is because of the difference in the velocity with which light passes through the two different media (say, air and water), which is measured by the **refractive index**.

☞ CONDUCTION, CONVECTION, AND RADIATION

There are three ways in which heat is transferred:

Conduction can occur in solids, liquids, or gases and means (more or less) that a cool thing is warmed up by coming into contact with a hot thing. The different levels of conductivity in metals are reflected in their uses in anything from the science lab to kitchenware: Copper, for example, is highly conductive, and therefore it works well for fast cooking (although it may react with certain foods, which is why copper-bottomed pans are often lined with tin); whereas cast iron heats slowly but then cooks evenly.

Convection occurs in liquids and gases and is the basis of the principle that hot air rises. A hot liquid or gas is generally less dense than a cool one; as the hot particles rise, cooler ones rush in underneath to take their place. As the hot particles rise, they cool and come down again, and so on.

Radiation involves the energy that all objects, hot or cold, emit. It is the only one of the three that works in a vacuum and is how the sun's rays manage to warm the Earth from such a far distance away.

Heat is not the only commodity that is transferred in these ways. There is also electrical conduction, mass convection (of which evaporation is an example), and electromagnetic radiation. So, strictly speaking, you should insert the words "heat" or "therma" in front of conduction, convection, and radiation if that is what you mean.

☞ PHYSICAL LAWS

Physics is based on properties that explain what matter and energy can or can't do; without these interactions the universe would probably fall apart. From the observation of the interactions, laws were developed. Some of the physical processes and phenomena are revealed in this section. But a few definitions might help first.

Mass is the quantity of matter a body contains. Newton defined it more precisely by bringing in inertia, which is "a property of matter by which it continues in its existing state of rest or uniform motion in a straight line, unless that state is changed by an external force." All this means is that a thing will sit still until you push it.

Force is calculated by multiplying mass by acceleration and concerns producing motion in a stationary body or changing the direction of a moving one.

Velocity is speed (the dictionary says, "measure of the rate of movement," but most people call that speed) in a given direction.

Acceleration is the rate of increase in velocity.

Work is the exertion of force overcoming resistance (which might be electrical resistance, or it could be physical resistance, such as friction).

And, regardless of what anyone else may tell you, in this context a **body** is a thing. The dictionary says, "an object or substance that has three dimensions, a mass, and is distinguishable from surrounding objects."

☞ THE LAWS OF THERMODYNAMICS

Thermodynamics is the study of heat and its relationship with other forms of energy, and it is important in the study of heat engines such as gas-driven motors and gas turbines.

The other key term here is **entropy,** which is defined as "a measure of the disorder of a system." A solid has less entropy than a liquid, since the constituent particles in a solid are in a more ordered state. The flow of energy maintatins order and life. Entropy states the opposite. Entropy takes over when energy ceases.

If you have managed to follow along this far, then you are ready for the three laws of thermodynamics:

1. Energy can change from one form to another, but it can never be created or destroyed.
2. In all energy exchanges, if no energy enters or leaves the system, the potential energy of the state will be less than that of the initial state.
3. As the thermodynamic temperature of a system approaches absolute zero, its entropy approaches zero.

The British scientist and author C. P. Snow came up with a great way of remembering the three laws:

1. You cannot win (you cannot get something for nothing, because matter and energy are conserved).
2. You cannot break even (you cannot return to the same energy state, because there is always an increase in disorder).
3. You cannot get out of the game (because absolute zero is unattainable).

Moving swiftly on.

☞ THE LAWS OF CONSERVATION OF ENERGY AND MASS

The most common of these laws states that energy in a closed system cannot be created or destroyed (it's similar to the first law of thermodynamics), and nor can mass. At a more advanced level, similar laws apply to electric charge, linear momentum, and angular momentum, but most people never get that far.

☞ NEWTON'S THREE LAWS OF MOTION

1. A body remains at rest or moves with constant velocity in a straight line unless acted upon by a force.
2. The acceleration (a) of a body is proportional to the force (f) causing it: $f = ma$, where m is the mass of the body in question.
3. The action of a force always produces a reaction in the body, which is of equal magnitude but opposite in direction to the action.

Newton also came up with a **law of gravity,** which states that the force between two bodies is directly proportional to the product of their masses and inversely proportional to the square of the distance between them. The universal gravitational constant that makes this equation work is called *G,* and its value is 6.673×10^{-11} newton m^2 per kg^2.

However, Einstein's general theory of relativity describes gravity more accurately.

☞ EINSTEIN'S THEORIES OF RELATIVITY

Before reviewing Einstein's general theory of relativity, take a look at his *special* theory of relativity. Before Einstein—that is, until the start of the 20th century—it was believed that the speed of light relative to an observer could be calculated in the same way as the relative speed of any other two objects (such as two cars driving at different speeds). Einstein's theory is based on the assumption that the speed of light in a vacuum is a constant (186,000 miles—or 2.998×10^8 m—per second), regardless if the observer is moving or at what speed. Furthermore, he suggested that as bodies increase in speed, they increase in mass and decrease in length (relative to the observer)—although this effect became noticeable only as objects neared the speed of light.

Relative to each observer, time moves at a slower rate. All this led him to the conclusion that mass and energy are two different aspects of the same thing, which led to the famous equation

$$E = mc^2,$$

where E is energy, m is mass, and c is the velocity of light.

So, back to gravity. The special theory of relativity concerned motion in which there was no acceleration—that is, a constant speed. The general theory extended this to consider accelerated motion. According to this, gravity is a property of space and time that is "curved" by the presence of a mass. Einstein posited that the motion of the stars and planets was controlled by this curvature of space in the vicinity of matter, and that light was also bent by the gravitational field of a massive body. Subsequent experiments have shown him to be correct.

☞ ELECTRIC CURRENT

There are also a handful of laws to do with electricity. Here's one of the more familiar:

Ohm's law states that the current (I) flowing through an element in a circuit is directly proportional to the voltage drop or potential difference (V) across it: $V = IR$, where R means resistance—anything that gets in the way of the flow of current. What this means, more or less, is that the greater the resistance (measured in ohms), the greater the voltage (measured in volts) required to push the current (measured in amps) through it.

☞ EQUATIONS OF MOTION

These are basic equations that describe the motion of a body moving with constant acceleration.

A body moving with constant acceleration (*a*) starts with an initial velocity (*u*) and achieves a final velocity (*v*) in a time of *t* seconds, covering a total distance *s*. If you know any three of these components, you can decipher the other two.

Acceleration can be expressed as

$$a = \frac{v - u}{t}.$$

Distance traveled (*s*) is simply time multiplied by average speed:

$$s = t\,\frac{(u + v)}{2}.$$

These two equations—one for calculating acceleration and the other for calculating distance—are essentially all that is known here, but some other equations can be obtained by combining them.

For example, eliminate v from both of them. The first equation can be recast as

$$v = u + at$$

(multiply everything by t, then add u to both sides) and the second as:

$$v = \frac{2s}{t} - u$$

(multiply everything by 2, divide by t, and deduct u from both sides).

This may sound complicated, but the point is to produce an equation that defines v. Just in case you want to calculate v, you understand.... But you also now have two equations beginning "v=," so you can put them together and deduce that:

$$u + at = \frac{2s}{t} - u,$$

which, after a bit of rearranging, is equivalent to

$$s = ut + \tfrac{1}{2}at^2.$$

This looks a bit more impressive, but it's not really telling you anything new.

Similarly, you could eliminate *u* from each of our original equations, yielding:

$$s = vt - \tfrac{1}{2}at^2.$$

Or eliminate *t* from them both to show that:

$$v^2 = u^2 + 2as.$$

So, to give an example, if a body traveling at 30 m/sec (*u*) accelerates at 2 m/sec/sec (*a*) for 10 sec (*t*), it reaches a velocity (*v*):

$$v = at + u = (2x10) + 30 = 50 \text{ meters per second}$$

$$s = ut + \tfrac{1}{2}at^2 = (30 \times 10) + (\tfrac{1}{2} \times 2 \times 10^2)$$
$$= 300 + 100 = 400 \text{ meters.}$$

Average speed is distance traveled (*s*) divided by *t*, which in this instance is $^{400}/_{10}$ = 40 m/sec. Which sounds reasonable, because it starts at 30 and ends up at 50.

Apparently, this isn't rocket science, unless you have a rate of acceleration equal to the force of gravity, in which case you are into the realm of projectiles and ballistics, which is, um, rocket science.

HISTORY

High-school history books are typically gargantuan tomes of no fewer than 1,500 pages. You probably never covered more than 10 chapters or so, but you still had to lug those monstrous compilations onto the bus each day. Today, with history just a click away, students can quickly locate a specific historical tidbit or surf for hours (or even days) collecting information on major historical events.

With thousands of years to cover, and many choices and opinions regarding the proper texts, this chapter can only scratch the surface. But one thing most people agree upon regarding history is the importance of its study. As writer and philosopher George Santayana stressed so insightfully, "Those who cannot remember the past are condemned to repeat it."

Notable U.S. Presidents

At the time of publication, there have been 44 presidents of the United States. Since there is not enough room to include a compete list, what follows are facts about some of the most notable ones, with their time in office noted following their name. (D = Democrat, R = Republican—parties that came into being around 1828 and 1854, respectively.)

George Washington (1789–97): commander-in-chief of the forces that rebelled against British rule in the 1770s, and president of the Constitutional Convention of 1787, which produced the blueprint of today's Constitution. Unanimously elected first President of the United States two years later. Probably didn't chop down a cherry tree or tell his father that he couldn't tell a lie, but the legend persists.

John Adams (1797–1801): another major figure in the War of Independence, known as the "colossus of the debate" over the Declaration of Independence. Became America's first vice president, then president after Washington's resignation.

Thomas Jefferson (1801–09): credited with drafting the Declaration of Independence and something of a polymath, with an interest in architecture, science, and gardening, to name but a few. Lived for 17 years after ceasing to be president and became a respected elder statesman.

James Madison (1809–17): "the father of the Constitution," having played a major role in the Constitutional Convention of 1787.

James Monroe (1817–25): promulgator of the Monroe Doctrine, which stated that "the European powers could no longer colonize or interfere with the American continents."

John Quincy Adams (1825–29): the son of John Adams. Secretary of State under Monroe, he may actually have written the Monroe Doctrine. Also an antislavery campaigner.

Abraham Lincoln (R, 1861–65): really *was* born in a log cabin. Gained national stature from his stance against slavery. His election to the presidency caused the Southern states to secede from the Union, thus beginning the Civil War. His famous Gettysburg Address—"Four score and seven years ago our fathers brought forth upon this continent a new nation, conceived in Liberty…"—further expressed his antislavery views, as did his campaign for reelection in 1864. He was shot by John Wilkes Booth five days after the surrender of the Confederate general Robert E. Lee, which effectively ended the Civil War.

Ulysses S. Grant (R, 1869–77): the leader of the Union army during the Civil War; presided over the reconstruction of the South.

James Garfield (R, 1881): assassinated by a disgruntled office-seeker after only four months in office.

William McKinley (R, 1897–1901): president during the Spanish-American War that saw the United States acquire Cuba and the Philippines. Assassinated by an anarchist in Buffalo.

Theodore Roosevelt (R, 1901–09): one of four U.S. presidents to be awarded a Nobel Peace Prize (for his role in ending the Russo-Japanese War). Expansionist policies included promoting the growth of the U.S. Navy and the building of the Panama Canal. A great advocate of the United States, entering the First World War.

Woodrow Wilson (D, 1913–21): avoided joining the war for several years, but in the end was forced "to make the world safe for democracy." His Fourteen-Point plan to prevent future wars formed the basis of the League of Nations (the fore-runner of the United Nations).

Warren Harding (R, 1921–23): campaigned on the issue of opposing U.S. membership of the League of Nations during Wilson's tenure; died in office under mysterious circumstances.

Calvin Coolidge (R, 1923–29): notoriously taciturn president whose economic policies were blamed for the 1929 Wall Street crash. Apparently, a woman who sat next to him at a dinner party bet him that she would get at least three words out of him in the course of the evening. "You lose" was the president's reply—and she did; he didn't say another word for the rest of the night.

Franklin D. Roosevelt (D, 1933–45): the longest-serving president in U.S. history. Stricken with polio and confined to a wheelchair throughout his presidency, he came to power at the height of the Great Depression and instituted the New Deal for economic recovery. He was president during most of World War II and died in office three weeks before Germany surrendered. His wife, Eleanor, was a noted diplomat and political adviser.

Harry S Truman (D, 1945–53): Roosevelt's vice president, who succeeded him in the last months of World War II and was responsible for the decision to drop atomic bombs on Nagasaki and Hiroshima. Also popularized the expression "The buck stops here."

Dwight D. Eisenhower (R, 1953–61): Nicknamed Ike, he was the Supreme Commander of the Allied forces during the 1944 Normandy landing. His presidency coincided with the height of the Cold War and the birth of the civil rights movement.

John F. Kennedy (D, 1961–63): the first Catholic to be elected president. He and his glamorous wife, Jackie, changed the image of the presidency. President during the Cuban Missile Crisis, which may be the nearest the world has ever come to nuclear war. Assassinated in Dallas by Lee Harvey Oswald, who was himself shot and killed by Jack Ruby two days later. The conspiracy theorists are still working on it.

Lyndon B. Johnson (D, 1963–69): Known as LBJ, he was Kennedy's vice president. The Civil Rights Act and the Voting Rights Act, which extended the voting rights of African Americans, were passed during his presidency, but Johnson is mostly remembered for his escalation of the Vietnam War and the subsequent protests.

Richard Nixon (R, 1969–74): the only U.S. president to resign under the threat of impeachment, following the scandal known as Watergate: The Democratic Party's headquarters at the Watergate Hotel had been robbed during the 1972 elections, and it became apparent that Nixon knew all about it and the subsequent cover-up. *Washington Post* journalists Bob Woodward and Carl Bernstein led the exposure—the story is told in their book *All the President's Men,* and a film based on the book was made.

Gerald Ford (R, 1974–77): the only president not to have been elected, even as vice president: Nixon appointed him after the elected vice president, Spiro Agnew, resigned over a tax scandal. Ford granted Nixon a presidential pardon for his role in Watergate.

Jimmy Carter (D, 1977–81): the peanut farmer from Georgia who brought social reform at home and was instrumental in arranging a peace treaty between Israel and Egypt. He will be most remembered for the chaos surrounding the taking of U.S. hostages in the American embassy in Iran. Carter won the Nobel Peace Prize in 2002 for his international peacekeeping efforts, work in human rights, and economic development.

Ronald Reagan (R, 1981–89): former Hollywood film star and long-term governor of California before becoming president. Introduced the anti-Russian Strategic Defense Initiative (known as Star Wars) but later reached an arms-reduction agreement with the USSR. Reagan ordered military action in Granada, an island north of Venezuela. His administration is also remembered for the Iran-Contra affair. In 1981 there was an unsuccessful assassination attempt against him that provoked his remark, "Honey, I forgot to duck."

George H. W. Bush (R, 1989–93): a former West Texas oil executive before becoming president, his political posts included director of the Central Intelligence Agency and vice president in Ronald Reagan's administration. He took the world into the first Gulf War and ordered military action in Panama, and was in office when the Berlin Wall fell and the Soviet Union collapsed. His popularity at home declined when he broke a campaign promise to lower taxes. Bush is the father of the forty-third president George W. Bush and Jeb Bush, former governor of Florida.

Bill Clinton (D, 1993–2001): young, charismatic, Clinton spent a lot of time in the headlines because of his alleged affair with a White House intern. Married to Hillary, who ran, unsuccessfully, for the 2008 democratic presidential nomination.

George W. Bush (R, 2001–2009): a former partner of the Texas Rangers baseball team and governor of Texas, Bush was elected president in 2000, receiving a majority of the electoral votes, but narrowly losing the popular vote. In his first term he enacted "No Child Left Behind," a measure later signed into law that aimed to close the gap between rich and poor student performance. After the September 11, 2001 attacks on the United States, he initiated a global war on terrorism and launched attacks on Afghanistan and Iraq.

Canadian Prime Ministers

Prime Minister Pierre Trudeau once said: "Living next to the Americans is like sleeping next to an elephant—no matter how friendly and even-tempered the elephant, one is affected by every twitch!" It takes a certain kind of character to cope with such sleeping arrangements, as well as the challenges that come with running the second largest (in area) country in the world. Here are the top politicians that Canadians voted in and out.

Sir John A. Macdonald (1867–73; 1878–91): a Scottish-born lawyer with a soft spot for hard drink, he shepherded the country from being a rump of four tiny provinces into a vast nation linked from sea to sea by a brand-new transcontinental railway. A champion of Canadian autonomy within the British Empire as well as the status of the French in public institutions, the Conservative PM is also remembered for the binge drinking that dogged him during his time in office.

Alexander Mackenzie (1873–78): emigrated from his native Scotland at age 20 in pursuit of the girl he loved. As the country's first Liberal head of government, Mackenzie established the Supreme Court and founded the Royal Military College. A staunch democrat proud of his working-class roots, the former stonemason turned down an offer of knighthood three times.

Sir John Abbott (1891–92) son of an Anglican priest and two-term mayor of Montreal. The Conservative also happened to be the great-grandfather of Hollywood actor Christopher Plummer.

John Thompson (1892–94): Conservative PM who suffered a stroke and promptly died during a visit to Windsor Castle. Queen Victoria was not amused.

Mackenzie Bowell (1894-96): forced to resign by his own cabinet ministers, this prominent Orangeman lived long and prospered, dying in his 95th year.

Sir Charles Tupper (1896): Conservative who served the shortest period in office of any prime minister: 69 days. On the other hand, his marriage to wife Frances Morse lasted the longest: 66 years.

Sir Wilfrid Laurier (1896–1911): once decreed: "The nineteenth century was the century of the United States. I think we can claim that Canada will fill the twentieth century." During the Liberal's 15 years as head of government, Laurier witnessed an era of unprecedented immigration, infrastructure expansion, and the creation of two new western provinces.

Robert Borden (1911–20): last prime minister to be born before Confederation, whose bold commitment to the war effort precipitated the Conscription Crisis. This cost the Conservative the support of many French-speaking Canadians. His face adorns the Canadian $100 bill.

Arthur Meighen (1920–21; 1926): the Ontario-born prime minister. The son of a farmer, he studied mathematics and physics at the University of Toronto. The Conservative was instrumental in creating the Canadian National Railways system.

Mackenzie King (1921–26; 1926–30; 1935–48): grandson of William Lyon Mackenzie, leader of the 1837 Rebellion in Upper Canada. As Canada's longest-serving prime minister, this Liberal led the country for 22 years. King was a bachelor who had a penchant for holding séances and talking to his dog. But he was also a capable politician and statesman. He steered the country through much of the Depression as well as World War II. A social reformer, his government brought in unemployment insurance and family allowances.

Richard Bennett (1930–35): elected on the eve of the Great Depression, he was Canada's only prime minister to be buried abroad. It took the Conservative several years to implement radical economic reforms, but by then it was too late for his government. After his defeat he moved to England, where he died.

Louis St. Laurent (1948–57): dubbed Uncle Louis for his folksy and avuncular campaigning style, he staked Canada's global role as an important middle power. His Liberal administration got the ball rolling on the Trans-Canada Highway and St. Lawrence Seaway, welcomed Newfoundland into Confederation, and oversaw Canadian participation in the Korean War.

John Diefenbaker (1957–63): set out to make Canadian citizenship more inclusive to people of diverse origins, with an emphasis on aboriginal peoples. The Progressive Conservative appointed the first female federal cabinet minister, Ellen Fairclough, and was an outspoken opponent of apartheid in South Africa. But economic and fiscal woes, as well as his decision to scrap the Avro Arrow jet project, led to his government's demise.

Lester Pearson (1963–68): considered to be the "inventor" of U.N. peacekeeping, for which he won the 1957 Nobel Peace Prize, his Liberal government initiated federal bilingualism, established a national pension plan, signed the Auto Pact with the United States, introduced universal Medicare, and unveiled a new national flag. A well-rounded athlete, Pearson played semipro baseball in Ontario and hockey while studying at Oxford.

Pierre Elliott Trudeau (1968–79; 1980–84): not only a swinging playboy, but also a no-nonsense gunslinger. When rioters hurled objects at him during a 1968 ceremony, he refused to withdraw to safety. When separatist terrorists took hostages in Quebec, he sent in the army. He stuck it to the Alberta oil barons during the energy crisis of the 1970s. He made mincemeat of his main opponent during the 1980 referendum on Quebec sovereignty. A Liberal, he brought in official bilingualism, the metric system, and—in his proudest moment—repatriated the Constitution, to which he added the Charter of Rights and Freedoms. Fidel Castro, his good friend, was among the pallbearers at his funeral.

Joe Clark (1979–80): dismissed as "Joe Who?" during his early years on the national stage, this Progressive Conservative politician astounded the pundits when he was elected Canada's youngest-ever prime minister at age 39.

John Turner (1984): dashing, dapper, and athletic, he inherited the prime minister's job after Pierre Trudeau retired. The Liberal is remembered for his tooth-and-nails crusade against the proposed free-trade deal with the United States.

Brian Mulroney (1984–93): won the largest majority government in Canadian history in 1994. The Progressive Conservative soon came under fire for his cozy friendship with U.S. president Bush, a revolving door of scandals, and ill-advised tinkering with the Constitution. Nevertheless, his administration hammered out the 1988 Free Trade Agreement with the United States and the 1992 North American Free Trade Agreement.

Kim Campbell (1993): Canada's first female prime minister, who voters never actually gave a mandate to rule. Instead, she briefly inherited the reigns of power, only to go down to a prompt and decisive defeat.

Jean Chrétien (1993–2003): eighteenth child of a paper-mill worker, he was a seasoned veteran of Liberal cabinets dating back to the 1960s. A brilliant, if rustic, campaigner, his long experience and political instincts won him three consecutive majority governments.

Paul Martin (2003–6): as a Liberal three-time finance minister, he has been credited with getting Canada's fiscal health into shape. The scion of a wealthy shipping family, he faced the electorate, but once as prime minister won a short-lived minority mandate.

Stephen Harper (2006–present): the current prime minister, he represents a Conservative party that removed the word Progressive from its official name. An influential back-room player whose survival skills brought him to the fore, Harper has consolidated power in the prime minister's office as rarely seen before.

Notable Kings and Queens of England

House	Name	Known for
Normandy	William I (1066–87)	Won Battle of Hastings, created the feudal system.
Plantagenet	Henry II (1154–89)	Son of Matilda, the one who conflicted with Thomas à Becket.
	Richard I (1189–99)	The Lionheart, fought the Crusades. Depicted as good king in Robin Hood stories.
	John (1199–1216)	Richard's brother, the wicked Prince John in Robin Hood. Forced to sign Magna Carta.
	Edward I (1272–1307)	Conquered most of Wales, built many castles, son was titled Prince of Wales. Died fighting the Scottish.
Lancaster	Henry IV (1399–1413)	Richard's cousin Henry Boling-broke. Battled Welsh prince Owen Glendower and Henry Percy of Northumberland.
	Henry V (1413–22)	Shakespeare's Prince Hal, has merry dealings with Falstaff but grows up to win the battle of Agincourt.
York	Edward IV (1461–83, briefly deposed 1470–71)	Great-great grandson of Edward III; brought back with help of cousin Richard Neville, who later betrayed him.
	Richard III (1483-85)	Uncle of Ed V; depicted by Shakespeare and others as wicked hunchback/mass murderer. Defeated at battle of Bosworth.
Tudor	Henry VII (1485–1509)	Defeated Richard III, taking the throne more by force than by lineage, effectively ending the War of the Roses.
	Henry VIII (1509–47)	Six wives: Catherine, Anne, Jane, Anne, Catherine, Catherine; often remembered as divorced, beheaded, died, divorced, beheaded, survived.

House	Name	Known for
Tudor (continued)	Mary I (1553–58)	Older sister of Edward VI, daughter of Catherine of Aragon. Overthrew Lady Jane Grey and had her beheaded.
	Elizabeth I (1558–1603)	Mary's sister, daughter of Anne Boleyn. Defeated the Spanish Armada. Beheaded Mary Queen of Scots, but since Liz had no heir, Mary's son became king.
Stuart	James I (1603–25)	Already James VI of Scotland, Mary's son. Oversaw the translation of the Bible.
	Charles I (1625–49)	Believed in the Divine Right of Kings. Did whatever he wanted and was beheaded as a result.
Stuarts, Restored	Charles II (1660–85)	The Merry Monarch, reintroduced theater. Ruled during the Great Plague and the Great Fire of London.
	Anne (1702–14)	First sovereign under a unified England and Scotland. Died without living children. Throne went to the Hanoverians.
Hanover	George I (1714–27)	Never really mastered English, lived in Hanover most of his life.
	George III (1760–1820)	The mad one who lost the American colonies after the Revolutionary War.
Saxe-Coburg-Gotha	Victoria (1837–1901)	Longest-reigning monarch. Her children married diplomatically; most royal houses of Europe are, in some way, descended from her.
Windsor	George V (1910–36)	King during WWI, the General Strike and Great Depression. Valuable political advisor.
	George VI (1936–52)	Brother of edward VIII. Ruled during WWII, wife Elizabeth known as Queen Mother.
	Elizabeth II (1952–)	The present queen. Mother of Prince Charles; former mother-in-law to Lady Di.

Major World Conflicts

Times may change, but the issues that incite wars among people around the world remain the same: Power, territory, religion, and resources are usually at the heart of the matter.

☞ 1066: BATTLE OF HASTINGS

The year 1066 was a busy one. King Edward the Confessor died on January 5, leaving four claimants to the throne. The legitimate heir, Edward's son Edgar, was a child and no one took much notice of him. Military expediency preferred the successful Saxon general Harold Godwin, but there was also the Norwegian king, Harald Hardrada, who invaded northern England and, on September 25, was defeated by Harold at Stamford Bridge, near York. Three days later an army led by William of Normandy (to whom Harold Godwin may or may not have promised allegiance in a visit to Normandy the previous year) landed at Pevensey in Sussex, some 249 miles (400 km) away. Harold marched to meet him, and the battle now known as Hastings took place on October 14. Harold was killed (tradition has it by an arrow in his eye), and on Christmas Day, William the Conqueror was crowned King William I.

☞ 1337–1453: HUNDRED YEARS WAR

A war between England and France. Primarily a dispute over territory because parts of France, notably the prosperous wine-growing areas of Gascony and Aquitaine, had come into English possession through a succession of strategic marriages. The battles include: Crécy (1346), at which Edward III's son, the Black Prince, "won his spurs;" Poitiers (1356), when the French king, John II, was captured and held for ransom; and Harfleur and Agincourt (both 1415), when English archers won the day. After Henry V's early death in 1422, a French resurgence inspired by Joan of Arc gradually pushed the English back, until in 1453 the French won a decisive victory at Castillon and reclaimed all of the southwest part of the country. Only Calais remained in English possession.

☞ 1455–85: WARS OF THE ROSES

A series of civil wars between the English royal houses of York and Lancaster. In a nutshell, Edward III had far too many descendants who thought they ought to be in charge. Key battles were, Wakefield (1460), in which Richard, Duke of York, leader of the opposition to the Lancastrian Henry VI, was killed; and Tewkesbury (1471), a Yorkist victory, shortly after which Henry VI died—probably murdered—in the Tower of London. Rivalry between the in-laws of the new (Yorkist) king, Edward IV, the numerous and opportunistic Woodvilles, and other members of the aristocracy ensured that conflict continued. It culminated in the Battle of Bosworth (1485), when Henry Tudor, a Lancastrian descended from an illegitimate son of Edward III's son, John of Gaunt, defeated and killed the Yorkist Richard III and became Henry VII.

☞ 1622-1917: THE AMERICAN INDIAN WARS

In the past, American history books have conveniently skimmed over or skipped the Indian wars altogether. A few early proprietors, such as William Penn, formed alliances with the Native American people, even learning to speak their language, but a large number of the early settlers encroached upon Indian territory, defied treaties, monopolized game, and practiced outright slaughter of the Native Americans. In some cases the Native Americans attacked first, but most often they felt threatened. The Pequot War of 1637, one of the earliest skirmishes, essentially eliminated the power of the Pequot tribe in present-day New England; most were killed, others were sold into slavery. The Indian wars were eventually fought in other parts of the East, the Great Plains, the Southwest, and in California. Some of the wars include Tecumseh (the Creek War), the Texas-Indian Wars, the Battle of Little Big Horn (Custer's Last Stand), the Wounded Knee Massacre, the Navajo and Apache conflicts, the California Indian wars, and many more. Native Americans were killed, relocated, or escaped to Canada. The 10th Cavalry Regiment, an African-American unit that the Native Americans termed Buffalo Soldiers, fought one of the last battles in 1917.

☞ 1759: THE BATTLE OF THE PLAINS OF ABRAHAM

A significant turning point in North American history, the British rout over French forces at the Battle of the Plains of Abraham near Quebec City on September 13 was an important milestone for the ascendant British Empire. This battle by land and sea that cost the lives of the commanding generals on both sides all but eradicated France's colonial role in the New World. It also helped set the stage for the American War of Independence less than two decades later.

☞ 1775–83: AMERICAN WAR OF INDEPENDENCE, OR THE REVOLUTIONARY WAR

The clue is in the title, really. The thirteen British colonies in North America revolted against British rule, specifically against taxation without representation. The Boston Tea Party (1773) was an act of direct action, which helped spark the American Revolution. Late on the night of April 18, 1775, a silversmith named Paul Revere recieved word that the British posed an imminent threat, which Longfellow preserved in the infamous poem *Paul Revere's Ride* ("Listen my children and you shall hear…"). Early battles at Lexington and Concord (the shot heard 'round the world) were followed by the Battle of Bunker Hill, which was really fought on Breed's Hill. The Declaration of Independence was signed in 1776, and battles followed across what are now the northeastern United States and eastern Canada. George Washington, the American commander-in-chief, led troops across the Delaware River to mount an attack upon the British and Hessian troops. This success at the Battle of Trenton (1776) marked the turning point of the war. France, Spain, and Holland all sided with the Americans—the Dutch gained control of the English Channel and threatened to invade Britain. Britain finally acknowledged American independence by the Treaty of Paris (1783).

☞ 1789: FRENCH REVOLUTION

The French finally had enough of the Bourbon kings and overthrew them, storming the state prison, the Bastille, on July 14, mobbing the palace of Versailles and eventually beheading King Louis XVI and his queen, Marie Antoinette. The revolutionaries proclaimed a republic, but the moderate

Girondins were ousted by the more extreme Jacobins. Power passed to the hands of the Committee of Public Safety (one of those names that you can just tell is going to lead to trouble). Georges Danton, initially one of the most important members of the committee, was superceded by a lawyer named Maximilien Robespierre, and the ensuing Reign of Terror saw the execution of thousands of alleged antirevolutionaries. Perhaps inevitably, Danton and Robespierre both also ended up on the guillotine.

☞ 1792–1815: NAPOLEONIC WARS

Napoleon Bonaparte rose to prominence in the aftermath of the French Revolution, and was in charge of the French army fighting the Austrians in Italy by 1796. Next he decided to break down the British Empire by conquering Egypt. Defeated by the British admiral Horatio Nelson at the Battle of the Nile (1799), he returned to France, overthrew the Executive Directory (the post-revolutionary government), became consul and then emperor in 1804—and he was 35 years old. The following year, he was again defeated by Nelson (at Trafalgar, where Nelson was killed) but did better on land, winning victories at Austerlitz, Jena–Averstedt, and Friedland and more or less conquering continental Europe. The British Duke of Wellington, Arthur Wellesley, defeated him in the Iberian Peninsula—a subsection of the Napoleonic wars known as the Peninsular War (1808–14), in the course of which Napoleon also found time to march on Moscow, losing about 400,000 of his 500,000-strong army in the harsh Russian winter. He was defeated again at Leipzig in 1813, forced to abdicate, and exiled to Elba, an island off the coast of Italy. He escaped, resumed power for the

"Hundred Days," and was finally defeated in 1815 at the battle of Waterloo, and exiled again, this time to the remote South Atlantic island of St. Helena, where he died in 1821.

☞ 1812–15: THE WAR OF 1812

Contrary to its name, this war lasted almost three years. The British were invading American ships and putting its sailors into servitude. And a British sea blockade on France during the Napoleonic Wars made trade difficult (although New England opposed the war and was trading with Britain and Canada). The British also didn't appreciate that forces within the United States were moving into the Northwest Territories and the Canadian border. However, British and Mohawk forces stood ready for a U.S. advance and many American soldiers were taken prisoner at the Battle of Beaver Dams. This war ended with the conclusion of the Napoleonic War when the British fleet pulled out of its blockade, and the Treaty of Ghent took effect in 1815. Since, technically, the United States was not defeated (although it took a beating), the war was considered a stalemate, with both sides going back to their corners and calling it a day. The United States considered the war a confirmation of its independence because they stuck together, once again, and fought bravely.

☞ 1846–48: THE MEXICAN-AMERICAN WAR

The bankrupt Mexican government had a loose hold on Texas and its northern and western provinces (the West) after it won its own independence from Spain. American settlers in the Texas region, such as a group led by Colonel Davy Crockett, fought a war of independence from Mexican forces in the area (remember the Alamo?). With many losses the Texas settlers eventually won this war and proclaimed annexation from Mexico in 1845, but Mexico did not recognize this secession. The Texans and Western states obtained support from the U.S. government. Although many Whigs in the United States opposed the war, many southern Democrats, who wished to gain territory and expand slavery, held the belief of Manifest Destiny, proclaiming that the United States was somehow divinely destined to expand from the Atlantic seaboard to the Pacific Ocean. Mexico and the United States disagreed regarding borders, and after more skirmishes and battles the United States declared war on Mexico in May 1846. Author Henry David Thoreau refused to pay his taxes as a protest to the war and was put in jail for a night as a result—an incident that inspired him to write an essay that was later dubbed "Civil Disobedience," which stated that individuals should not allow the government to sway or overrule their own sense of conscience, especially in true matters of injustice. Ultimately, the United States won the war and signed the Treaty of Guadalupe Hidalgo, which required Mexico to secede not only Texas but also parts of Colorado, Arizona, New Mexico, and Wyoming as well as all of California, Nevada, and Utah in return for $15 million.

☞ 1861–65: AMERICAN CIVIL WAR

Eleven breakaway Confederate states objected to the antislavery sentiments of the North. These sentiments (and eventual policies) had their roots in the Abolitionist Movement, which was spearheaded by Northern Transcendentalists such as

Ralph Waldo Emerson, Henry David Thoreau, and Louisa May Alcott, and in large part by Harriet Beecher Stowe's novel, *Uncle Tom's Cabin*.

The Southern plantations had become well off from the extremely profitable combination of slavery and the Cotton Gin (Eli Whitney's then recent invention). This fact, combined with Southern fears regarding the North's control of the banking system, would lead to the idea of states' rights, from which was born the Confederacy of the Southern states.

A few decades earlier, a geographic border divided the North from South, and it became known as the Mason-Dixon Line. The Confederate secession was led by Jefferson Davis, and the war began with a Confederate attack on Fort Sumter, South Carolina (the first state to secede from the Union). Later key encounters included the Confederate victory at Bull Run, Confederate General Stonewall Jackson's campaign in Shenandoah, and the Union victories in the Seven Days' Battle and at Gettysburg (where Lincoln delivered the famous Gettysburg Address).

The Battle of Gettysburg lasted for three days and is still considered the largest battle in the history of the Western Hemisphere. The casualties of the war were horrific, with as many as 23,000 dead and wounded at the Battle of Antietam alone, which to this day remains the single bloodiest day in American history. After this battle, President Lincoln announced the Emancipation Proclamation, which freed "all people." After Union general William T. Sherman's brutal march through the South in 1864 and the capture of Atlanta and Savannah, much of the South would soon be in Union control. Within months Confederate general Robert E. Lee (who commanded the feared army of Northern Virginia), would surrender to future president Ulysses S. Grant at Appomattox Court House. Following the Union victory and the assassination of Abraham Lincoln, there was a painful reconstruction period in the South, where some cities, such as Vicksburg, would not celebrate the Fourth of July until 1938.

☞ 1880–81 and 1899–1902: BOER WARS

These were revolutionary wars fought by the Afrikaners (Boers, descended from Dutch settlers) of South Africa against British rule. The first, in which the Boers were led by Paul Kruger, gained a degree of independence for Transvaal, which became known as the South African Republic. The second involved lengthy Boer sieges of Ladysmith and Mafeking. Lord Horatio Kitchener was one of the leaders of the British forces; Robert Baden-Powell, who went on to found the Boy Scouts, distinguished himself in the siege of Mafeking. British public and political opinion was polarized by the second Boer War, and it led to a lot of rising and falling of governments.

☞ 1914–18: WORLD WAR I

The principal players were an alliance of Britain, France, Russia, and others (the Allied Powers, united by the Entente Cordiale and later the Triple Entente), against Germany, Austro-Hungary, and Turkey (the Central Powers); the United States joined in 1917. The complicated causes included the Allies' fear of German expansion in Europe and various colonies, particularly in Africa; and a conflict of interest between Russia and Austro-Hungary in the Balkans.

Although war was looming for years, it was sparked by the assassination of the Archduke Franz Ferdinand, heir to the Austro-Hungarian throne, by a Serb nationalist, Gabriel Princip. Austro-Hungary declared war on Serbia, Russia backed the Serbs, and you can guess the rest. Much of "The Great War" took place on what is known as the Western Front in the trenches of northeastern France and Belgium after Germany's thwarted attempt to invade France and take over Paris. It is most notable for the horrific loss of life: over a million men in the Battle of the Somme alone, with Ypres and Passchendaele not much better. On the Eastern Front the Gallipoli Campaign in Turkey killed many Australians and New Zealanders. The Central powers not only suffered great loss of life but were losing resources and support on the homefront, which led them to agree to the armistice treaty and subsequently the Treaty of Versailles, which ended the fighting.

Some of the provisions of the treaty required Germany and its allies take full responsibility for the war, pay reparations, and essentially redraw the map of Europe. Austria-Hungary was sliced into Austria, Hungary, Czechoslavakia, and Yugoslavia. The Ottoman Empire was distributed among the Allied Powers (with the Turkish core remaining as the Republic of Turkey). The western frontier of the Russian Empire became Estonia, Finland, Latvia, Lithuania, and Poland. As a result of the treaty, the League of Nations (later replaced by the United Nations) was founded to help countries settle disputes through negotiation, diplomacy, and the global improvement of the quality of life.

☞ 1917: RUSSIAN REVOLUTION

Actually two revolutions—one in February and one in October of the same year. The first, sparked by a shortage of food, led to the abdication of the Romanov czar Nicholas II; the second involved the Bolsheviks (led by Vladimir Lenin and Trotsky) seizing power, executing most of the royal family, and establishing the first communist state. A civil war between the "Red" Bolsheviks and the anticommunist "White" Russians lasted until 1921. After Lenin died in 1924, Trotsky lost a power struggle with Stalin, went into exile in Mexico, and was murdered there.

☞ 1939–45: WORLD WAR II

Hitler rose to power in Germany in the early 1930s and proceeded to take over various parts of Europe. Britain and France had promised to protect Polish neutrality, so they were forced to declare war when Germany invaded Poland. The Berlin, Rome, Tokyo pact bound Germany, Italy, and Japan together, known as the Axis powers.

Hitler's invasion of France led to the evacuation of hundreds of thousands of Allied forces, many of them in small boats, from Dunkirk, in 1940; Britain now faced the threat of invasion and months of bombing (the Blitz). The war in the air that followed (1940–41) is known as the Battle of Britain. The previously neutral United States began selling arms and goods to Great Britain, provided it sent its own ships to U.S. ports for "cash and carry."

In 1940 the United States implemented a series of embargoes against Japan, and in September of that same year, the United

States agreed to swap American destroyers for British bases. In December 1941 the Japanese bombed the Hawaiian naval base at Pearl Harbor, bringing the United States into the war and opening up a whole new theater of conflict in the Pacific.

Exactly six months after Pearl Harbor, the U.S. Navy defeated a Japanese attack of the Midway Islands, sinking four Japanese carriers and a warship. This defense severely weakened Japanese Naval power, turning the tide in the United State's favor. The Battle of the Japanese island, Iwo Jima, constituted another hard-fought victory for the Allied forces and was a stepping-stone toward the Japanese heartland. The Japanese had built an elaborate bunker and tunnel system on the island through Mount Suribachi. Allied forces used flamethrowers and grenades to clear them out. Eventually the Japanese ran out of water, food, and supplies. Most of the 21,000 Japanese soldiers fought to their deaths, and one in four U.S. soldiers died during the attack—over 26,500. One of the most reproduced photographs in history is the flag raising by U.S. soldiers on the top of the mountain, which was converted into a statue at Arlington Cemetery and a war memorial in Harlingen, Texas. Three of the six flag raisers would die soon after the photograph was taken.

After Iwo Jima, another major win for the Allied forces—the Battle of Okinawa—took more lives than the atomic bombs later dropped on Hiroshima and Nagasaki. Kamikazes, or suicide aviation bombers, sunk almost 34 Allied ships and crafts of all kind, damaging 368; the fleet lost 763 aircraft. The cost of this battle in lives, time, and material weighed heavily on the decision to drop the atomic bombs six weeks later, which forced the Japanese to surrender.

Far away, Germany made the mistake of attacking western Russia in July of 1942. The Russians held out in Stalingrad and launched a counteroffensive in the bloodiest battle in human history, with combined casualties of over 1.5 million. The Nazis were held up in the winter on their way to Moscow, some freezing to death. The Germans were ill-equipped and ill-prepared for winter conflict. Stalingrad continued until February 1943, when the last German forces surrendered. This paved the way for the Normandy (D-Day) landings in June 1944, the turning point for Germany, which surrendered in May 1945.

The Holocaust. Prior to and during the war, the German country became involved in state-supported genocide of Jewish people (the Holocaust or Shoah). Many German nationalists held deep-seated resentment, hatred, and prejudice against the Jewish people. Before World War II the Depression hit Germany hard, especially because of reparations required after World War I. Germans blamed communists for WW I, calling it a Judeo-Bolshevist conspiracy and even went so far as to blame Jewish Bankers for the Treaty of Versailles. Many Germans resented Jewish successes and felt that the Jewish people were taking German jobs. Hitler believed in supremacy of the German/Aryan race and considered Jewish, Polish, gay, Gypsies, Slavs, Russian, and mentally challenged people as subhuman. Hitler preached hatred, and the ignorant masses followed, looking for a scapegoat for their desperate situation. Some believed the propaganda that the Jews were being jailed for their "crimes," whereas others simply went along in fear of the Nazis as they essentially brutally beat up or killed anyone who opposed their power.

☞ 1950–53: THE KOREAN WAR

After WWII Korea was divided into the communist Northern half and the American-occupied South, with the dividing line at the 38th parallel. This war began when the North Korean communist army, armed with Soviet tanks, invaded South Korea. Although the territory was not strategically important to the United States, a deep-seated fear of communism led to the country's involvement in what was termed a police action, so Congress did not need to make an official declaration of war. General Douglas MacArthur and his U.S. and U.N. troops orchestrated an invasion of Inchon and then recaptured Seoul, passing the 38th parallel to the Northern side, which prompted China to send in troops to protect its interests in Manchuria. MacArthur continued to push northward until he was relieved of his duties by President Truman, a politically unpopular move since MacArthur was a WWII war hero. Both sides tried to negotiate a peace treaty but disagreed over many of the provisions, so fighting continued. In 1953 at Panmunjom, a treaty was signed that brought about a cease-fire and returned the divided line to its prewar coordinates. The war would later inspire the novel and subsequent film and television series *M*A*S*H,* about the doctors and support staff stationed at the 4077th Mobile Army Surgical Hospital, which was located near Ouijongbu during the war.

☞ THE COLD WAR

Difficult to date because it wasn't really a war, but a period of intense mutual distrust between former World War II Allies—the United States, U.K., and France on the one hand and the

USSR on the other—at its height during the 1950s. Winston Churchill coined the term "iron curtain" for the ideological and political barrier that separated east from west. Tensions began to diminish during the 1970s and 1980s, especially with the introduction by Mikhail Gorbachev of the policies of *glasnost* (openness) and *perestroika* (reconstruction—specifically of the economy), which led to the breakup of the USSR.

☞ 1959–75: THE VIETNAM WAR

Much of the fighting occurred between 1964 and 1975 in South Vietnam and bordering areas of Cambodia and Laos. Several bombing runs over North Vietnam also occurred.

The United States, Australia, New Zealand, and South Korea all joined forces with the Republic of Vietnam to fight the North, with its communist-led South Vietnamese guerrilla movement and the National Liberation Front backed by USSR-supplied weaponry.

The seeds of the Vietnam War were planted during the First Indochinese War, when the communists, under Ho Chi Minh, fought the French for independence. After a socialist state was established in the North, mass killings of "class enemies" followed. Eventually, a U.S.-backed government in the South launched its own anticommunist campaign. However, the South's autocratic and nepotistic president, Ngo Dinh Diem, had trouble with insurgencies. The CIA apparently alerted generals in the South that the United States would support a coup, and Diem was eventually assassinated. This caused chaos in the South, and the Viet Cong gained ground.

At this point U.S. president John F. Kennedy increased U.S. forces in the area to help train troops. Three weeks after Diem's death, Kennedy was also assassinated. The Vietnamese War was fraught with controversy; some Americans strongly feared a communist scourge, whereas others did not feel that the United States should police the world, toppling regimes out of fear, causing even more unrest. President Nixon ordered a suspension of the action in 1973 and soon afterward signed the Paris Peace Accords, which ended U.S. involvement in the conflict. After that, the North ignored the cease-fire agreement, invaded the South, taking Saigon (being renamed Ho Chi Minh City), and forming the Socialist Republic of Vietnam. Many supporters of the South were jailed or executed.

☞ 1991: THE GULF WAR

The Gulf War involved the high-tech conflict between Kuwait and U.N.-led forces against Iraq in order to remove Iraq forces that overran Kuwait in a surprise assault. The Iraqis had several claims for the attack, including that the Kuwaitis were stealing their oil through slant drilling on the border, and that Kuwait had been part of the Ottoman Empire's province of Basra. This war was largely fought from the air and from tanks, with U.N. forces grossly outnumbering the Iraqi forces. U.N. forces liberated Kuwait and attacked southern Iraq. The troops pulled out after Iraq agreed to a U.N. resolution requiring the Middle Eastern country to destroy major weapons, not develop new ones, and cease its support of terrorists groups.

☞ **2003–PRESENT: THE IRAQ WAR**

The U.S. sought to remove the corrupt Iraqi government and military establishment from power. The American government claimed that the Iraqis were hiding weapons of mass destruction. And it also hoped to protect and secure U.S. interests in the Middle East, which many people believe to be oil. Many U.N. allies opposed the war, especially the Arab countries, but an abbreviated coalition was sent into Iraq nonetheless, toppling the Saddam Hussein regime. Through the years, a long and continued war in Iraq has lost popularity with most U.S. citizens, but the plan to exit the country was not as well executed as the plan to enter, and many fear the inevitable civil unrest that may ensue upon U.S. departure. Others fear that pouring manpower and trillions of dollars into a war that could last for many years could have futile and catastrophic consequences to a nation that needs to concentrate its money and human resources into conservation and clean and renewable energy.

African American History

Another scantly covered period in American history involves the mass atrocities committed against Africans; they were kidnapped, captured, and sold into slavery. Revolts ensued but were quashed. African Americans persisted and held strong against their persecutors, eventually gaining freedom after the Civil War and affecting major positive changes in the United States and Canada. This small section cannot do justice to the major obstacles that were overcome and the progressive advances made by the African American community. Slavery was finally abolished in 1865 by the 13th Amendment of the

Constitution, and less than 150 years later Barack Obama, of half-Kenyan ancestry, announced his candidacy for president of the United States.

☞ SLAVERY

In 1619 a Dutch trader exchanged Africans for food in the marketplace of Jamestown, Virginia. By the 1660s a race-based slave system became popular with tobacco planters in the American South, who at the time also enslaved Native Americans; slavery soon spread among the colonies. Slaves were not treated as people but as property; they were mistreated, punished harshly, and killed. In the 1700s England's abolitionists, and later the Quakers, within the colonies sought to petition government against slavery. The American abolitionist movement began to gain ground. In 1793 Eli Whitney patented his invention, the cotton gin, increasing demand and production of U.S.-grown cotton. Although this proved positive for the economy, it caused a resurge in slavery trade, especially in the cotton-growing South, since farmers needed more workers to glean the cotton. In the North small progress was being made, and in 1830 the first National Negro Convention was held in Philadelphia, where one point of discussion involved emigration to Canada.

☞ THE UNDERGROUND RAILROAD

The date marking the start of this movement remains unknown. During the 19th century Canada played a key role in the battle to abolish slavery, with at least 30,000 slaves escaping by secret routes to flee enslavement in the American South.

This political movement crossed the racial and geographic borders and exemplified Thoreau's concept of civil disobedience, which also planted the seeds for the women's suffrage movement. In 1790, Philadelphia became Underground-Railroad Central for the Northern states, since it contained a large number of emancipated black individuals and Quakers. In fact, Harriet Tubman originally escaped to Philadelphia before conducting 13 missions for the Underground Railroad to free slaves; she would later serve as a Union spy in the Civil War, and then struggled for the women's suffrage.

As a youngster, a man named John Brown traveled northeastern Ohio guiding fugitives and vowed to dedicate his life to the freedom of slaves. In 1847 he laid out his plans to raid slave plantations and route the freed people through the Appalachian Mountains to a safe haven near Lake Placid, New York. Brown would free slaves by any means necessary. He met violence with more violence, meeting his own brutal fate during an unsuccessful raid at Harper's Ferry in 1859.

A year later the Southern States seceded from the Union, followed by the American Civil War, where emancipated blacks fought bravely in the Union Army for their own freedom.

Other Important Historical Dates

This small section just didn't fit anywhere else, but most of us will remember at least something about these notable events:

☞ 1215: MAGNA CARTA, OR THE GREAT CHARTER
Signed by King John at Runnymede, this was the first successful attempt to control the power of the English monarchy.

☞ 1453: FALL OF CONSTANTINOPLE

You might not think it was a big deal (after all, cities were falling all over the place all of the time), but this was when the Muslim Ottoman Empire took over the Byzantine, or Christian, capital of the Eastern Roman Empire, and all those scholarly monks fled into Western Europe, taking their books with them. In other words, it marked the start of the Renaissance—which, in its narrowest sense, means a rebirth in interest in classic literature, art, and architecture.

☞ 1605: GUNPOWDER PLOT

A failed attempt by a group of provincial English Catholics to blow up the Protestant king, James I, and the Houses of Parliament. Somebody let it be known, and Guy Fawkes was caught in the cellars under the Palace of Westminster with a load of gunpowder.

☞ 1620: PILGRIM FATHERS

A group of Puritans, persecuted in England because of their religion, set sail from Southampton in the *Mayflower* and in due course established a colony in Plymouth, Massachusetts.

☞ EARLY 18TH CENTURY ONWARD: AGRICULTURAL REVOLUTION

Larger, enclosed fields, inventions such as Jethro Tull's planting drill, and the concept of crop rotation pioneered by Viscount "Turnip" Townshend improved agricultural methods and increased food yield, which made it possible to feed the increasing numbers of people not working on the land following the Industrial Revolution.

☞ 1750 ONWARD: INDUSTRIAL REVOLUTION

The invention of Arkwright's water-powered spinning frame, Hargreaves's spinning jenny, and Crompton's mule revolutionized the production of yarn and therefore cloth, leading to the development of factories and mass production.

Explorers

Since this chapter has been talking about fighting over many regions of the world, here is a quick rundown of people who discovered some of them.

Eric the Red and **Leif Eriksson** (late 10th–11th century, Norwegian): father and son. Eric, brought up in Iceland, was the first European to settle in Greenland; Leif, blown (a long way) off course on his way from Iceland to Greenland, became the first European to reach America. He landed at a place he called Vinland, which may have been modern-day Newfoundland or Nova Scotia.

Bartolomeu Dias (*c.* 1450–*c.* 1500, Portuguese): trade routes to India were the big thing after the Turks blocked off the land route. Dias made an attempt at doing it by sea, being the first to round the Cape of Good Hope at the bottom of Africa. But he named it the Cape of Storms, which may suggest why his crew made him turn back before they got farther than Mozambique.

Christopher Columbus (1451–1506, Italian): born in Genoa but had his voyages sponsored by Ferdinand and Isabella of Spain. The idea was to reach the East (that is, Asia) by sailing west, thus proving beyond all doubt that the Earth was round. Of course, America got in the way. Columbus never actually reached mainland North America, but he did discover the Bahamas, Hispaniola, Guadeloupe, Jamaica, and Puerto Rico, among others. His ships were the *Niña,* the *Pinta,* and the *Santa Maria.*

Amerigo Vespucci (1454–1512, Italian): discovered the mouth of the Amazon and the River Plate, which made him important enough to have a continent or two named after him.

Vasco da Gama (*c.* 1469–1525, Portuguese): persisted where Dias had failed and made it to Calicut in India.

Francisco Pizarro (*c.* 1478–1541, Spanish): the conqueror (or *conquistador*) of Peru and destroyer of the Incan Empire.

Ferdinand Magellan (*c.* 1480–1521, Portuguese): leader of the first expedition to sail around the world, although he was murdered in the East Indies. Like Columbus, he was trying to reach the East by sailing west, and this took him through the Straits of Magellan at the southern tip of South America.

Hernán Cortés (1485–1547, Spanish): did for the Aztecs in Mexico (whose emperor was Montezuma) much the same as Pizarro had done in Peru.

Francis Drake (1540–96, English): best known of the Elizabethan seafarers who were in constant battle with the Spaniards over control of the Caribbean (the Spanish Main) and its riches. Drake—in a ship called the *Pelican,* later renamed the *Golden Hind*—was the first Englishman to sail around the world. He was also pivotal in the English defeat of the Spanish Armada.

James Cook (1728–79, British): one of the great navigators of all time, made three expeditions to the Pacific in an attempt to discover the supposed great southern continent. He became the first European to land in New Zealand and also charted parts of Australia and Antarctica. His famous ships were the *Endeavour* and the *Resolution*. He is also remembered for devising a diet of limes—high in vitamin C, which protected his men against scurvy (the source of the nickname "limey" for the British). He was murdered in Hawaii.

Robert Falcon Scott (1868–1912, British): failed by a matter of days to become the first person to reach the South Pole, and died, with the rest of his party, in the course of the return journey. One of his companions was Captain Oates, who—knowing that his weakness was endangering the lives of the others—went out into the blizzard saying, "I may be some time."

Roald Amundsen (1872–1928, Norwegian): the one who made it to the South Pole—and back again. He was also the first to sail through the Northwest Passage, the sea route from Pacific to Atlantic along the north coast of North America.

GEOGRAPHY

"Geography is about maps," said E. Clerihew Bentley, and although geographers would take offense to that definition, a lot of what we learned as a kid was about the stuff that filled maps. The last section of this chapter should really be classed as paleontology, but nobody told us that at the time.

The Countries of the World

The world is divided into seven continents: Europe, Asia, North America, South America, Africa, Australia, and Antarctica. It's a matter of debate to which continent you assign various island nations, because a continent is by definition a continuous landmass. The islands of the Pacific are usually grouped together as Oceania, so for the purpose of this list, I am going to use that convention and place Australia under that heading, too. And I'm going to create a continent called Central America and include in it all the islands of the Caribbean, as well as the stretch of mainland south of Mexico.

Antarctica contains no countries—instead, it is a stateless territory protected from exploitation by an international treaty.

The countries listed here (with their capitals, continents, and any change of name since 1945) are the 192 members of the United Nations, the most recent being Montenegro, which split from Serbia in 2006; Switzerland, that long-term bastion of neutrality, finally succumbed in 2002. And they are given in the alphabetical order used by the United Nations, which provides such delights as The Former Yugoslav Republic of Macedonia, coming under T. SU or Y after a country's name means that it was formerly part of the Soviet Union or Yugoslavia.

Country	Capital	Continent
Afghanistan	Kabul	Asia
Albania	Tirana	Europe
Algeria	Algiers	Africa
Andorra	Andorra la Vella	Europe
Angola	Luanda	Africa
Antigua & Barbuda	St. John's	N. America
Argentina	Buenos Aires	S. America
Armenia (SU)	Yerevan	Asia
Australia	Canberra	Oceania
Austria	Vienna	Europe
Azerbaijan (SU)	Baku	Asia
Bahamas	Nassau	C. America
Bahrain	Manama	Asia
Bangladesh *formerly East Pakistan*	Dhaka	Asia
Barbados	Bridgetown	C. America
Belarus (SU)	Minsk	Europe
Belgium	Brussels	Europe
Belize	Belmopan	C. America
Benin *formerly Dahomey*	Porto Novo	Africa
Bhutan	Thimphu	Asia
Bolivia	La Paz	S. America

Country	Capital	Continent
Bosnia & Herzegovina (Y)	Sarajevo	Europe
Botswana *formerly Bechuanaland*	Gaborone	Africa
Brazil	Brasilia	S. America
Brunei Darussalam	Bandar Seri Begawan	Asia
Bulgaria	Sofia	Europe
Burkina Faso *formerly Upper Volta*	Ouagadougou	Africa
Burundi *formerly joined with Rwanda to form Ruanda-Urundi*	Bujumbura	Africa
Cambodia *known as Kampuchea from 1976–89*	Phnom Penh	Asia
Cameroon	Yaoundé	Africa
Canada	Ottawa	N. America
Cape Verde	Praia	Africa
Central African Republic	Bangui	Africa
Chad	N'Djamena	Africa
Chile	Santiago	S. America
China	Beijing	Asia
Colombia	Bogota	S. America
Comoros	Moroni	Africa
Congo, Republic of the *formerly the French Congo*	Brazzaville	Africa
Costa Rica	San José	C. America
Côte d'Ivoire *formerly the Ivory Coast*	Yamoussoukro	Africa
Croatia (Y)	Zagreb	Europe
Cuba	Havana	C. America
Cyprus	Nicosia	Europe

Country	Capital	Continent
Czech Republic *used to be joined to Slovakia to form Czechoslovakia*	Prague	Europe
Democratic People's Republic of Korea *(North Korea to you and me)*	Pyongyang	Asia
Democratic Republic of the Congo	Kinshasa	Africa
Denmark	Copenhagen	Europe
Djibouti *formerly the French Territory of the Afars and the Issas*	Djibouti City	Africa
Dominica	Roseau	C. America
Dominican Republic*	Santo Domingo	C. America
Ecuador	Quito	S. America
Egypt	Cairo	Africa
El Salvador	San Salvador	C. America
Equatorial Guinea	Malabo	Africa
Eritrea *gained independence from Ethiopia in 1993*	Asmara	Africa
Estonia (SU)	Tallinn	Europe
Ethiopia	Addis Ababa	Africa
Fiji	Suva	Oceania
Finland	Helsinki	Europe
France	Paris	Europe
Gabon	Libreville	Africa
Gambia	Banjul	Africa
Georgia (SU)	Tbilisi	Asia

* Easily confused: Dominica is one of the Lesser Antilles islands in the southeastern Caribbean; the Dominican Republic, farther north but still in the Caribbean, shares the island of Hispaniola with Haiti and forms part of the Greater Antilles.

Country	Capital	Continent
Germany *from 1949-90 was divided into West (Federal Republic) and east (Democratic Republic) with capitals Bonn and Berlin respectively*	Berlin	Europe
Ghana	Accra	Africa
Greece	Athens	Europe
Grenada	St. George's	C. America
Guatemala	Guatemala City	C. America
Guinea *formerly French Guinea*	Conakry	Africa
Guinea-Bissau *formerly Portuguese Guinea*	Bissau	Africa
Guyana *formerly British Guiana*	Georgetown	S. America
Haiti	Port-au-Prince	C. America
Honduras	Tegucigalpa	C. America
Hungary	Budapest	Europe
Iceland	Reykjavik	Europe
India	New Delhi	Asia
Indonesia	Djakarta	Asia
Iran	Tehran	Asia
Iraq	Baghdad	Asia
Ireland	Dublin	Europe
Israel	**	Asia
Italy	Rome	Europe
Jamaica	Kingston	C. America

** Israel proclaimed Jerusalem as its capital in 1950, but the U.S., like nearly all other countries, maintains its embassy in Tel Aviv.

Country	Capital	Continent
Japan	Tokyo	Asia
Jordan	Amman	Asia
Kazakhstan (SU)	Astana	Asia
Kenya	Nairobi	Africa
Kiribati *formerly Gilbert Islands*	Tarawa	Oceania
Kuwait	Kuwait City	Asia
Kyrgyzstan (SU)	Bishkek	Asia
Laos	Vientiane	Asia
Latvia (SU)	Riga	Europe
Lebanon	Beirut	Asia
Lesotho *formerly Basutoland*	Maseru	Africa
Liberia	Monrovia	Africa
Libya	Tripoli	Africa
Liechtenstein	Vaduz	Europe
Lithuania (SU)	Vilnius	Europe
Luxembourg	Luxembourg City	Europe
Madagascar	Antananarivo	Africa
Malawi *formerly Nyasaland*	Lilongwe	Africa
Malaysia *created in 1963 from the Federation of Malaya, the states of Sarawak and Sabah in Borneo, and briefly, Singapore*	Kuala Lumpur	Asia
Maldives	Malé	Asia
Mali	Bamako	Africa
Malta	Valletta	Europe
Marshall Islands	Delap-Uliga-Darrit	Oceania
Mauritania	Nouakchott	Africa

Country	Capital	Continent
Mauritius	Port Louis	Africa
Mexico	Mexico City	N. America
Micronesia, Federated States of	Palikir	Oceania
Moldova (SU)	Chisinau	Europe
Monaco	Monaco	Europe
Mongolia	Ulan Bator	Asia
Montenegro (Y)	Podgorica	Europe
Morocco	Rabat	Africa
Mozambique	Maputo	Africa
Myanmar *formerly Burma; the capital until 2006 was Rangoon/Yangon*	Nay Pyi Daw	Asia
Namibia *formerly South West Africa*	Windhoek	Africa
Nauru *formerly Pleasant Island*	Yaren	Oceania
Nepal	Kathmandu	Asia
Netherlands	Amsterdam	Europe
New Zealand	Wellington	Oceania
Nicaragua	Managua	C. America
Niger	Niamey	Africa
Nigeria	Abuja	Africa
Norway	Oslo	Europe
Oman	Muscat	Asia
Pakistan	Islamabad	Asia
Palau *formerly Belau*	Koror	Oceania
Panama	Panama City	C. America
Papua New Guinea	Port Moresby	Oceania

Country	Capital	Continent
Paraguay	Asunción	S. America
Peru	Lima	S. America
Philippines	Manila	Asia
Poland	Warsaw	Europe
Portugal	Lisbon	Europe
Qatar	Doha	Asia
Republic of Korea *(the South)*	Seoul	Asia
Romania	Bucharest	Europe
Russian Federation (SU)	Moscow	Europe/Asia
Rwanda *formerly joined with Burundi to form Ruanda-Urundi*	Kigali	Africa
Saint Kitts & Nevis	Basseterre	C. America
Saint Lucia	Castries	C. America
Saint Vincent & the Grenadines	Kingstown	C. America
Samoa	Apia & Pago Pago	Oceania
San Marino	San Marino	Europe
São Tomé & Príncipe	São Tomé	Africa
Saudi Arabia	Riyadh	Asia
Senegal	Dakar	Africa
Serbia (Y)	Belgrade	Europe
Seychelles	Victoria	Africa
Sierra Leone	Freetown	Africa
Singapore *became independent of the Malaysian Federation in 1965*	Singapore	Asia

Country	Capital	Continent
Slovakia *used to be joined to the Czech Republic to form Czechoslovakia*	Bratislava	Europe
Slovenia (Y)	Ljubljana	Europe
Solomon Islands	Honiara	Oceania
Somalia	Mogadishu	Africa
South Africa	Pretoria	Africa
Spain	Madrid	Europe
Sri Lanka *formerly Ceylon*	Colombo	Asia
Sudan	Khartoum	Africa
Suriname *formerly Dutch Guiana*	Paramaribo	S. America
Swaziland	Mbabane	Africa
Sweden	Stockholm	Europe
Switzerland	Berne	Europe
Syria	Damascus	Asia
Tajikistan (SU)	Dushanbe	Asia
Thailand	Bangkok	Asia
The Former Yugoslav Republic of Macedonia	Skopje	Europe
Timor-Leste (East Timor)	Dili	Asia
Togo	Lomé	Africa
Tonga	Nuku'alofa	Oceania
Trinidad & Tobago	Port-of-Spain	C. America
Tunisia	Tunis	Africa
Turkey	Ankara	Europe/Asia
Turkmenistan (SU)	Ashgabat	Asia
Tuvalu *formerly Ellice Islands*	Funafuti	Oceania

Country	Capital	Continent
Uganda	Kampala	Africa
Ukraine (SU)	Kiev	Europe
United Arab Emirates	Abu Dhabi	Asia
United Kingdom of Great Britain & Northern Ireland	London	Europe
United Republic of Tanzania *formed in 1964 from a union of Tanganyika and Zanzibar*	Dodoma	Africa
United States of America	Washington	N. America
Uruguay	Montevideo	S. America
Uzbekistan (SU)	Tashkent	Asia
Vanuatu *formerly New Hebrides*	Port Vila	Oceania
Venezuela	Caracas	S. America
Vietnam *from 1954–76 divided into North and South, with Hanoi the capital of the North and Saigon (now Ho Chi Minh City) of the South*	Hanoi	Asia
Yemen	San'a	Asia
Zambia *formerly Northern Rhodesia*	Lusaka	Africa
Zimbabwe *formerly Southern Rhodesia, then from 1964–79 Rhodesia; until 1979 the capital was called Salisbury*	Harare	Africa

The 50 United States of America

Listed below are the 50 states with their nicknames, their capitals, and the date they entered the Union. Those marked with an asterisk are the original 13 colonies that declared themselves independent from British rule in 1776. Those marked with two asterisks seceded from the Union during the Civil War and formed the Confederate States of America; all had been readmitted by 1870.

State	Nickname	Capital	Date
Alabama **	Yellowhammer State	Montgomery	1819
Alaska	The Last Frontier	Juneau	1959
Arizona	Grand Canyon State	Phoenix	1912
Arkansas **	Natural State	Little Rock	1836
California	Golden State	Sacramento	1850
Colorado	Centennial State	Denver	1876
Connecticut *	Constitution State	Hartford	1788
Delaware*	First State	Dover	1787
Florida **	Sunshine State	Tallahassee	1845
Georgia * **	Peach State	Atlanta	1788
Hawaii	Aloha State	Honolulu	1959
Idaho	Gem State	Boise	1890
Illinois	Prairie State	Springfield	1818
Indiana	Hoosier State	Indianapolis	1816

State	Nickname	Capital	Date
Iowa	Hawkeye State	Des Moines	1846
Kansas	Sunflower State	Topeka	1861
Kentucky	Bluegrass State	Frankfort	1792
Louisiana **	Pelican State	Baton Rouge	1812
Maine	Pine Tree State	Augusta	1820
Maryland *	Old Line State	Annapolis	1788
Massachusetts *	Bay State	Boston	1788
Michigan	Great Lakes State	Lansing	1837
Minnesota	North Star State	St. Paul	1858
Mississippi **	Magnolia State	Jackson	1817
Missouri	Show-me State	Jefferson City	1821
Montana	Treasure State	Helena	1889
Nebraska	Cornhusker State	Lincoln	1867
Nevada	Silver State	Carson City	1864
New Hampshire *	Granite State	Concord	1788
New Jersey *	Garden State	Trenton	1787
New Mexico	Land of Enchantment	Santa Fe	1912
New York *	Empire State	Albany	1788
N. Carolina * **	Tar Heel State	Raleigh	1789
North Dakota	Peace Garden State	Bismarck	1889
Ohio	Buckeye State	Columbus	1803
Oklahoma	Sooner State	Oklahoma City	1907
Oregon	Beaver State	Salem	1859
Pennsylvania *	Keystone State	Harrisburg	1787

State	Nickname	Capital	Date
Rhode Island *	Ocean State	Providence	1790
S. Carolina * **	Palmetto State	Columbia	1788
South Dakota	Mount Rushmore State	Pierre	1889
Tennessee **	Volunteer State	Nashville	1796
Texas **	Lone Star State	Austin	1845
Utah	Beehive State	Salt Lake City	1896
Vermont	Green Mountain State	Montpelier	1791
Virginia * **	The Old Dominion	Richmond	1788
Washington	Evergreen State	Olympia	1889
West Virginia	Mountain State	Charleston	1863
Wisconsin	Badger State	Madison	1848
Wyoming	Equality State	Cheyenne	1890

The District of Columbia is a federal district, not a state, sharing its boundaries with the city of Washington, D.C.

The Canadian Provinces and its Territories

In 1867 Canada became a self-governing dominion. The country is made up of seven provinces and three territories, the difference being that the provinces receive their power from the Monarchy, and the territories from the federal government. The territories are marked with an asterisk.

Province	Nickname	Capitol	Year
Alberta	The Princess Province	Edmonton	1905

Province	Nickname	Capitol	Year
British Columbia	The Pacific Province	Victoria	1871
Manitoba	The Keystone Province	Winnipeg	1870
New Brunswick	The Loyalist Province	Fredericton	1867
Newfoundland and Labrador	The Rock	St. John's	1949
Northwest Territories*		Yellowknife	1870
Nova Scotia	Canada's Ocean Playground	Halifax	1867
Nunavit*		Iquluit	1999
Ontario		Toronto	1867
Prince Edward Island	The Garden Province	Charlottetown	1873
Quebec	The Beautiful Province	Quebec	1867
Saskatchewan	The Wheat Province	Regina	1905
Yukon*	Land of the Midnight Sun	Whitehorse	1898

The World's Highest Mountains

All the mountains in the world that top 26,244 feet (8,000 m) are in the Himalayas, which is frankly a bit boring for a book like this, but what can you do?

Mountain	Country	Feet	Meters
Everest	China/Nepal	29,029	8,848

Mountain	Country	Feet	Meters
K2 (Godley Austen)	China/Kashmir	28,251	8,611
Kanchenjunga	India/Nepal	28,209	8,598
Lhotse	China/Nepal	27,940	8,516
Makalu	China/Nepal	27,825	8,481
Cho Oyu	China/Nepal	26,906	8,201
Dhaulagiri	Nepal	26,811	8,172
Manaslu	Nepal	26,759	8,156
Nanga Parbut	Kashmir	26,660	8,126
Annapurna	Nepal	26,503	8,078
Gasherbrum	China/Kashmir	26,470	8,068
Broad Peak	China/Kashmir	26,414	8,051
Xixabangma	China	26,286	8,012

There are another 20 that are above 22,966 feet (7,000 m), all still in Asia; then we shift to South America for Aconagua in Argentina, which is 22,835 feet (6,960 m).

And 19 more above 20,341 feet (6,200 m), all in the Andes, before it is worth even glancing elsewhere.

Here is a list of the top three from the other continents:

Mountain	Country	Feet	Meters
NORTH AMERICA			
McKinley	U.S. (Alaska)	20,322	6,194

Mountain	Country	Feet	Meters
Logan	U.S.	19,551	5,959
Citlaltepetl	Mexico	18,701	5,700
AFRICA			
Kilimanjaro	Tanzania	19,341	5,895
Mount Kenya	Kenya	17,057	5,199
Ruwenzori	Uganda/Zaire	16,762	5,109
ANTARCTICA			
Vinson Massif		16,066	4,897
Mount Kirkpatrick		14,856	4,528
Mount Markham		14,268	4,349
EUROPE			
Mont Blanc	France/Italy	15,771	4,807
Monte Rosa	Italy/Switzerland	15,203	4,634
Dom	Switzerland	14,911	4,545
OCEANIA			
Mount Wilhelm	Papua New Guinea	14,790	4,508
Aoraki *(formerly Mount Cook)*	New Zealand	12,313	3,753
Mount Balbi	Solomon Islands	8,002	2,439

The World's Largest Bodies of Water

The four principal oceans of the world with areas in square miles (sq km) are:

OCEANS

Ocean	Square miles	Sq km
Pacific	69,374	179,679
Atlantic	35,665	92,373
Indian	28,539	73,917
Arctic	5,440	14,090

SEAS

Sea	Location	Square miles	Sq km
South China	between mainland Asia & the Philippines	1,149	2,975
Caribbean	east of Central America	1,068	2,766
Mediter-ranean	between Europe and Africa	971	2,516
Bering	at the very north of the Pacific, between Alaska and Russia	875	2,268
Gulf of Mexico	south of the eastern U.S., east of Mexico	596	1,543
Sea of Okhotsk	south of eastern Russia, north of Japan	590	1,528

Sea	Location	Square miles	Sq km
East China & Yellow	east of mainland China, north of South China, and south of the Okhotsk	482	1,249
Hudson Bay	Canada	475	1,232
Sea of Japan	between Japan and eastern Asia	389	1,008
North	east of the UK, bounded on the east by Denmark	222	575

The deepest point in the world is the Mariana Trench (in the Pacific, east of the Philippines), at 36,161 feet (11,022 m).

The World's Longest Rivers

The world's longest rivers are more fairly divided than its mountains, so here are the 17 that are longer than 2,175 miles (3,500 km), with the countries they mostly flow through:

River	Location	Miles	Km
Nile	Egypt	4,145	6,670
Amazon	Brazil	4,008	6,450
Yangtze	China	3,964	6,380
Mississippi–Missouri	U.S.	3,748	6,020
Yenisey–Angara	Russia	3,448	5,550
Huang He	China	3,395	5,464
Ob–Irtysh	Russia	3,361	5,410

River	Location	Miles	Km
Zaire/Congo	Zaire/Congo	2,901	4,670
Mekong	Vietnam/Cambodia	2,796	4,500
Paraná–Plate	Argentina	2,796	4,500
Amur	Russia	2,734	4,400
Lena	Russia	2,734	4,400
Mackenzie	Canada	2,634	4,240
Niger	Nigeria/Niger/Mali	2,597	4,180
Murray–Darling	Australia	2,330	3,750
Volga	Russia	2,299	3,700
Zambezi	Mozambique/ Zimbabwe/Zambia	2,199	3,540

If you counted the Mississippi and Missouri as two separate rivers, they would both still find a place on this list, as would the Ob and Irtysh. The Yenisey on its own would also qualify.

Geological Time

The largest subdivision of geological time is an **era**, which can be divided into **periods** and then into **epochs**. The major divisions tend to be marked by mass extinctions, with smaller ones indicated by smaller extinctions and/or climate change. There have been three main eras; anything earlier than this was referred to as Precambrian.

☞ PALEOZOIC ERA, FROM ABOUT 600–250 MYA (MILLION YEARS AGO)

Paleozoic literally means *ancient life*. Life on Earth had existed for perhaps 4,000 million years before this, but it consisted largely of single-celled creatures such as algae and bacteria. The Cambrian period, the first part of the Paleozoic, is when bigger creatures—some of them with backbones—began to emerge, although they were still living in the sea. The Paleozoic was followed by the Permian extinction, when 95 percent of all life on Earth—plants and animals on both land and sea—died. Just like that. Just when they were beginning to get the hang of it. (To be fair, the period of extinction lasted millions of years, so "just like that" is an exaggeration, but scientists still don't know for sure why it happened.)

Anyway, it paved the way for…

☞ MESOZOIC ERA, FROM ABOUT 250–65 MYA

Mesozoic means *middle life*. This was the age of the dinosaurs, and it was divided into three periods:

- **Triassic** (*c*. 250–220 mya): the time of the first dinosaurs, small and agile to start with but poised to take over the world.
- **Jurassic** (*c*. 220–155 mya): when giant herbivores such as *Apatosaurus* (which used to be called Brontosaurus) and *Diplodocus* ruled.
- **Cretaceous** (*c*. 150–65 mya): dominated by *Tyrannosaurus rex*, but also the time when plants first produced flowers.

Then along came the Cretaceous–Tertiary (known as the KT) extinction, when the Earth may or may not have been hit by a meteorite. Nothing quite as bad as the Permian but still enough to wipe out the dinosaurs, and following that...

☞ CENOZOIC ERA, FROM ABOUT 65 MYA TO THE PRESENT

Cenozoic means *recent life*. This is when mammals and birds took over. It is sometimes divided into the Tertiary and Quaternary periods and then subdivided into these epochs:

- **Palaeocene** (65–55 mya): when the first large mammals emerged to fill the gaps left by the dinosaurs.
- **Eocene** (55–35 mya): a period of great warmth, when the first grasses started to grow.
- **Oligocene** (35–25 mya): when mammals and flowering plants began to greatly diversify.
- **Miocene** (25–5.5 mya): when the common ancestor of human beings and primates emerged.
- **Pliocene** (5.5–2 mya): when that same common ancestor came down from the trees.
- **Pleistocene** (2 million–11,750 years ago—this is where you enter the Quaternary period if you belong to that school of thought.): mammoths and Neanderthal man came and went, but *Homo sapiens* may be here to stay.
- **Holocene** (11,750 years ago–present, but see below): the emergence of agriculture and thus of the first civilizations.

There is a suggestion that the Holocene period finished in the year 1800 and that human impact since the time of the Industrial Revolution justifies us designating a new period, the Anthropocene.

GENERAL STUDIES

This chapter covers various subjects that didn't fit elsewhere in the book: mythology, art, music—all the subjects that weren't included in the exams but you had to learn a bit of anyway.

World Religions

There are, of course, lots of them and lots of subdivisions within them, but here is a little about the five really big ones, starting with the oldest.

☞ JUDAISM

Monotheistic religion whose beginnings are lost in the mists of time. Its adherents are called Jews, their god is eternal and invisible, and trusting in God's will is a fundamental tenet. Jewish law as revealed by God is contained in the Torah, which comprises the first five books of the Christian Old Testament. The Wailing Wall in Jerusalem is a sacred site.

☞ HINDUISM

Polytheistic, about 5,000 years old, and followed primarily in India. One of its tenets is that one's actions lead to the reward or punishment of being reincarnated in a higher or lower form of life. The aim is to be freed from this cycle and attain the state of unchanging reality known as Brahman. The three principal creator gods are Brahma, Vishnu, and Shiva, but

Krishna (an incarnation of Vishnu) is also widely worshipped. The main scriptures are the Vedas. The Ganges River is seen as a goddess of purity and pilgrims come to the holy city of Varanesi (Benares) to bathe in the river. The cow is a sacred symbol of fertility.

☞ BUDDHISM

Founded in the 6th century B.C. by Gautama Siddhartha, known as the Buddha or "Awakened One." There are no gods in Buddhism; its adherents follow the philosophy expressed in the Buddha's Four Noble Truths—that existence is characterized by suffering, that suffering is caused by desire, that to end desire is therefore to end suffering, and that this may be achieved by following the Eightfold Path to the ideal state of nirvana.

☞ CHRISTIANITY

Monotheistic religion that grew out of Judaism 2,000 years ago and is based on the belief that Jesus Christ is the son of God. The holy book is the Bible, divided into the Old and New testaments; the New Testament is the one concerned with the teachings of Christ and his apostles. The church divided initially into Eastern (Orthodox) and Western (Roman Catholic) branches. The Catholic Church still recognizes the Pope as leader and Rome as a holy city, but a major rift beginning in the 16th century led to the emergence of the Protestants and many subsequent subdivisions. Jerusalem is the traditional site of Christ's burial and resurrection.

☞ ISLAM

Monotheistic religion whose god is called Allah, founded in the 7th century A.D. by the one prophet, Mohammed. The holy book—the Koran or Qur'an—contains the revelations that Allah made to Mohammed. The holy cities are Mecca, birthplace of Mohammed, and Medina, where he is buried. All able-bodied Muslims who can afford it are expected to make a pilgrimage (*hadj*) to Medina at least once in their lives. The Dome of the Rock in Jerusalem is the oldest intact Muslim temple in the world and is built over the point from which Mohammed traditionally ascended to heaven.

☞ THE TEN COMMANDMENTS

Given to Moses by God on Mount Sinai (remember Charlton Heston and those massive tablets?), these are a basic code of conduct for both Jews and Christians.

1. Thou shalt have no other gods before me.
2. Thou shalt not make unto thee any graven image, or any likeness of any thing that is in heaven above or that is in the earth beneath, or that is in the water under the earth.
3. Thou shalt not take the name of the Lord thy God in vain.
4. Remember the Sabbath day and keep it holy.
5. Honor thy father and thy mother.
6. Thou shalt not kill.
7. Thou shalt not commit adultery.
8. Thou shalt not steal.
9. Thou shalt not bear false witness against thy neighbor.
10. Thou shalt not covet thy neighbor's house, thou shalt not covet thy neighbor's wife, nor his manservant, nor his maidservant, nor his ox, nor his ass, nor any thing that is thy neighbor's.

Roman Numerals

I = 1	C = 100
V = 5	D = 500
X = 10	M = 1,000
L = 50	

From there, the Romans could make up any number they wanted—except, interestingly enough, zero, because they didn't have a symbol for it. They made the other numbers by adding (putting letters at the end) or subtracting (putting them at the beginning).

For example:

I = 1
II = 2
III = 3 but IV (for example, 1 before 5) = 4

Similarly,

V = 5
VI = 6
VII = 7
VIII = 8 but IX (1 before 10) = 9

The same principle applies with the big numbers, so you end up with something like XLIV (44, because it is 10 before 50 and 1 before 5) and CDXCIX (499, made up of 100 before 500, 10 before 100, and 1 before 10). You would have thought 499 might be ID (1 before 500), but it isn't.

The Seven Wonders of the World

The Seven Wonders of the Ancient World, described in an old encyclopedia as "remarkable for their splendor or magnitude," were:

- The Hanging Gardens of Babylon
- The Mausoleum at Halicarnassus
- The Lighthouse of Alexandria
- The Colossus of Rhodes
- The Temple of Artemis at Ephesus
- The Statue of Zeus at Olympia
- The Great Pyramid of Giza

Of the seven, only the Great Pyramid is still in existence.

A Bit of Classical Mythology

There are lots of Greek and Roman gods, as well as enough mythological characters and demigods to fill a book on their own, but these are some you might remember:

Greek Name	Roman Equivalent	God of...
Zeus	Jupiter	father of the gods, also god of thunder
Hera	Juno	his wife and sister, goddess of marriage
Apollo	Apollo	god of hunting and of healing, who was consulted at the Oracle of Delphi
Ares	Mars	god of war
Aphrodite	Venus	goddess of love
Artemis	Diana	goddess of hunting and the moon

Greek Name	Roman Equivalent	God of…
Hermes	Mercury	messenger of the gods, who wore the winged sandals and helmet
Athena	Minerva	goddess of war and wisdom
Hephaestus	Vulcan	god of fire
Poseidon	Neptune	god of the sea
Demeter	Ceres	goddess of corn and the harvest
Dis	Pluto	god of the underworld

Famous Artists

This was meant to be a Top 20, but the list kept growing. There are so many artists that have contributed to the wonderful world of art we know today that I found I couldn't leave any of these names out.

Sandro Botticelli (1445–1510, Italian): best known for *The Birth of Venus* (Venus with flowing hair, standing in a shell).

Leonardo da Vinci (1452–1519, Italian): painter, sculptor, inventor, and all-around polymath—one of the great figures of the Renaissance. Among many of his celebrated works are *Mona Lisa* and *The Last Supper.*

Michelangelo Buonarotti (1475–1564, Italian): painter—most famous for the ceiling of the Sistine Chapel in the Vatican—and sculptor of the statue of *David* in Florence.

Raphael (1483–1520, Italian): painter of many versions of the Madonna and Child; and of frescoes, notably *The School of Athens* for the Sistine Chapel.

Titian (*c.* 1490–1576, Italian): greatest painter of the Venetian school. His religious and mythological subjects include *Assumption of the Virgin* and *Bacchus and Ariadne*.

Hans Holbein the Younger (*c.* 1497–1543, German, latterly in England): court painter to Henry VIII, responsible for the flattering portrait of Anne of Cleves, which encouraged the king to marry her.

Pieter Brueghel the Elder (1525–69, Flemish): famous for scenes of peasant life and landscapes.

El Greco (Domenikos Theotokopoulos, 1541–1614, Greek living in Spain): used distinctive elongated figures in his paintings of saints and in *The Burial of Count Orgaz*.

Peter Paul Rubens (1577–1640, Flemish): greatest of the Baroque artists, based mainly in Antwerp. Painted the ceiling of the Banqueting Hall in Whitehall, London, but is best remembered for depictions of abundantly fleshy women.

Frans Hals (*c.* 1581–1666, Dutch): best known for portraiture. Painter of *The Laughing Cavalier*.

Diego de Velázquez (1599–1660, Spanish): court painter to Philip IV, producing many portraits of his patron and his family, notably *Las Meninas*. Also *The Rokeby Venus*, painted where the goddess is lying naked on a bed, facing away from the viewer, and looking at herself in a mirror.

Rembrandt van Rijn (1606–69, Dutch): prolific portraitist and self-portraitist; creator of *The Night Watch*, the most famous painting in the Rijksmuseum in Amsterdam.

Jan Vermeer (1632–75, Dutch): based in Delft and noted for his skillful use of light; painted everyday scenes of women reading or writing letters or playing musical instruments. Best known for his oil on canvas, *Girl with a Pearl Earring.*

Canaletto (Giovanni Canal, 1697–1768, Italian): famous for his views of Venice, but also spent time in London and painted scenes of the Thames.

William Hogarth (1697–1764, British): engraver; hard-hitting social satires such as *The Rake's Progress* and *Gin Lane.*

Francisco de Goya (1746–1828, Spanish): painter, notably of the portraits *Maja Clothed* and *Maja Nude*, and the dramatic *Shootings of May 3rd 1808*, inspired by Spanish resistance to French occupation.

J(ohn) M(allord) W(illiam) Turner (1775–1851, British): prolific painter of landscapes and maritime scenes, most famously *The Fighting Téméraire.* His use of color and light and his portrayal of weather inspired the French Impressionists Monet and Renoir.

John Constable (1776–1837, British): painter of landscapes, notably *The Haywain.*

Edouard Manet (1832–83, French): established before the Impressionists, he adopted some of their techniques but was never quite one of that school. Famous works include *Déjeuner sur l'Herbe* (the one where the men are fully dressed and the women are not) and *A Bar at the Folies-Bergère.*

James McNeill Whistler (1834–1903, American, working in England): painter, notably of *The Artist's Mother*; also known as a wit. When Oscar Wilde remarked, "How I wish I'd said that," Whistler responded, "You will, Oscar, you will."

Edgar Degas (1834–1917, French): Impressionist who painted all those ballet dancers.

Paul Cézanne (1839–1906, French): post-Impressionist and precursor of cubism, based in Provence. In addition to landscapes, famous works include *The Card Players* and various groups of women bathing.

Claude Monet (1840–1926, French): most important painter of the Impressionist movement, famous for the "series" paintings that studied the effect of light at different times of day and year on the same subject: Rouen cathedral, haystacks and poplars. Lived latterly at Giverny, outside Paris, now a much visited garden, and painted a series of the waterlilies (*nymphéas*) there.

Auguste Rodin (1840–1917, French): sculptor, most famously of *The Kiss*, *The Thinker*, and *The Burghers of Calais*.

Pierre-Auguste Renoir (1841–1919, French): Impressionist, best known for *Les Parapluies* and *Le Moulin de la Galette* (a bar in Montmartre).

Paul Gauguin (1848–1903, French): the one who went to Tahiti and painted the people there.

Vincent van Gogh (1853–90, Dutch, working mainly in France): cut off part of his ear and subsequently committed suicide. Self-portraits, *The Potato Eaters*, *Sunflowers*, *The Starry Night*.

John Singer Sargent (1856–1925, American): portrait painter of the stars, including Ellen Terry, John D. Rockefeller, and various young ladies of fashion.

Henri de Toulouse-Lautrec (1864–1901, French): the little one. Lived in Montmartre and painted music halls, cafés, and their habitués. Works include *At the Moulin Rouge* and *La Toilette*.

Pablo Picasso (1881–1973, Spanish, working mostly in France): arguably the greatest and certainly the most versatile painter of the 20th century. After the famous "rose" and "blue" periods of his early years, he was fundamental to the development of cubism, expanded the technique of collage, became involved with the surrealists, designed ballet costumes, and did a bit of pottery. His greatest painting is probably *Guernica*, a nightmarish portrayal of the horrors of the Spanish Civil War.

Salvador Dalí (1914–89, Spanish): surrealist and notable egomaniac. Studied abnormal psychology and dream symbolism and reproduced its imagery in his paintings. Also worked with the surrealist film director Luis Buñuel (*Le Chien Andalou*) and designed the dream sequence in Alfred Hitchcock's *Spellbound*. His painting of the Last Supper is the one that shows the arms and torso of Christ floating above the disciples at the table.

Jackson Pollock (1912–56, American): abstract expressionist painter who believed that the act of painting was more important than the finished product. His paintings are therefore highly colorful and chaotic to the point of frenzy. And often huge.

Famous Composers

I was much more disciplined with this list—my Top 20 actually has 20 people in it.

Antonio Vivaldi (1678–1741, Italian): composed operas and church music galore but is now mostly remembered for *The Four Seasons*, a suite of violin concertos.

Johann Sebastian Bach (1685–1750, German): highly esteemed and vastly influential composer—without him there might have been no Haydn, no Mozart, and no Beethoven. Wrote mostly organ music, church music, and orchestral music, such as the *Brandenburg Concertos*, the *St. Matthew Passion, The Well-Tempered Clavier,* and *Jesu Joy of Man's Desiring*. Came from a famous musical family and had many children, including the composers Carl Philip Emmanuel and Johann Christian; the latter moved to London and became known as the English Bach.

George Frideric Handel (1685–1759, German, working in England): successful in Germany before moving to England when George I became king; wrote the *Water Music* for him. Also wrote a number of operas and developed the English oratorio, of which *Messiah* (which contains the *Hallelujah Chorus*) is the best known; composed the anthem *Zadok the Priest* for the coronation of George II.

Franz Josef Haydn (1732–1809, Austrian): "Papa Haydn," another vastly prolific composer, credited with the development of the classical symphony (he wrote 104 of them, including the *London* and the *Clock*) and the four-movement string quartet.

Wolfgang Amadeus Mozart (1756–91, Austrian): infant prodigy and all-around genius. Composer of 41 symphonies, including the *Jupiter;* operas, including *Don Giovanni* and *The Magic Flute*; innumerable concertos, sonatas, solo piano pieces, and chamber music. Not bad for someone who died at 35.

Ludwig van Beethoven (1770–1827, German): wrote nine symphonies, but the ones we all know are the Fifth (da-da-da-DAH) and the Ninth (the *Choral Symphony*, whose last movement includes the glorious *Song of Joy*—amazing to think that he was already deaf by this time and never heard it performed). Also wrote *Für Elise*, a piano piece studied laboriously by generations of budding pianists. And lots of other stuff, including one opera, called *Fidelio.*

Gioachino Rossini (1792–1868, Italian): known mostly for operas, including *La Cenerentola, The Barber of Seville,* and *William Tell,* which boasts the world's most famous overture.

Franz Schubert (1797–1828, Austrian): wrote about 600 songs (*lieder*) and *The Trout* piano quintet. This ambitious career seems odd, then, that he would ever leave anything unfinished. But when we talk about the *Unfinished Symphony,* we tend to mean Schubert's Eighth.

Frédéric Chopin (1810–49, Polish): wrote some beautiful tear-jerking stuff for the piano, much of it influenced by Polish folk music: mazurkas, polonaises, waltzes, and short romantic pieces called nocturnes, a term he popularized.

Franz Liszt (1811–86, Hungarian): virtuoso pianist, possibly the best there has ever been, as well as a prolific composer. His best-known works are probably the *Hungarian Rhapsodies.* His daughter Cosima became Mrs. Richard Wagner.

Richard Wagner (1813–83, German): was once said that he had wonderful moments but bad quarters of an hour. Fans of his work use words like "a masterpiece" and "greatest achievement in the history of opera," but given that the four "musical dramas" that comprise the *Ring* cycle run for a total of nearly 16 hours, I am never going to find out firsthand.

Giuseppe Verdi (1813–1901, Italian): wrote rather shorter operas, notably *Rigoletto, La Traviata, Don Carlos,* and *Aida.*

Pyotr Tchaikovsky (1840–93, Russian): best known as a composer of ballet music (*The Nutcracker Suite, Swan Lake,*

The Sleeping Beauty) but also wrote the wonderfully loud and patriotic *1812 Overture* after Napoleon had been forced to retreat from Moscow.

Edward Elgar (1857–1934, English): responsible for the *Enigma Variations*, including *Pomp and Circumstance* ("Land of Hope and Glory").

Giacomo Puccini (1858–1924, Italian): another one for the opera buffs—*La Bohème, Tosca, Madama Butterfly, Turandot.* My reference book says he "lacks the nobility of Verdi" but makes up for it in dramatic flair and skill. And he certainly wrote tunes.

Arnold Schoenberg (1874–1951, Austrian): wrote only a few tunes but invented a form of music called atonality and, later, serialism, which are bywords for "unlistenable" to many people.

Gustav Mahler (1860–1911, Austrian): became widely known after Tom Lehrer wrote a song about his wife, Alma, but he was also a great conductor and wrote some good music, too. This included nine finished symphonies and an unfinished one, all on a grand scale, and a song-symphony called *Das Lied von der Erde* ("The Song of the Earth").

Gustav Holst (1874–1934, English): best known for the *Planets* suite, which has seven parts—Earth was not deemed worthy of inclusion and Pluto was not discovered yet. Which is convenient in light of recent events.

Igor Stravinsky (1882–1971, Russian): composed the *Firebird Suite* specifically for Diaghilev's Ballets Russes and followed this with *Petrushka* and *The Rite of Spring*. His style was always experimental, and he turned to neoclassicism and later to serialism, but he was never in the same league as Schoenberg for making people reach for the "off" button.

Sergei Prokofiev (1891–1953, Russian): included because of *Peter and the Wolf*, a symphonic fairy tale that I listened to at school and that crops up on TV every so often. *The Oxford Dictionary of Music* says that it is "delightful in itself and a wonderful way of instructing children (and others) how to identify orchestral instruments." Oh, and he wrote other things, too, starting when he was about three: symphonies, ballets (*Romeo and Juliet, Cinderella*), operas, film music (*Alexander Nevsky*), and more.

The Planets

When I was at school, learning the planets was pretty straightforward. There were nine planets in our solar system. Starting at the Sun and working outward, we learned of Mercury, Venus, Earth, Mars, Jupiter, Saturn, Uranus, Neptune, and Pluto. And there were sundry mnemonics to help you remember, along the lines of My Very Educated Mother Just Served Us Nine Pizzas.

Then they began making new discoveries. Most important, in 2003, they discovered an icy body that was larger than Pluto, which brought the whole definition of a planet into question. After much controversy a conference of the International Astronomical Union in 2006 deemed that Pluto no longer qualified. The icy body became known as Eris—after the Greek goddess of discord, which was very appropo, given all the trouble she had caused.

So there are now officially eight major planets—the first eight on the original list—with Pluto and Eris demoted to the status of minor planets or ice dwarfs.

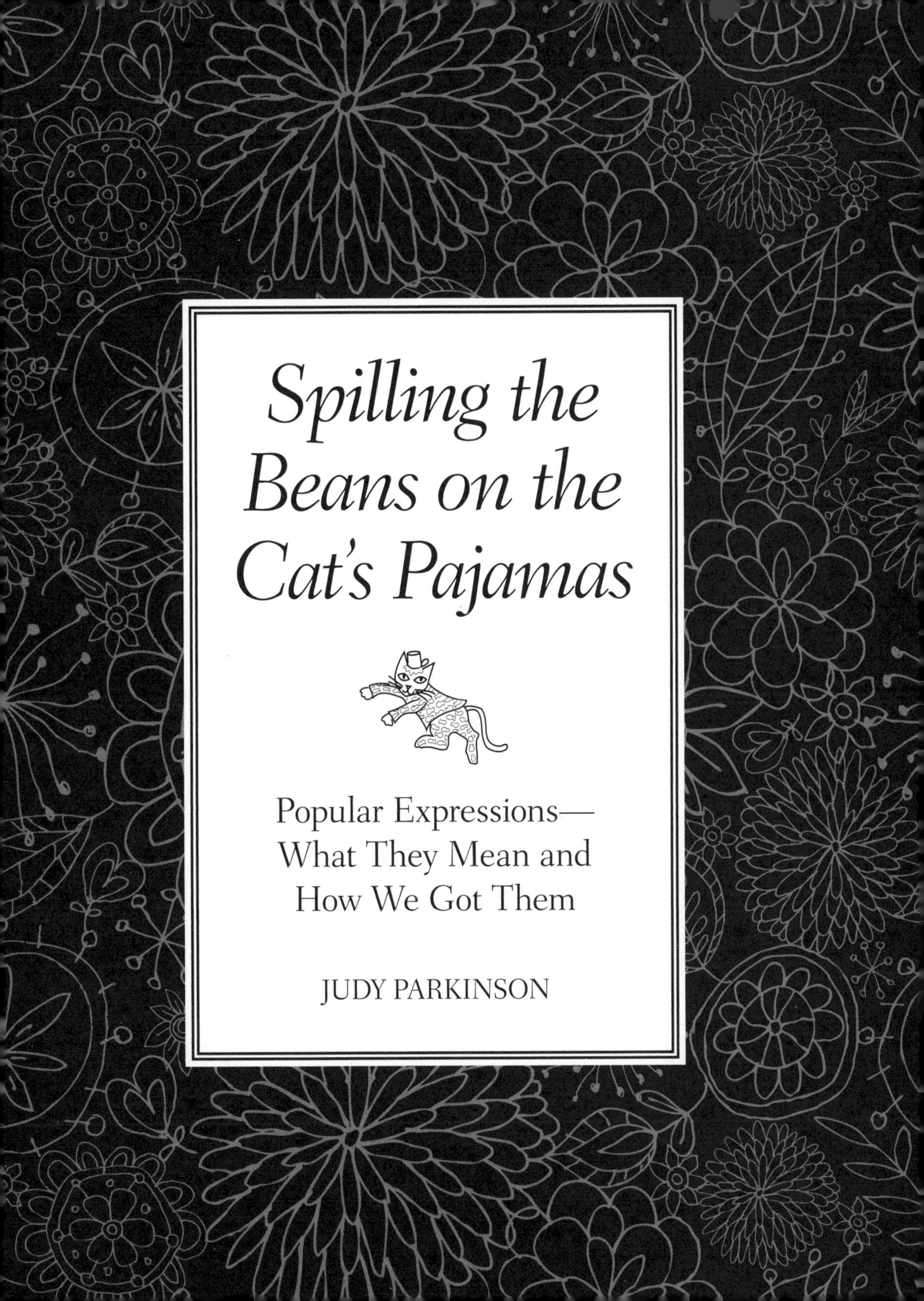
Spilling the Beans on the Cat's Pajamas
Popular Expressions—
What They Mean and
How We Got Them
JUDY PARKINSON

INTRODUCTION

The English language has flourished over the centuries. Our ever-flexible language often revives phrases that we thought had "bitten the dust"—and new words and expressions creep into the lexicon all the time. There's a different "flavor of the month" for each generation.

So "strike while the iron's hot": If you want "to bone up" on the origins of some of the curiosities of the English language, look through these pages and you'll be "in seventh heaven." This book is "the cat's whiskers" and "the cat's pajamas," all rolled into one, as it "spills the beans" on the origins of all these expressions and many more.

I will "make no bones" about it, and I won't "beat around the bush" (after all, don't forget I'm "talking turkey" here): This book contains some fascinating and remarkable stories about our best-loved and most colorful phrases. The staples of our language—those familiar, well-worn expressions and clichés—originate from the most diverse sources. From main street to Homer, from advertising to social networking websites, from the army to the air force, from stage to screen…it's an "all-singing, all-dancing," around-the-world trip through our language's history.

If you've ever gone "over the top," you can thank the military. "Walk the plank" and "shake a leg" are both nautical terms, and I wouldn't be "rubbing salt in the wound" to say that that's another one. The world of sport, meanwhile, provides rich pickings. "To throw in the sponge" and "to come up to scratch" are both boxing terms, and baseball has allowed us "to take a rain check." But that's for another time. Look no further; you'll be "as pleased as Punch."

~ A ~

ADD INSULT TO INJURY

To hurt, by word or deed, someone who has already suffered an act of violence or injustice. The expression has been in use for centuries.

During the Augustan era, the so-called Golden Age of Latin literature, Phaedrus translated Aesop's fables into Latin verse, peppering them with anecdotes of his own. He quotes the fable about a bald man who tried to swat a fly that had bitten him on the head, but who missed the insect and instead slapped himself hard on the head.

Seeing this the fly then remarked, "You wished to kill me for a mere touch. What will you do to yourself since you have added insult to injury?"

ALIVE AND KICKING

Active and in good health. The expression was coined in the late eighteenth century and probably referred originally to a healthy baby, either while still in the womb or just after birth.

ALL CATS LOVE FISH, BUT FEAR TO WET THEIR PAWS

A traditional saying, dating back to at least the sixteenth century, used to describe a person who is eager to obtain something of value, but who is not bold enough to make the necessary effort or to take the risk.

It is to this saying that William Shakespeare referred in Macbeth (1:7):

> Letting "I dare not" wait upon "I would,"
> Like the poor cat i' the adage.

ALL IN A DAY'S WORK

Said of an unusual or unexpected task that can be obligingly included in the normal daily routine.

The expression was common by the eighteenth century and may stem from the nautical use of the term "day's work," which referred to the reckoning of a ship's course during the twenty-four-hour period from noon one day to noon the next.

A character in Sir Walter Scott's novel *The Monastery* says, "That will cost me a farther ride...but it is all in the day's work."

ALL OVER BUT THE SHOUTING

This expression is firmly rooted in the world of sports and was first used in print by nineteenth-century sportswriter Charles James Apperley in 1842. It means that victory is in the bag, only the cheering of the crowd at the end of the game or contest remains to come.

The phrase may perhaps be derived specifically from boxing—the shouting being the noisy appeal from the supporters of one of the boxers against the referee's decision.

It is also often applied to political elections in which the outcome is certain, even before the ballot papers have been counted.

ALL SINGING, ALL DANCING

This piece of popular phraseology was inspired by the first Hollywood musical, *Broadway Melody*, in 1929—the era in which sound first came to the movies, which was advertised with posters proclaiming:

The New Wonder of the Screen!
ALL TALKING
ALL SINGING
ALL DANCING
Dramatic Sensation!

The phrase caught on immediately, and two rival studios used the same sales pitch in the same year for *Broadway Babes* and *Rio Rita*.

In about 1970, the computing world adopted the phrase to hype up new software, so that by the mid 1980s, every kind of organization seemed to boast that their computers and systems packages had some quality that was "all singing, all dancing."

Subsequently, the expression has been linked with anything from savings plans, pensions and mortgages to machines—especially electronically controlled machines—of almost any kind.

A saying with a similar meaning is the older phrase "All the bells and whistles," which also describes that all-important "wow" factor.

ALL TARRED WITH THE SAME BRUSH

Everyone in the group shares the same failings; they're all sheep of the same flock. This old saying alludes to the methods used by farmers to mark their sheep. A brush dipped in tar was applied to the wool as a form of branding.

The phrase is now often used when people feel they have been lumped in with others and judged unfairly as a result.

ALL THAT GLITTERS IS NOT GOLD

Appearances are not what they seem. A saying that must have been in use for a thousand years or more and a favorite of poets, it is thought to be Latin in origin. It is a well-known note of prudence in Shakespeare's *The Merchant of Venice* (2:7):

> All that glisters is not gold,
> Often have you heard that told.

This implies that the proverb dates from earlier wisdom; certainly it was used by Geoffrey Chaucer in *The Canterbury Tales*, for in "The Canon's Yeoman's Tale," he wrote:

> However, all that glitters is not gold,
> And that's the truth as we're often told.

Many other writers have referenced it, including Thomas Gray in his "Ode on the Death of a Favourite Cat, Drowned in a Tub of Gold Fishes," but perhaps the most cynical use is that of Ogden Nash, who observed in "Look What You Did, Christopher":

> All that glitters is sold as gold.

ANNUS HORRIBILIS

A particularly bad or miserable year, the phrase being Latin for "horrible year." It owes its popularity to Queen Elizabeth II, who used it in a speech at a banquet in the Guild Hall, London, in 1992—the year that saw the divorce of the Princess Royal, the separations of the Prince and Princess of Wales and of the Duke and Duchess of York, and the devastating fire at Windsor Castle.

The next day, the punning headline writers **had a field day** (see page 248), with *The Sun* proclaiming on the front page, "One's Bum Year."

"Annus horribilis" was a play on a phrase with the opposite meaning—annus mirabilis, which was first used as the title of a poem by John Dryden to describe the year 1666, which he saw as an example of miraculous intervention by God.

It has ever since been used to describe particular years full of wonders or achievements; 1759 was one such for the British, in which they achieved a string of military successes (in British naval history, 1759 is also known as the "Year of Victories").

ANOTHER NAIL IN THE COFFIN

A depressing phrase that is applied to a development that makes a situation progressively worse. It refers to something that accelerates the failure of something or someone. The final nail can be compared with the "last straw" (see **clutching at straws**, page 220).

The phrase "another nail in the coffin" was also adopted by smokers. As early as the 1920s, they referred to cigarettes as "coffin nails," and this expression became the stock response whenever someone accepted yet another cigarette.

At the time, they were referring to the hazards of a smoker's cough; the links between smoking, cancer and heart disease were only recognized later (when cigarettes earned another nickname—"cancer sticks").

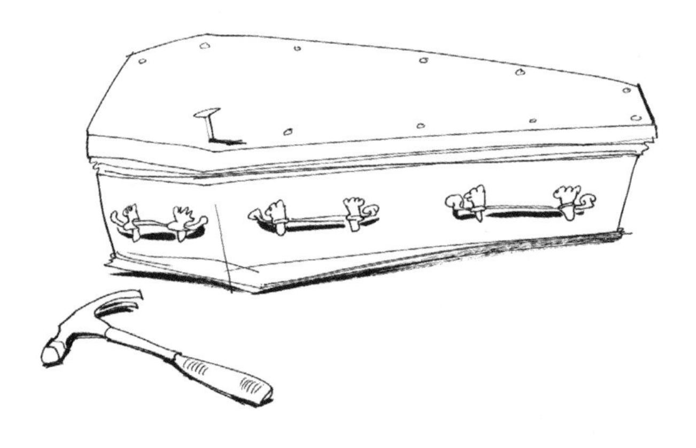

ANTS IN ONE'S PANTS

Said of an excessively restless or over-eager person.

The expression was popularized by Hugh S. Johnson, a dynamic former U.S. Army general who was in charge of the National Recovery Administration (NRA) in 1933–34, when the national reconstruction policies of President Franklin D. Roosevelt's "New Deal" were implemented.

He said of the NRA general counsel Donald Richberg: "Donald's agitation is just a symptom of the ants of conscience in his pants."

THE APPLE OF ONE'S EYE

"The apple of one's eye" is what one cherishes most. The pupil of the eye has long been referred to as the "apple" because it is perfectly round and was originally thought to be solid.

Because sight is so precious, someone who was called this as an endearment was similarly precious, with the result that the phrase took on the figurative sense we still retain.

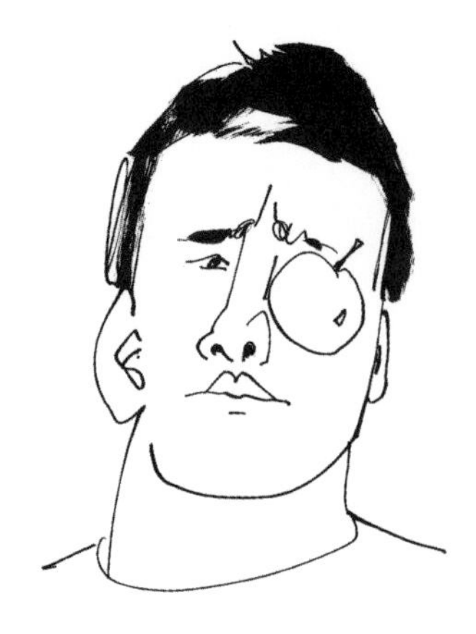

The Bible employs the phrase many times, including:

> Keep me as the apple of the eye, hide me under the shadow of thy wings.
>
> Psalms 17:8

Examples of the saying's use can also be found in the works of King Alfred, dating from the end of the ninth century.

Our modern word for the physical "apple of one's eye," "pupil," comes from Latin and appeared in English in the sixteenth century. It is figurative in origin; the late Latin original was pupilla, "little doll."

The word might have been applied to the dark central portion of the eye within the iris because of the tiny doll-like image of oneself that can be seen when looking into another person's eye.

AROUND ONE'S EARS

This colloquialism means to be in a very troublesome situation. It is a shortened form of the saying "to bring a hornets' nest down around one's ears." Similarly, "down around your ears" is often used.

The expression "to stir up a hornets' nest" implies the same degree of trouble as the phrase above—and suggests perhaps deliberate provocation, too.

ASK SOMETHING POINT BLANK

To ask a direct question. This is a sixteenth-century phrase from the sport of archery. The targets had a white (blanc in French) central spot, so the arrows were pointed at the white; that is, point blanc.

In military and artillery usage, "point blank" is a range at which there is no fall of shot due to gravity—in other words, a very close range. (Any projectile from a firearm "drops" from the point of aim as the range increases, which in turn means that the farther the target, the higher the weapon has to be aimed above it.)

~ B ~

BACK TO SQUARE ONE

To begin again, or, less formally, "Back to where you started, sunshine!" This colloquialism possibly derives from board games like snakes and ladders, in which players, through bad luck or poor judgment, have to move their pieces back to the starting point.

The meaning of the expression, "back to square one" is similar to "back to the drawing board," which means to go back and rethink a complete project or scheme. Aircraft designers during the Second World War used this phrase when a concept or even a whole design for a new machine proved unworkable and had to be started all over again.

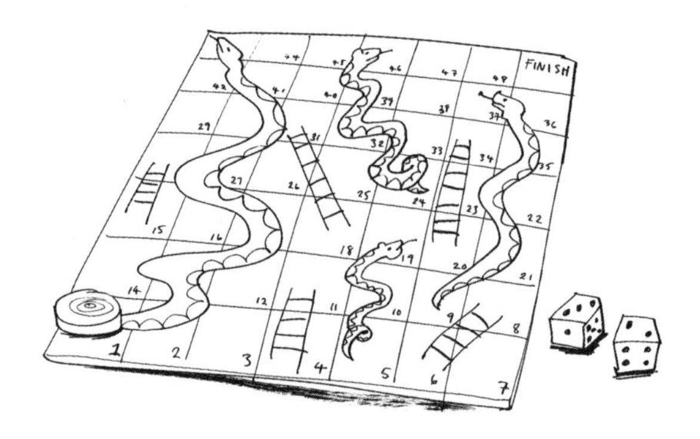

BAKER'S DOZEN

A baker's dozen is 13, one more than the standard dozen.

This phrase is widely held to date back to medieval England. Henry III (1216-1272) instituted a reign called the *Assize of Bread and Ale* that called for the severe punishment of any bakers caught shortchanging customers. English bakers developed the habit of including an extra loaf of bread when asked for a dozen to ensure that if one were stolen, dropped, or lost, they wouldn't be accused of shorting their customers.

BALLPARK FIGURE

An estimate, or a budget figure, which might better be described as a "guesstimate."

The phrase "in the same ballpark" was originally used when two figures, the projected and the real figure, were reasonably close. Over time, the term has evolved so that the estimated figure itself is now known as a "ballpark figure."

BARKING MAD

Used to suggest raving insanity, this phrase is frequently shortened to simply "barking." The expression emerged at the beginning of the twentieth century.

Its derivation stems from its link with rabid or mad dogs, whose wild howls and yaps audibly betrayed their diseased state.

BARK UP THE WRONG TREE

To be totally off the mark, to waste energy following the wrong course of action, or to have one's attention diverted off the subject in hand.

The phrase dates back to the 1800s and neatly puns a dog's bark with tree bark. The phrase's origins stem from the American sport of raccoon hunting. The hounds of the hunting pack are trained to mark the tree in which the raccoon they are

pursuing takes shelter, and then to howl at its base until their master arrives to shoot the animal. The hounds may bark up at the wrong tree, however, if the raccoon has managed to evade them.

The expression first became popular in the early nineteenth century, appearing in the works of James Hall, Davy Crockett—himself a great raccoon hunter—and Albert Pike.

BASKET CASE

A derogatory slang term used to describe a mentally-ill person who is unable to function properly. Recently the term has also come to be used in referring to poorly run and failing organizations.

The term originated in the U.S. military in World War I and was slang for soldiers who had lost both arms and both legs and because of this needed to be carried in a basket by others. Ironically, the term became widely known through a bulletin aiming to curtail its use. The U.S. Command on Public Information in March 1919, on behalf of Major General M. W. Ireland, the U.S. Surgeon General wrote:

"The Surgeon General of the Army...denies...that there is any foundation for the stories that have been circulated...of the existence of "basket cases" in our hospitals."

BEAT AROUND THE BUSH

To approach a matter indirectly or in a roundabout way. The expression has evolved from early hunting methods for catching birds. One team of hunters would approach the birds hiding in the undergrowth from the sides, so as to drive them into the path of another team, who would catch them with nets as they took off.

This task of literally beating the bushes in which the birds take shelter is still an important part of pheasant shooting today.

A BEE IN ONE'S BONNET

To be obsessed with a particular idea or notion, as though mentally all abuzz.

The expression, in the form of the variant "to have bees in the head," implying scattiness, was in circulation in the sixteenth century, for a reference to bees and crazed thought was recorded by the English poet, Court musician and entertainer John Heywood in 1546 in one of his collections of English proverbs.

It is thought that bees first met bonnets in the poem "Mad Maid's Song" by Robert Herrick, written in 1648:

For pity, sir, find out that bee,
Which bore my love away.
I'll seek him in your bonnet brave,
I'll seek him in your eyes.

BETWEEN THE DEVIL AND THE DEEP BLUE SEA

Caught between two evils or dangers, in a dilemma with nowhere to turn. The saying may be of nautical origin, the "devil" being a term for a seam in the hull of a ship that ran along the waterline.

A commonly used modern phrase with a similar meaning is "between a rock and a hard place."

> *"Between the devil and the deep blue sea" could also have been inspired by the ancient phrase "to steer or sail between Scylla and Charybdis."*
>
> *In Homer's* Odyssey*, Scylla was a six-headed monster who lived in a cavern overlooking a narrow channel off the coast of Sicily; she seized sailors from every passing ship with each of her six mouths.*
>
> *On the opposite rock, Charybdis, another monster, lived under a huge fig tree, from where she sucked in and regorged the sea, forming a treacherous whirlpool.*
>
> *In the poem, Odysseus sailed between these two perils, losing his ship in the whirlpool and the crew to Scylla. Only he survived—by clinging to the fig tree.*

BEWARE GREEKS BEARING GIFTS

Sometimes expressed as "I fear Greeks even when they offer gifts" (Virgil, *Aeneid*, 29–19 BC), this saying has its roots in the story of Helen of Troy (see **the face that launched a thousand ships**, page 237) and the Trojan War.

After a ten-year siege of the city of Troy by the Greeks, one of the remaining Greek besiegers (the Odysseus of the previous entry) devised an ingenious plan to invade the city. He hid all his men in a huge wooden horse, which was left outside the city gates, and then the Greeks abandoned their posts. The Trojans mistakenly took the horse to be a tribute from their beaten enemy and in celebration took the gift to the heart of their stronghold.

When night fell, the Greek soldiers poured out of the horse and—having the element of surprise—were victorious in the final battle.

THE BIG APPLE

The well-known nickname for New York City.

The name was first coined in the 1920s by John J. Fitz Gerald, a reporter for the *Morning Telegraph*, who used it to refer to the city's racetracks and who claimed to have heard it used by black stable hands in New Orleans in 1921.

Black jazz musicians in the 1930s took up the name to refer to the city, especially Harlem, as the jazz capital of the world.

The epithet was then revived in 1971 as part of a publicity campaign to attract tourists to New York.

The sentiment behind "The Big Apple" is likely to be the idea of an apple as a symbol of the best, as in **the apple of one's eye** (see page 187), meaning someone or something that is very precious.

In the eighteenth century, the writer and politician Horace Walpole referred to London as "The Strawberry," being impressed by its freshness and cleanliness compared with foreign cities; he named his estate at Twickenham, Middlesex, Strawberry Hill, and founded there the Strawberry Hill Press.

THE BIG ENCHILADA

The leader, the top man or woman, the boss.

The phrase crops up in the infamous Watergate tapes, referring to the then U.S. Attorney-General, John Mitchell, who led President Nixon's re-election campaign in 1972. Mitchell was later indicted on charges that he had conspired to plan the burglary of the Democratic National Committee's headquarters in the Watergate complex in Washington, D.C., and had then obstructed justice and perjured himself during the subsequent cover-up. He was convicted in 1974.

"The big enchilada" is a modernized version of earlier phrases that became popular in the mid 1970s, such as "big gun" or "the big cheese," both of which are used to describe VIPs, especially in business; a group of them may sometimes be facetiously described as *les grands fromages*.

BIG-STICK DIPLOMACY

A political catchphrase that describes diplomatic negotiations backed up by the threat of military force.

The term was brought to public attention in 1901 when then U.S. Vice-President Theodore Roosevelt revealed in a speech his fondness for the West African proverb "Speak softly and carry a big stick, you will go far." (Later, as President, he employed this philosophy successfully in the Alaskan boundary dispute of 1902–04.)

THE BIRDS AND THE BEES

A euphemism for human procreation that was probably inspired by songwriter Cole Porter, thanks to his 1954 composition, "Let's Do It":

> Birds do it, bees do it,
> Even educated fleas do it,
> Let's do it, let's fall in love.

The phrase was used, often by embarrassed parents or teachers, as a means of avoiding dangerous words like "sex" or "sexual intercourse"; nowadays, it tends to be used ironically.

BITE THE BULLET

To undertake the most challenging part of a feat of endurance, to face danger with courage and fortitude, to behave stoically or to knuckle down to some difficult or unpleasant task.

The expression originated in field surgery before the use of anesthetics. A surgeon about to operate on a wounded soldier would give him a bullet to bite on, both to distract him from the pain and to make him less likely to cry out.

BITE THE DUST

To fall down dead.

The Scottish author Tobias Smollett was the first to put this expression in print in 1750, in his translation of Alain-René Le Sage's *Adventures of Gil Blas of Santillane*; while in Samuel Butler's 1898 translation of Homer's *The Iliad*, Achilles has the line:

> Grant that my sword may pierce the shirt of Hector about his heart, and that full many of his comrades may bite the dust as they fall dying round him.

Another version of the phrase—"lick the dust"—had the same meaning and appeared in the original (1611) edition of the King James Bible.

The phrase was in common use during the Second World War, especially in the RAF; today, it is more often used to describe the failure of an idea, plan or task than death or injury.

TO THE BITTER END

To the last extremity, to the final defeat, or to the death. An affliction can be borne until the bitter end, meaning to the last stroke of bad fortune.

'Bitter end" is a mid-nineteenth-century nautical term for the end of a rope or chain secured in a vessel's chain locker. When there is no windlass (winch), such cables are fastened to bitts—that is, pairs of bollards fixed to the deck—and when the rope is let out until no more remains, the end is at the bitts: the "bitter end."

However, the phrase appears in the Old Testament in the context that we use today, and some etymologists believe that this is the true source of the expression:

> Her end is bitter as wormwood, sharp as a two-edged sword.
>
> Proverbs 5:4

BLACKMAIL

The crime of forcing or coercing a victim into a particular action by threatening to reveal substantially true information about a person to a family member, associates, or the public that would either embarrass, socially damage, or incriminate the victim.

The term originated in 19th century Scotland and northern England where clan chieftains ran protection rackets against Scottish farmers.

BLOOD, SWEAT AND TEARS

An emphatic description of the effort required to complete a challenging task. It is a concise form of a phrase used by Winston Churchill in his first speech to the House of Commons upon taking over as Prime Minister, on May 13, 1940.

Yet Churchill may have been inspired by a number of sources; some three centuries earlier, John Donne wrote in "An Anatomy of the World" (1611), "Mollify it with thy tears, or sweat, or blood"; while Lord Byron observed in *The Age of Bronze* (1823):

> Year after year they voted cent per cent,
> Blood, sweat and tear wrung millions—why? For the rent!

At the time of Churchill's assumption of the highest political office, British morale was at a low ebb: German forces had overrun Denmark, Holland and Belgium, and were in the process of conquering Norway and France. The prospect of victory over Germany looked increasingly unlikely.

Churchill's actual words were, "I have nothing to offer but blood, toil, tears and sweat," and he revisited this phrase several times during the war years.

BLOW HOT AND COLD

To be inconsistent, to have fluctuating opinions, or simply to be unable to make up one's mind.

The expression has its origins in the Aesop's fable that describes the experience of a traveler who accepted the hospitality of a satyr (one of the gods of the forest, a creature who is part goat and part man).

The chilly traveler blew on his cold fingers to warm them—and then blew on his hot broth to cool it. The indignant satyr ejected him because he blew both hot and cold with the same breath.

BLUE BLOOD

A translation of the Spanish phrase, "sangre azul," which is used to indicate nobility or noble descent. The phrase is said to have derived from some of the aristocratic families of Castile who boasted that they were purebred, having no link with the Moors, who had longed controlled the country, or any other group. A mark of this pure breeding, they claimed, was that their veins showed more clearly blue through their fairer skin. By the 19th century, the phrase had come into wide use in English.

A BONE TO PICK

This is a desire to discuss a difference of opinion, settle a misunderstanding about something disagreeable, or express a complaint. The bone is probably the bone of contention, metaphorically tossed between two dogs fighting over it.

Usage goes back to the middle of the sixteenth century, but the expression may well have come from an earlier phrase, "to have a crow to pluck," which was used at least a hundred years earlier; the crow in this instance symbolizing discord.

In Howell's Proverbs (1659) the phrase "to have a goose to pluck with you" is used in the same sense.

BONE UP ON

To study intensively, to engage in serious research into a particular subject, or to revise a subject comprehensively.

Some sources suggest that the phrase is an allusion to whalebone in a corset, which sculpts the shape and stiffens the garment, as a metaphor for the gaining of "hard knowledge."

Others believe it came from the Victorian practice of using bone to polish leather, and that it indicated a polishing or refinement of knowledge.

However, in the nineteenth century a publishing firm owned by Henry Bohn produced English translations of Greek and Latin classics that were widely used by students cramming for their exams—and it is possible that the expression "to Bohn up" may have evolved into "bone up."

BORN ON THE WRONG SIDE OF THE TRACKS

To be born on the wrong side of the tracks is a disadvantage, as it was the part of town deemed to be both socially and environmentally inferior.

The expression originated from when railway lines ran through the centers of towns. Poor and industrial areas were often located to one side of the railroad tracks because the prevailing wind would blow smoke from the railway and smog in that direction, leaving the better-off neighborhoods unpolluted.

The phrase is now used to refer to anyone who comes from a poor or rough background.

THE BOTTOM LINE

The main point of an argument, the basic characteristic of something, the actual value of a financial deal, or the nub or truth of the matter.

The phrase itself is an accounting term, and refers to the figure at the end of a financial statement, indicating the net profit or loss of a company.

"The bottom line" gained wide currency as a phrase during the 1970s, possibly because of its frequent use by Secretary of State Henry Kissinger. He spoke of "the bottom line" as the eventual outcome of a negotiation—ignoring the distraction of any inessential detail.

BREAK A LEG!

The theater is notoriously superstitious, and among actors it is deemed bad luck to wish a colleague "good luck" before going on stage. Instead, this phrase—a traditional, if somewhat black, euphemism—is employed to wish someone luck in a performance, especially on opening night.

There are a number of possible sources for the expression and the earliest recorded use is in fact German; Luftwaffe pilots in the Second World War would send each other off to fight with the cheery saying "*Hals und Beinbruch*," meaning "break your neck and leg."

The phrase was also used in English around this time to mean "make a strenuous effort," so it may have simply been an instruction to put on the best show you possibly could.

A more fanciful explanation is that the saying came from the assassination of President Abraham Lincoln in his private box at Ford's Theatre, Washington, D.C., on April 14, 1865.

The murderer, John Wilkes Booth, a reputable Shakespearean actor, escaped after firing the shot by leaping down on to the stage, breaking his leg in the process.

THE BUCK STOPS HERE

A declaration meaning "this is where ultimate responsibility lies."

The most likely origin for the phrase is the poker table, where a buckhorn knife was placed before the player whose turn it was to deal. "Passing the buck" meant passing responsibility on to the next player.

The phrase was made famous by U.S. President Harry S. Truman, who had it handwritten on a sign on his desk at the White House to remind himself and those around him that he alone had the ultimate responsibility for every decision of his administration.

Some twenty-five years later, President Jimmy Carter had the legend reinstated with the same idea in mind.

BUSINESS AS USUAL

This self-explanatory expression was widely used in Britain in the Second World War, and especially during the London Blitz and the blitzes on other major cities, when shops and businesses continued to open in spite of bomb damage. In the capital, "Business as usual" and "London can take it" were commonly scrawled defiantly on the walls of damaged buildings.

Winston Churchill popularized the phrase in 1941 in a speech at the Guild Hall in London when he said, "The maxim of the British people is: 'Business as usual.'"

BY THE SKIN OF ONE'S TEETH

By the narrowest margin. There are several metaphors with the meaning "only just" and many allude to body parts (for example, "by a hair's breadth'), emphasizing the physical danger of a given situation from which one might have just escaped.

"By the skin of one's teeth" specifically is a (slightly misquoted) biblical phrase that means to have suffered "a close shave":

> My bone cleaveth to my skin, and to my flesh, and I am escaped with the skin of my teeth.
>
> Job 19:20

CALL OFF ALL BETS

A summons to cancel all wagers, deriving from the racetrack and the betting shop; for instance, a bookmaker may call off all bets if he suspects that a race or other contest has been rigged.

In a widening of its meaning, the phrase is used to mean rejecting a complicated or disadvantageous issue.

In slang of the 1940s, however, it meant "to die"—indeed, the most final way of calling off all bets.

CAN'T HOLD A CANDLE TO

To be unable to measure up to someone. The phrase dates back to the time before electricity when part of the duty of an apprentice was to hold a candle so that the more experienced workmen would able to see what they were doing. If an apprentice could not even perform this low level task adequately, his status was quite low.

Sir Edward Dering used a similar phrase "to hold the candle" in his The fower cardinal-vertues of a Carmelite fryar, 1641:

"Though I be not worthy to hold the candle to Aristotle."

CARRY A TORCH

To suffer unrequited love. Since the late 1920s, this phrase has been used to describe a long-standing emotional attachment that is either undeclared or not returned.

The torch represents the flame of undying love, and this symbolism may come from depictions of Venus, the goddess of love, holding a burning torch.

A "torch singer" is (usually) a female who sings sentimental love songs. It is thought that the expression "torch song," in this sense, may have been coined by Broadway nightclub singer Tommy Lyman in the 1930s.

CASE THE JOINT

A slang expression from the criminal fraternity meaning to inspect or reconnoiter a building before attempting to rob it or break into it for some other nefarious purpose.

"Joint" in this context means "a building": an early twentieth-century colloquialism for a sleazy dive where opium could be smoked or, during the Prohibition era (1920–33), where illicit spirits could be bought and drunk. The word "joint" has since come to be generally applied disparagingly to almost any disreputable establishment.

CAST THE FIRST STONE

To be first to criticize, to find fault, to start a quarrel, or to cast aspersions on someone's character. In biblical times, the barbaric custom of capital punishment was to pelt heretics, adulteresses and criminals with stones and rocks in a public place.

The phrase is from John 8:7, spoken by Jesus to the Scribes and Pharisees who brought before him a woman caught in adultery. They said that according to the law of Moses, she should be stoned to death, to which Jesus replied: "He that is without sin among you, let him first cast a stone at her."

CAST PEARLS BEFORE SWINE

To offer something precious or of quality to someone who is perceived to be too ignorant or uncultured to understand or appreciate it. To show, for example, a brilliant idea or a work of art to an unappreciative audience or to the kind of person known as a Philistine.

(Philistines were warlike immigrants to Philistia in ancient Palestine, who fought the Israelites for possession of the land, and came to be stigmatized as an uneducated, heathen enemy; the term has since by extension come to mean anyone unreceptive or hostile to culture, especially someone who is smugly and boorishly so.)

The phrase itself comes from the New Testament (Matthew 7:6): "Give not that which is holy unto the dogs, neither cast ye your pearls before swine, lest they trample them under their feet."

CAT GOT YOUR TONGUE?

A question directed at a silent partner in a conversation to ask why they're not speaking.

The earliest written example appeared in 1911, according to the *Oxford English Dictionary*, but it may have been around since the mid-nineteenth century.

As to the phrase's origins, numerous theories abound; none firmly proved. Some argue that it must stem from ancient Middle Eastern punishment techniques, when liars" tongues were ripped out and then fed to kings" cats; while others cite the much-feared whip the "cat-o'-nine-tails" as the source of the phrase, insinuating that this nasty weapon, used to flog sailors, forced them into silence—both through fear and pain.

THE CAT'S PAJAMAS

This colloquialism first surfaced in the 1920s to describe something or someone superlatively good or top-notch and has retained its meaning for almost a hundred years.

Alternative sources suggest that the phrase may come from an early nineteenth-century English tailor E. B. Katz, who apparently made the finest silk pajamas, though there is little evidence to prove this is true.

"The cat's whiskers" and "the bee's knees" are phrases with similar meaning. In the 1920s, people played with phrases that linked animals to humans, and so we find "the kipper's knickers," "the snake's hips," "the elephant's instep" and so on.

In the last twenty years, modern imagination has taken this idea further, and we now have more ribald phrases such as the popular British term, "the dog's bollocks" (which is sometimes abbreviated to just "the dog's").

CATCH-22

A Catch-22 situation is a lose-lose situation; whichever alternative you choose, you can't win.

It is the title of Joseph Heller's highly regarded satirical novel published in 1955. The story centers on Captain Yossarian of the 256th U.S. Army Air Force bombing squadron in the Second World War, whose main aim in life is to avoid being killed. The best way for a pilot to achieve this was to be grounded due to insanity...

> There was only one catch and that was Catch-22, which specified that concern for one's own safety in the face of dangers that were real and immediate was the process of a rational mind. Orr [another pilot] was crazy and could be grounded. All he had to do was to ask and as soon as he did, he would no longer be crazy and would have to fly more missions.

CATCH FORTY WINKS

A colloquial term for a short nap or a doze.

Just why shutting one eye forty times has come to mean a quick snooze is unclear, but it could have something to do with the fact that the number forty appears frequently in the scriptures and used to be thought of as a holy number.

Moses was on the Mount for forty days and forty nights; Elijah was fed by ravens for forty days; the rain of the Flood fell for forty days, and another forty days passed before Noah opened the window of the ark. Christ fasted for forty days, and he was seen forty days after his Resurrection.

Busy people and politicians who work late into the night maintain their faculties by taking "power naps" to recharge their batteries.

A CHIP ON ONE'S SHOULDER

To display an inferiority complex, to perceive oneself as an underdog, to have a grievance, often unjustifiably.

The expression is believed to have originated in about 1840 and may allude to a game of dare, in which a man challenges another to dislodge a chip—as in piece of wood—he carries on his shoulder.

A chip is also a figurative term for consequences, and so the phrase may be a warning to an adversary not to aim too high.

There is an ancient proverb, "Hew not too high lest chips fall in thine eye." By the late sixteenth century, this health-and-safety warning had become something of a challenge, a dare to a fearless woodcutter to look high up without regard to any falling chips of wood.

CLAM UP

To refuse to talk, to stop talking, to become silent. People are generally said to "clam up" when they are trying to defend themselves.

The phrase takes its origins from the closed shell of a live clam. At high tide, clams open their shells a little to allow seawater to filter through, so that they can feed. When the tide goes out, they close their shells tightly to retain the water and protect themselves from predators.

CLEAN ROUND THE BEND

Completely crazy or eccentric. The phrase was described by F. C. Bowen in the *Oxford English Dictionary* in 1929 as "an old naval term for anybody who is mad."

The word "clean" is used in many different ways to describe something complete, pure, unmarked or unreserved—for instance, "clean bowled," "to make a clean break" or "to make a clean breast of it."

CLEAR THE DECKS

To remove everything not required, especially when preparing for action; to prepare for some task by removing the extraneous or irrelevant.

This is a nautical phrase and alludes to a sailing ship preparing for battle, when anything in the way of the guns and their crews, or that might burn or splinter, or that was not lashed down, was removed from the usually cluttered decks so that no untethered articles would roll about and injure the seamen during the battle.

This saying is used in many contexts, such as clearing the table of food and dishes or preparing the house to receive guests.

"Deck" appears in many commonly used phrases, among them "to hit the deck"—to fall over, usually to escape injury—or "to deck someone" (to hit them and knock them to the floor).

CLIMB ON THE BANDWAGON

To declare support for a popular movement or trend, usually without believing in the movement or trend.

The expression is believed to have originated in the South, probably dating from the first presidential campaign of William Jennings Bryan in 1892, when candidates for political office would parade through the streets, led by a band of musicians performing on a large horse-drawn dray.

As a publicity stunt, the local candidate would mount the wagon as it passed and ride through his constituency in an attempt to gain personal support from the voters. Perhaps unsurprisingly, Bryan never won the presidency, losing to McKinley in 1896 and 1900, and to Taft in 1908.

The phrases "Get on the bandwagon!" and "Jump on the bandwagon!" are also often used.

CLOAK AND DAGGER

Any operation that involves some intrigue, especially the melodramatic undercover activities of those involved in espionage or other secret work.

Cloak-and-dagger plays were swashbuckling adventures popular in the seventeenth century. In France, a performance of this type was known as a *comédie de cape et d'épée* and this is the direct source of the English phrase, "cloak and dagger."

> *The name also appears in the Spanish* comedias de capa y espada, *literally "comedies of cloak and sword," particularly those by the Spanish dramatists Lope de Vega and Calderón, although their plays were dramas of merely domestic intrigue.*

ON CLOUD NINE

To be on cloud nine means to be in a state of elation, very happy indeed, or feeling "as high as a kite."

This fanciful twentieth-century expression comes from the terminology used by the U.S. Weather Bureau. The Bureau divides clouds into classes, and each class into nine types.

Cloud nine is cumulonimbus, a cumulus cloud that develops to a vast height, with rounded masses of white vapor heaped one on the other; the upper parts resembling the shapes of domes, mountains or towers, while the base is practically horizontal.

CLUTCHING AT STRAWS

Someone in desperate circumstances will reach out and grab hold of anything, however flimsy or inadequate, in the hope of surviving the situation.

It was first used in print by Sir Thomas More in 1534, in his *Dialogue of Comfort Against Tribulation*.

The word "straw" has been used as a metaphor for years, representing the insubstantial or groundless, as in a "man of straw," someone financially insecure or with a poor credit rating. We also have "the last straw (that broke the camel's back)," that little extra burden which makes something no longer bearable (as with the camel's load, tipping the balance of tolerance).

COCK-AND-BULL STORY

A rambling or incredible tale; a tall story invented as an excuse; a lie.

There are various possible explanations for the derivation of this term. In the coaching days of the seventeenth century, the London coach changed horses at the Bull Inn and the Birmingham coach at the Cock Inn. The waiting passengers of both coaches would exchange stories and jokes. The "Cock-and-Bull" story is said to have originated from this scenario.

The phrase may derive, however, from ancient fables in which cocks and bulls and other animals conversed. In his Boyle Lecture of 1692, Richard Bentley stated:

> That cocks and bulls might discourse, and hinds and panthers hold conferences about religion.

While in his novel *Tristram Shandy* (1759), Laurence Sterne wrote:

> "L—d!" said my mother. "What is all this story about?"
> "A Cock and Bull," said Yorick—"And one of the best of its kind, I have ever heard."

Today both words are commonly employed separately in a slang or vulgar context. "Bull" is used as in "what a load of bull," politely avoiding saying the word "bullshit," while "cock" speaks for itself.

> *A Scottish satire or lampooning story is known as a "cocka-lane," which is taken directly from the French phrase of the same meaning as "cock and bull":* coq et l'âne *(cock and ass, donkey or fool).*

COLD ENOUGH TO FREEZE THE BALLS OFF A BRASS MONKEY

This means that the weather is extremely cold, and although the expression sounds delightfully vulgar, it was not in fact originally a reference to monkeys' testicles.

A brass monkey is a type of rack in which cannonballs were stored. Being brass, the "monkey" contracted in cold weather, resulting in the cannonballs being ejected.

The expression has also mutated to a shortened form, again a comment on the temperature, as "brass-monkey weather."

COME OUT OF THE CLOSET

To declare one's homosexuality, to come out into the open about it. The term was used by the gay rights organization the Gay Liberation Front from about 1969, but the idea of "coming out" had first been encouraged by German gay-rights advocate Karl Heinrich Ulrichs in 1869.

In the days when homosexuality was a criminal offense, gay men had to hide the nature of their sexual preferences. They became known as closet queens, the closet being a private room.

When antihomosexual laws were repealed, the need for secrecy receded and gay men were able "to come out"—although many, fearful of society's disapproval, remained "in the closet."

The expression is now often used generally to mean "to declare one's real position."

The phrase "to come out" is also used to describe debutantes, upper-class young women making their official debut in society.

COME UP TO SCRATCH

To be good enough to pass a test; to make the grade. This is a colloquialism from the boxing ring dating back to the nineteenth century.

Under the London Prize Ring Rules introduced in 1839, a round in a prizefight ended when one of the fighters was knocked down. After an interval of thirty seconds, the floored fighter was given eight seconds to make his way, unaided, to a mark scratched in the center of the ring.

If he failed to reach the mark, he had not "come up to scratch" and was declared the loser of the bout.

COUCH POTATO

Slang from the late 1980s, used to describe someone who indulges in the habit of lounging at home watching television, eating and drinking, but never exercising.

The expression is now used in most English-speaking countries, particularly with the increase in the number of television channels to choose from.

Perhaps the potato featured in the metaphor because the blemishes on its skin are known as "eyes"; or possibly because it is the tuber of the potato plant, punning with "the tube"—the television.

CROSS THE RUBICON

To take an irrevocable step, to burn one's bridges, to go beyond the point of no return.

The Rubicon was a small river, possibly the present-day Fiumicino, which formed the border between ancient Italy and Cisalpine Gaul, the province allocated to Julius Caesar. When Caesar crossed this stream in 49 BC, he went beyond the limits of his own province and became an invader in Italy, making the outbreak of war between Pompey and the Senate inevitable.

"The Rubicon" is now often used alone as a description of "the point of no return."

CRY ALL THE WAY TO THE BANK

The expression "to cry all the way to the bank" was a popular catchphrase in the 1950s. It is an ironic comment, usually made about someone who has done something questionable, or produced something kitsch or tasteless or for some reason generally disapproved of, while making a great deal of money from it.

It is thought to have been first used by the high-camp pianist and entertainer Liberace in 1956, after critics had savaged his performance at a Madison Square Gardens concert. Liberace was the highest-paid entertainer in the United States during the 1960s and 1970s, and his income averaged $5 million a year for more than twenty-five years.

CUT THE MUSTARD

A zesty and confident phrase meaning to do something well and efficiently, to prove oneself beyond all expectations at completing a task or occupation.

The expression probably derives from mustard as slang for "the best"; a line from O. Henry's *Cabbages and Kings* (1894) reads:

> I'm not headlined in the bills, but I'm the mustard in the salad just the same.

"To cut," in this phrase, might refer to the harvesting of the plant, but it also might be used as in the expressions to "cut a dash," "cut up rough" or "cut capers."

CUT YOUR COAT ACCORDING TO YOUR CLOTH

This metaphorical proverb dates back to the sixteenth century and is all about good housekeeping and living within one's means. It is sensible advice to keep to one's budget and restrict expenditure to the amount of one's income.

It is often shortened, becoming simply "to cut your coat."

CUTE AS A BUTTON

To be charming, pretty, or attractive in a dainty way, almost always with the connotation of being small.

This often used simile sounds odd when you think about it. After all, how is it that a button is cute? That's debatable. Some say the "button" referred to here is not the kind you find on a shirt but actually the flower bud on a bachelor's button. Others insist the phrase refers to the button quail, an adorable little gray, fluffy bird.

DEAR JOHN LETTER

A "you're dumped" note from a wife or girlfriend breaking the news that the relationship with the recipient is over.

The expression originated during the Second World War. The unfortunate objects of Dear John letters were usually members of the armed forces overseas, whose female partners at home had made new liaisons, proving that absence sometimes does not make the heart grow fonder.

The name "John" was often used to signify "everyman" at the time; "John Doe" was the name given to any man whose real name was unknown or had to be kept anonymous.

THE DOG DAYS OF SUMMER

Very hot and oppressive summer days. The Romans called the hottest weeks of the summer *caniculares dies,* and not because dogs are thought to go mad in the heat (although Noël Coward did write in 1932 that "mad dogs and Englishmen go out in the midday sun").

The theory was that the days when the Dog Star, Sirius—the brightest star in the firmament—rose with the sun were the hottest and most sultry. It is an ancient belief that the combined heat of Sirius and the sun produced the stifling weather from about July 3rd to August 11th.

We also now use the phrase "dog days" to describe any period of stagnation.

DON'T COUNT YOUR CHICKENS BEFORE THEY'RE HATCHED

Don't assume something is certain before it is proved to be so. The phrase has been around for thousands of years, since it appears in Aesop's fable of "The Milkmaid and Her Pail."

There are probably more versions of this proverb than any other. "The man that once did sell the lion's skin / While the beast liv'd, was kill'd with hunting him," wrote Shakespeare in Henry V *(1598–9; 4:3), while a Hindu proverb urges, "Don't bargain for fish which are still in the water," and an ancient Egyptian saw cautions, "Do not rejoice over what has not yet happened."*

DON'T LOOK A GIFT HORSE IN THE MOUTH

(see also **straight from the horse's mouth,** page 317)

This references the method of assessing the age of a horse by inspecting the length of its teeth. The meaning is: Do not question the value of something given to you. It is very bad form to inspect a gift for faults or defects, so be grateful for anything received. As the old saying goes: "It's the thought that counts."

The phrase is an old proverb that has been in use for hundreds of years. It was discovered in the writings of St. Jerome, one of the Latin Fathers of the fourth century, who identified it as a common proverb. The saying also occurs in French, German, Italian, Spanish and other European languages, emphasizing the centuries-long dominance of the horse until the coming of the automobile.

DRESSED TO THE NINES

To be dressed flamboyantly.

Some say that the phrase originated as tailors used to traditionally use nine yards of material to make a fine suit.

It is also worth noting that the shorter phrase, "to the nines," was used in the 18th century meaning achieving perfection or the highest standards. For example from William Hamilton's Epistle to Ramsay, 1719:

> The bonny Lines therein thou sent me,
> How to the nines they did content me.

DROP OF A HAT

On signal, instantly, without delay.

The expression alludes to the frontier practice of dropping a hat as a signal for a boxing or wrestling match to begin, usually the only formality observed. Athletics or horse races also used to be started by the fast downward sweep of a hat.

There are many sayings including the word "hat," such as "hats off to him," "as black as your hat," and "I'll eat my hat," all of which probably originated in the days when dress codes and social etiquette were more formal, requiring people in polite society to cover their heads.

EASY AS PIE

Making a pie is not easy and this expression must apply to the eating of it. It originates in the nineteenth-century, when sweet pie was a common dish and the word "pie" was associated with simple pleasures.

An easy task can also be described as a "piece of cake," which is also easy to obtain and eat, as opposed to baking it.

EAT HUMBLE PIE

To make a humble apology or to submit oneself to a certain degree of humiliation, to climb down from a position one has assumed, to be obliged to take a lower station.

Here, "humble" could be a play on the word "umble," the umbles being the offal—the heart, liver and entrails—of an animal, usually the deer, considered a delicacy by some, although most thought them only fit for the servants.

Though the word humble has a different derivation, the closeness of the two words could be one of the reasons the phrase evolved as it did. For when the lord of the manor and his family dined on venison at high table, the huntsman and lower orders of the household took lower seats and partook of the umbles made into a pie.

James Russell Lowell observed in 1864:

> Disguise it as you will, flavor it as you will, call it what you will, umble pie is umble pie, and nothing else.

EGG ON ONE'S FACE

To be embarrassed or humiliated by something you have done.

The phrase has been used in the United States for over fifty years, and it seems to be a simple analogy that has become an idiom in itself. Just as if you were to eat your eggs sloppily and end up with them on your face, when you do something ineptly, you wind up looking foolish and embarrassing yourself.

AT THE ELEVENTH HOUR

Just in the nick of time, at the last moment, before the end of the day.

The allusion is to Jesus's parable of the laborers hired to work in the vineyard in which those starting work at the eleventh hour—that is, late in the afternoon at about five o'clock—were paid the same as those who had "borne the burden and heat of the day" (Matthew 20:1–16).

The Allies' armistice with Germany, ending the First World War, came into effect at the eleventh hour of the eleventh day of the eleventh month in 1918.

EVERY CLOUD HAS A SILVER LINING

In every situation, no matter how seemingly hopeless and gloomy, there is always some redeeming brightness to be found if one takes the trouble to look for it—"while there's life, there's hope."

This optimistic guidance to look on the bright side has been around since Roman times (although one Latin proverb reads, "After the sun, the clouds").

The phrase is thought to have its origins in Milton's *Comus* (1634): the lady lost in the wood resolves not to give up hope and says:

Was I deceived or did a sable cloud
Turn forth her silver lining on the night?

EVERY DOG HAS ITS DAY

This is a commonly used phrase that seems to have first appeared in English in the writings of R. Taverner in 1539 and subsequently in those of Shakespeare:

Let Hercules himself do what he may,
The cat will mew, and dog will have his day.

Hamlet (1600; 5:1)

It means that everyone will have a chance one day; everyone will have a moment of success or of being important eventually. This sentiment has been expressed for thousands of years.

The Latin proverb reads Hodie mihi—cras tibi, *"Today to me, tomorrow to thee." And another ancient old wives" tale states that: "Fortune visits every man once, she favors me now, but she will favor you in your turn."*

As a further example, Peter Pindar wrote in his Odes to Condolence *(1792):*

Thus every dog at last will have his day—
He who this morning smiled, at night may sorrow,
The grub today's a butterfly tomorrow.

AN EYE FOR AN EYE

Punishment equal to the crime, retaliation in kind, or simply getting even. The justification for this form of retribution comes from the Old Testament:

> Eye for eye, tooth for tooth, hand for hand, foot for foot.
>
> Exodus 21:24

Jesus referred to these words in the New Testament and put his own spin on their message, creating another commonly used expression, "to turn the other cheek":

> Ye have heard that it hath been said, An eye for an eye, and a tooth for a tooth: But I say unto you, That ye resist not evil: but whosoever shall smite thee on thy right cheek, turn to him the other also.
>
> Matthew 5:38–9

F

THE FACE THAT LAUNCHED A THOUSAND SHIPS

The face is that of the legendary beauty, Helen of Troy, and the ships were the Greek fleet, which sailed for Troy to avenge the King of Sparta.

In Greek legend, Helen was the daughter of Zeus and Leda, and wife of Menelaus, King of Sparta. She eloped with Paris, Prince of Troy, and the angry Menelaus sent a thousand ships to lay siege to the city of Troy. The fabled Helen is now an archetype of female beauty.

The phrase itself was first written by Christopher Marlowe:

> Was this the face that launched a thousand ships,
> And burned the topless towers of Ilium?
>
> *Doctor Faustus* (first published 1604)

A FEATHER IN ONE'S CAP

A personal achievement or honor to be proud of. The feather is a proud and visible emblem of victory and the gesture of putting a feather in your hat is almost universal in one form or another.

There is an ancient custom, widespread in Asia, among Native Americans and throughout Europe, of adding a feather to one's headgear to mark each enemy killed. Even today, a sportsman who kills his first woodcock puts a feather from the bird in his hat.

At one time in Hungary, the only people who could wear feathers were those who had killed Turks.

When General Charles Gordon, known as "Chinese Gordon," quelled the Taiping Rebellion in 1864, he was honored by the Chinese government with the "yellow jacket and peacock's feather."

FIDDLE WHILE ROME BURNS

To delay or vacillate or do nothing during an emergency or crisis—an allusion to Nero's reputed behavior during the burning of Rome in AD 64.

Nero Claudius Caesar was the infamous Roman emperor whom his contemporaries believed to be the instigator of the fire that destroyed most of the city. As the blaze raged, it is said that he sang to his lyre and recited his own poetry, while enjoying the spectacle from the top of a high tower.

Many historians doubt his complicity, however, and Nero himself blamed the Christians.

FIFTEEN MINUTES OF FAME

Meaning to have short-lived fame, of the type that is now quite possible in the modern, media-driven, celebrity-obsessed age. The expression comes from the celebrated words of Andy Warhol, first published in a catalog for an exhibition of his work in Stockholm in 1968. Pop artist Warhol was concerned, among other subjects, with the nature of celebrity, and he wrote, "In the future, everyone will be world famous for fifteen minutes."

The phrase struck a chord and is often now shortened to "he's had his fifteen minutes."

IN FINE FETTLE

To be in good order or condition—"fettle" is an old word meaning condition, order or shape. Nowadays, it rarely appears on its own, being usually heard in the alliterative phrase.

In the past, we might have heard "good fettle" or "bad fettle," and in *John Barleycorn* by Jack London, published in 1913, he wrote:

> Those fifty-one days of fine sailing and intense sobriety had put me in splendid fettle.

The origin of the word "fettle" is somewhat obscure. It probably comes from the Old English fetel for a belt, so "fettle" first meant to gird oneself up, as for a heavy task.

The word was most typically used as a verb meaning to put things in order, tidy up, arrange, or prepare. Such as in Anne Brontë's *Agnes Grey* (1847), in the Yorkshire dialect speech of a servant:

> But next day, afore I'd gotten fettled up—for indeed, Miss, I'd no heart to sweeping an' fettling, an' washing pots; so I sat me down i' th' muck—who should come in but Maister Weston.

In northern English dialects, "fettle" is sometimes used in the sense of making or repairing something. In Australia, a "fettler" is a railway maintenance worker.

It is also used in some manufacturing trades—in metal casting and pottery it describes the process of knocking the rough edges off a piece.

FLAVOR OF THE MONTH

A generic advertising phrase of the mid 1940s attempting to persuade shoppers to buy a new flavor of ice cream each month and not just stick to their usual choice.

Since then, it has been used to describe any short-lived fashion, craze or person that is quickly dropped after a period of being in demand.

THE FULL MONTY

Everything, the lot, the complete works. Said of anything done to the utmost or fullest degree.

The origin of the expression is uncertain. It may derive from the "full amount"; or the Spanish card game *monte* (literally mountain or heap of cards); or it may refer to the full, three-piece, "Sunday best" suit from the men's outfitters Montague Burton.

The phrase became even more popular after the release of the hit 1997 film *The Full Monty*, directed by Peter Cattaneo. The movie followed a fictitious group of unemployed factory workers from Sheffield, England, who raise money by staging a strip act at a local club and taking off "the full monty."

AT FULL TILT

At full speed or with full force.

The expression probably originated in the fourteenth century, when "tilting at the quintain" was a popular sport among medieval knights. A dummy head, often representing a Turk or Saracen, was fastened to rotate around an upright stake fixed in the ground. At full speed, the knight on horseback tilted toward the head with his lance. If he failed to strike it in the right place, it would spin round and strike him in the back before he could get clear.

Tilting at the quintain remained a rustic sport, especially popular at wedding celebrations, until the mid-seventeenth century.

The similar phrase "to tilt at windmills" has a rather different meaning, namely "to battle fanciful enemies." The reference is to the crazed knight Don Quixote (in Miguel de Cervantes's novel, Don Quixote, *1605), who imagined the windmills to be giants and advanced to attack.*

GIVE SHORT SHRIFT

To treat someone peremptorily and unsympathetically, without heeding any mitigating arguments, or simply to make short work of something.

Shrift is defined as a confession to a priest. "Short shrift" originally referred to the limited amount of time given to a convict between condemnation, confession and absolution, and then finally execution.

GIVE THE THIRD DEGREE

To subject one to uncomfortably detailed questioning to get to the bottom of an inquiry, whether it be criminal or general.

One possible source of the phrase is Free Masonry, where the third degree is the highest level of membership. Those wishing to be considered as Master Masons must sit an intensive exam with interrogatory-style questions.

The term is applied to the use by the police of exhaustive questioning to extract a confession or incriminating information from a suspect, criminal, accomplice or witness.

"Third-degree treatment" is also used as a euphemism for torture.

GOOD OL' BOY NETWORK

This is the network of social connections established through the private-school system that were traditionally used to get on in life.

The old-school tie worn by former pupils of various private schools was a distinguishing mark, recognized by members of the same privileged class. That recognition would lead to favorable support and opportunities.

Today the old-boy network is seen in a negative light as a way of preserving the social elite.

GO OFF HALF-COCKED

To be unsuccessful at doing something due to inadequate preparation, or being in too much of a hurry—reminiscent of the phrase "more haste less speed."

The term is related to hunting and shooting and originates from the eighteenth century, when a musket that was cocked halfway had the hammer set in the safety position to prevent accidental discharge. However, the mechanisms were sometimes faulty and the gun would fire, much to the surprise of the musketeer.

Modern sporting guns cannot in fact "go off" at half-cock accidentally, as they no longer have a half-cock mechanism.

GOODY TWO SHOES

A goody two shoes is someone who is virtuous in a coy or sentimental way.

In 1765 a fable called the *History of Little Goody Two Shoes* was published. A variation on the Cinderella story, it is about a poor orphan girl who has only one shoe. She is so delighted when a rich gentleman gives her a pair of shoes that she keeps repeating that she has two shoes:

> She ran out to Mrs. Smith as soon as they were put on, and stroking down her ragged Apron thus, cried out, "Two Shoes, Mame, see two Shoes." And so she behaved to all the People she met, and by that Means obtained the Name of Goody Two-Shoes.

GRAND SLAM

A sweeping success or total victory.

This phrase surprisingly has its origins in a game of cards and not sports as one might guess. In the card game, contract bridge, the term refers to a high score involving winning all the tricks in a hand, and it contrasts with a "small slam." Now popularly used in a variety of sports, including golf and tennis, it used when a single player wins several major championship contests. In baseball, it refers to a home run with three runners on base.

THE GREEN-EYED MONSTER

To be jealous of or to covet someone's beauty, achievements, attainments or wealth. The metaphor is commonly reduced to the expression "to be green with envy." The monster was identified by Shakespeare in *Othello* (3:3):

> O! beware, my lord, of jealousy;
> It is the green ey'd monster which doth mock
> The meat it feeds on.

However, to accuse someone of having "green in their eye" is to suggest that they are inexperienced or easily bamboozled, as in "greenhorn," which means to be a novice, green behind the ears; like the green horns of a young horned animal.

Shakespeare again, in *Antony and Cleopatra* (1:5):

> My salad days,
> When I was green in judgment...

THE HAIR OF THE DOG

This phrase refers to a remedy usually administered to someone with a hangover, after an overindulgence of alcohol the night before. The theory is that the very thing that causes the malady is the best cure or means of relief, so another drink in the morning is considered by some the best pick-me-up (by others a recipe to make one feel worse, not better).

The general principle that "like cures like" comes from Roman times, expressed in Latin as *similia similibus curantura.* The peculiar "hair of the dog" phrase perhaps originated in the sixteenth century. Back then, if one was bitten by a mad dog (which was likely to be suffering from rabies), it was accepted medical practice to dress the wound with the burnt hair of the dog, as an antidote.

Amazingly, this cure was recommended for dog bites for about two hundred years before its efficacy was finally brought into question.

HAVE A FIELD DAY

A figurative expression for a day or occasion or time of particular excitement, often a day away from the usual routine.

The phrase is in fact a military term for a day when troops have maneuvers, exercises or reviews—out in the field. (The military refer to the area or sphere of operations as "the field.")

The term is now used more generally to mean a time of enjoyment, or making the most of things; we might say that the tabloid newspapers would "have a field day" if they got hold of a particularly salacious story.

In the U.S. Navy, "a field day" is a day devoted to cleaning the ship in preparation for inspection.

Students, meanwhile, enjoy field trips, on which they travel away from school, particularly to study geography.

HEEBIE JEEBIES

An expression of intense apprehension, anxiety, or depression.

To give someone the heebie jeebies is to make that person uncomfortably nervous.

The first known use of the phrase was in the 1920s during a period when nonsensical rhyming phrases, such as, "the bee's knees," seemed all the rage. Cartoonist Billy DeBeck is widely cited as coining this particular one in a 1923 cartoon of his in the October 26th edition of the *New York American*:

> You dumb ox—why don't you get that stupid look offa your pan—you gimme the heeby jeebys!

HERE'S MUD IN YOUR EYE!

A drinking toast, the sentiments of which could be read either way. One interpretation is that it is to wish good fortune, as it was used in the trenches of the First World War when soldiers would naturally rather mud was thrown in their eye than anything more lethal.

Another, somewhat less good-natured, theory comes from horse racing, in which, with one's own horse out in front, it will be kicking mud into the eyes of the slower runners behind.

The phrase itself is thought to originate from a Bible story—featured in chapter nine of the Gospel of St. John—when Jesus puts mud in the eyes of a blind man and restores his sight.

HOIST WITH ONE'S OWN PETARD

To be beaten with one's own weapons, or to be caught in one's own trap. The modern equivalent relates to the sport of soccer, "to score an own goal."

Shakespeare coined the phrase when he wrote these lines for Hamlet:

> For 'tis the sport to have the engineer
> Hoist with his own petard.
>
> *Hamlet* (1600; 3:4)

In 1600, a petard was a newly invented explosive device used for blowing up walls, barricades or gates with gunpowder. It was a metal bell-shaped grenade filled with five or six pounds of gunpowder, dug into a trench and set off by a fuse.

The devices were often unreliable and went off unexpectedly, and the engineer who fired the petard might be blown up by the explosion. So the expression, in which "hoist" means to be lifted up, is an understated description of being blown up by your own bomb.

The name of the device came from the Latin petare, *meaning to break wind; the phrase is perhaps an ironic comment on the noise of the explosion.*

HUE AND CRY

A noisy commotion over some crowd gathering spectacle.

The phrase must have been in use since the beginning of the last millennium because the Norman French word *huer* means "to shout."

Until the beginning of the nineteenth century, "hue and cry" was the old legal term for an official outcry made when calling out for assistance, "with horn and with voice," in the pursuit of a suspected criminal escaping arrest. All able-bodied men were legally required to join the pursuit—if they refused, they risked being held liable for any theft committed by the fleeing felon. Thieves failing to respond to the "hue and cry" were liable to greater penalties once they were caught.

We now chiefly use the phrase to describe the way the news media clamor for someone to be held responsible for high-profile crimes or political mistakes.

HUNG, DRAWN AND QUARTERED

The correct order for this form of torturous capital punishment was that the victim was "drawn, hanged, drawn, beheaded and quartered." The crime that merited this sort of penalty was high treason.

The guilty were to be "drawn" to the place of execution on a hurdle or dragged along by horse's tail. Yet "drawn" also meant to be disembowelled, and this was added to the punishment in between the hanging stage and the beheading stage.

This expression is also sometimes shortened to just "drawn and quartered."

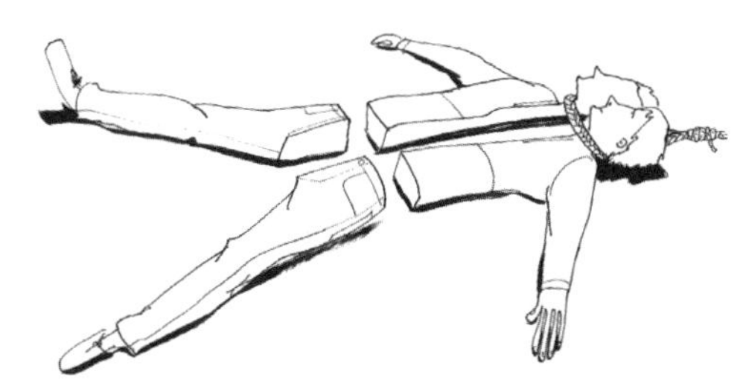

☙ I ❧

IT'S ALL GREEK TO ME

"It's all Greek to me" is used to mean that something is completely unintelligible to the speaker, Greek being a particularly tricky language to grasp because of its different alphabet.

The saying may have started out as an Anglicized version of the Latin phrase *Graecum est; non legitur*, meaning "It is Greek; it cannot be read," which was often used by monk scribes in the Middle Ages, when Greek was falling out of use.

It was probably popularized by Shakespeare's Julius Caesar, in which Casca says, "For mine own part, it was Greek to me" (1:2).

IT'S AN ILL WIND

Similar in spirit to "every cloud has a silver lining," this ancient nautical proverb suggests that some good can come from most misfortunes. The full phrase is, "It's an ill wind that blows nobody any good," meaning that only the very worst situations are universally bad, and that hardships usually bring benefits eventually.

It was already widely used by 1546, when John Heywood included it in his book of English proverbs. In 1591, Shakespeare wrote in *Henry VI*: "Ill blows the wind that profits nobody" (2:5).

IT TAKES TWO TO TANGO

A frequently used axiom that comes from the 1952 song of this title by Al Hoffman and Dick Manning:

> There are lots of things you can do alone!
> But it takes two to tango.

This satisfyingly alliterative phrase is often used in a sexual context when one partner is accused of seducing the other; it implies willingness on both sides. In general, it indicates that in any troublesome situation in which two people are involved, the blame should usually be shared between them.

It is also now used more widely in the fields of business and politics to imply that, in order to achieve agreement between two groups, both may have to compromise.

JUMP OUT OF THE FRYING PAN INTO THE FIRE

To leap from one bad predicament to another which is as bad or even worse.

In English, the phrase can be traced back to about 1530 when, in the course of a religious argument, Sir Thomas More, Henry VIII's Lord Chancellor and author of *Utopia,* said that William Tyndale, translator of the Bible into English, had "featly conuayed himself out of the frying panne fayre into the fyre."

Unfortunately, both men met a gruesome end. Sir Thomas More was hanged as a traitor in 1535 for refusing to approve the marriage between Henry VIII and Anne Boleyn, while Tyndale was publicly strangled and burned as a heretic in 1536.

Most languages have an equivalent phrase for "to jump out of the frying pan into the fire"; the French have tomber de la poêle dans le feu—*"fall from the frying pan into the fire'—from which the English is probably translated. The ancient Greeks had, "out of the smoke into the flame"; the Italians and Portuguese, "to fall from the frying pan into the coals"; and the Gaelic is, "out of the cauldron into the fire."*

KEEP ONE'S POWDER DRY

To be prepared for action, but preserve one's resources until they are really needed. The phrase comes from a saying attributed to Oliver Cromwell, and the powder is, of course, gunpowder, which will not ignite if wet, or even damp.

During his savage Irish campaign of 1649, Cromwell is said to have concluded a speech to his troops, who were about to cross the River Slaney before attacking Wexford, with the rousing words, "Put your trust in God, my boys, and keep your powder dry."

There is no contemporary recording of his use of this phrase, however, and it is possible that it was coined later by the soldier and historian Valentine Blacker in his poem "Oliver's Advice," which attributed the line to Cromwell.

KEEPING UP WITH THE JONESES

This phrase defines twentieth-century materialism as the never-ending struggle to keep up with the apparent affluence of one's neighbors, paying particular attention to the cars they drive, the vacations they take, the schools their children attend and all sorts of other lifestyle indicators.

Arthur R. Momand ("Pop"), whose strip cartoon was first published in the *New York Globe* in 1913, probably invented the phrase, which he used as his cartoon's title. The strip was based on Momand's own experiences of living beyond his means in a prosperous neighborhood—and his realization that all his neighbors were doing the same as he.

KISS THE BLARNEY STONE

A popular term used of someone who speaks in persuasive or seductive terms; the verb "to blarney," meaning to employ persuasive flattery, and the noun "blarney," for "flattering talk," have the same derivation.

The provenance for this expression can be found, literally, at Blarney Castle, near Cork, in southwest Ireland. Set high in the south wall of the castle is an almost inaccessible triangular stone bearing the inscription, *Cormac McCarthy fortis me fieri fecit.*

The tradition of kissing this Blarney Stone to improve one's eloquence and persuasive abilities—which can only be done by hanging, with one's feet securely held, head-down from the castle's battlements—dates from the eighteenth century.

The story behind the Blarney Stone's legacy is that in 1602, McCarthy, Lord of Blarney, was defending the castle against the English, who were fighting to force him to surrender the fortress and transfer his allegiance to the English crown.

However, McCarthy smooth-talked the British emissary, Sir George Carew, with flattery and sweet promises and stood his ground, much to the fury of Queen Elizabeth I.

It is said that the Queen herself coined the term "blarney" to describe the worthlessness of McCarthy's promises.

KISS OF DEATH

This phrase derives from Judas Iscariot's kiss given to Christ in the Garden of Gethsemane before he betrayed him (Luke 23:48 and Matthew 26:49). It's also known as a "Judas kiss," meaning an insincere act of courtesy or false affection.

In Mafia circles, a kiss from the boss may indeed be a fatal omen.

The phrase is often used today in political or business contexts, meaning that certain associations or actions may prove to be the undoing of a person or organization, or the downfall of a plan or project.

KITCHEN-SINK DRAMA

A type of drama popular in the 1950s, in which the plot centers on the more sordid aspects of working-class or lower-middle-class domestic life. Much of the action takes place in the kitchen or at the kitchen sink, which presumably is a metaphor to suggest drudgery and the dullness of dirty dishwater.

Plays such as *Look Back in Anger* (1956; this play gave rise to the phrase, "angry young men") by John Osborne used such squalid settings to emphasize their message of protest against the established values of the time.

More recently, Joanna Trollope's stories of domestic dramas and upheavals feature the lives of the middle-class country set. Her books are known as "Aga sagas," because much of the action takes place near the comfort of this famous stove, seen in most country kitchens ***worth their salt*** (see page 332).

THE LAND OF NOD

In the Bible, this was the land to which Cain was exiled after he had slain Abel (Genesis 4:16), but in modern usage, the phrase refers to the unknown place we go to in our dreams.

Jonathan Swift, the famous satirist, was the first to use the phrase in its figurative context in his little-known work, *Complete Collection of Genteel and Ingenious Conversation* (1731–38)—usually referred to as *Polite Conversation*—in which he wrote that he was "going to the land of Nod," meaning that he was going to sleep.

"To nod off" also means "to fall asleep," though this term is largely derived from the fact that the head tends to nod forward when one feels drowsy.

LICK INTO SHAPE

To take a failing object or faltering venture and turn it into something that works effectively.

Centuries ago it was held that bear cubs were born shapeless and had to be properly formed by their mother's licking. The origin of this phrase dates back to a 1413 translation of Guilleville's *The pylgremage of the sowle:*

> Bears are born foul and misshapen and are subsequently formed into their natural shape by the licking of their father and mother.

LIE ON A BED OF NAILS

A situation or position, usually self-inflicted, that is fraught with a multitude of difficult problems.

The phrase refers to the spiked bed of the Hindu *sadhu* (ascetic or holy man), on which he chooses to sleep as a mark of spiritual devotion. But while the spikes may not hurt the *sadhu,* they would be unbearable for most normal mortals.

The saying is sometimes used in its variant form, "to lie on a bed of thorns"; both are used to describe painful situations that people have created for themselves.

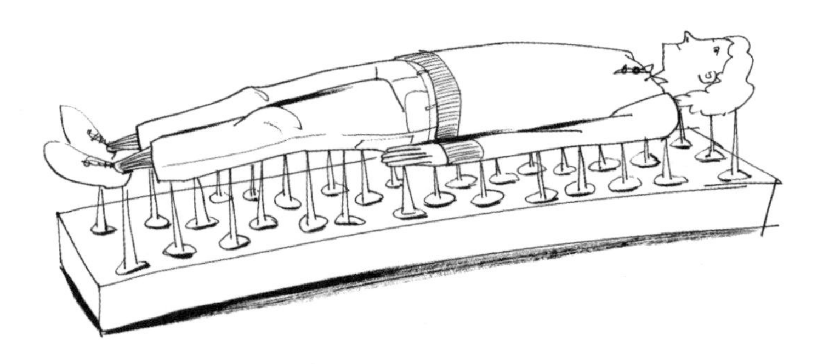

IN THE LIMELIGHT

To be in the limelight is to be the center of attention.

Limelight itself is an intense white light made by heating a piece of lime in a flame of burning oxygen and hydrogen. Thomas Drummond began using this process to create a bright light in the 1820s. It then became a widely used in theaters to illuminate the stage. Naturally the actors on stage were the center of attention, they were said to be in the limelight.

LIKE A BAT OUT OF HELL

Moving extremely quickly or suddenly.

Clearly referring to the rapid darting movement of bats, this phrase came into use at the turn of the twentieth century when Charles Earle Funk remarked that bats avoid light as if it were cast by the fires of hell.

LITTLE RABBITS HAVE BIG EARS

A twentieth-century Australian modification of the old proverb "little pitchers have great ears." The "ear" of a pitcher is the handle, which is often ear-shaped. The phrase "asses as well as pitchers have big ears" is also common.

They all mean that grown-ups should watch their language when talking in front of small children, who often pick up many a hint that the speaker might wish to have passed unnoticed.

LIVE LIFE IN THE FAST LANE

This is a metaphor meaning to live dangerously, indulgently and expensively, and dates from the late 1970s, probably coined by newspaper headline writers.

The fast lane is the inner lane of a highway, where traffic overtakes or travels at high speed. It is naturally associated with fast cars, and in an advertisement for Toshiba computers in 1989 the strapline read, "Jackie Stewart lives life in the fast lane—like any businessman really." (Stewart was three times the Formula 1 World Champion.)

The opposite metaphor, of course, is to be stranded on the hard shoulder of life.

M

MAD AS A HATTER

A renowned simile ever since Lewis Carroll's *Alice in Wonderland* (1865), although it can be found in W. M. Thackeray's *Pendennis* (1850) and is recorded as early as 1836.

The likely reason for linking hat-makers with madness is that hatters used the chemical mercurous nitrate in the making of felt hats, and its side effects can produce trembling symptoms such as those suffered in St. Vitus's Dance.

It is believed that Lewis Carroll based his character on Theophilus Carter, a furniture dealer who was known locally as the "mad hatter" because he wore a top hat and devised fanciful inventions such as an alarm-clock bed, which tipped the sleeper to the floor when it was time to wake up.

It has also been suggested that the original mad hatter was Robert Crab, a seventeenth-century English eccentric, who gave all his belongings to the poor and ate only dock leaves and grass.

MAD AS A MARCH HARE

Lewis Carroll also refers to the madness of the March hare in *Alice in Wonderland:*

> The March hare will be much the most interesting and perhaps, as this is May, it won't be raving mad—at least not so mad as it was in March.

The phrase comes from the observation that hares run wild in March, the beginning of their rutting season, exhibiting excitable behavior such as racing and "boxing."

The phrase first appeared in print in the late fourteenth century in Chaucer's *Canterbury Tales*, and has remained popular ever since.

MAKE A BEELINE FOR

To make a beeline for something is to go directly toward it.

In observing the behavior of bees, we see that when a forager bee finds a source of nectar, it returns to its hive and communicates its location to the other bees. Remarkably, after receiving this information, the other bees are then able to fly directly to the nectar.

MAKE DO

An official morale-boosting slogan that has a special resonance for people of a certain age. The phrase, originally "make do and mend," was designed to encourage thrift and the repairing of old garments and furniture, rather than buying a brand-new replacement and using up scarce resources.

It was in common use by 1943 and set the tone for life during the Second World War, and for many years after while food and clothing continued to be rationed.

The slogan struck a chord in the collective psyche, and although it may seem somewhat quaint to younger members of today's consumer society, the economic downturn has led to something of a revival in old-fashioned frugality.

MAKE HAY WHILE THE SUN SHINES

To act promptly when the opportunity presents itself and make use of favorable circumstances (see **strike while the iron's hot,** page 317). It has a similar seize-the-day meaning to the phrases "one today is worth two tomorrows," and, as seen on a postcard, "there's many a lemon dries up unsqueezed."

The phrase originated when many people worked on the land, and appeared in the sixteenth century. Before the days of the baler, cut hay was tossed about with a pitchfork before being gathered in, and then had to be left to dry in the fields, which meant that rain would spoil it.

In more recent times, it has come to be used as a justification for having fun or relaxing whenever the opportunity presents itself.

MAKE NO BONES

To be honest and direct without any risk that the statement may be misunderstood, but also sometimes used to mean to have no scruples about something.

One often cited source for this phrase is the world of gambling. Dice were often known as "bones" because they were originally made from animal bone. Yet there is no further evidence to link the phrase to dice.

It is more likely that it has its roots in the older expression "to find bones in something," which was used from the fifteenth century. That phrase came from the fact that finding bones in a bowl of broth was considered troublesome, so to find bones in something came to mean to take issue with it.

MEND FENCES

To rebuild a previously good relationship with someone you have had a disagreement with.

This expression is likely derived from the mid-seventeenth century proverb, "Good fences make good neighbors."

N

NAUGHTY BUT NICE

Between 1981 and 1984 the British National Dairy Council used this alliterative and somewhat suggestive slogan in a campaign to promote fresh cream cakes and the phrase is now used for anything that is a little bit wicked but enormously pleasurable.

The novelist Salman Rushdie claimed on the BBC's *Desert Island Discs* that he had created the phrase when he was an advertising copywriter in London, but his claim was refuted by others who had worked on the account.

The phrase was certainly not new even then, since it was the title for a 1939 film about a classical-music professor who accidentally wrote a popular song, and the film starred Dick Powell and Ronald Reagan.

It has also been used as an oblique phrase implying sexual intercourse since about 1900.

NECESSITY IS THE MOTHER OF INVENTION

An imperative need will force one to summon extra creative forces to devise a solution, or to create something, to alleviate a problem.

The phrase is thought to have been used in some form by Plato in the fourth century BC in *The Republic,* but it first appeared with the modern wording in a 1671 comedy by William Wycherley.

More modern derivations of the phrase are "A guilty conscience is the mother of invention" and "Boredom is the mother of invention." And in a twist by one Thorstein Veblen, "Invention is the mother of necessity."

However, Daniel Defoe wrote in Serious *Reflections of Robinson Crusoe* (1720):

> Necessity makes an honest man a knave.

THE NINETEENTH HOLE

The bar at the golf clubhouse. The standard golf course has eighteen holes, so the golfer who has played badly can drown his sorrows at the nineteenth. The term was first used by golfers in the 1920s.

NO HOLDS BARRED

Without rules or restrictions, often specifically referring to fighting, such as wrestling, hand-to-hand fighting, or martial arts.

The phrase originates with professional wrestling, and the holds referred to here are wrestling holds. Each type of wrestling has a specific set of rules attached to it. The sport has long been an Olympic one, administered by FILA, the sport's governing body. A match where no holds are barred is one where all of these rules and regulations have been lifted, and the fight is free form.

NO NEWS IS GOOD NEWS

The absence of information justifies continued optimism; that is, if all's quiet, then there is no cause for alarm. The phrase probably dates back to the early seventeenth century; in 1616, King James I wrote: "No newis is bettir than evill newis."

The word "news," now understood as a singular noun, was still plural up to the nineteenth century, as seen in this letter from Queen Victoria to the King of the Belgians, August 20, 1861: "The news from Austria are very sad, and make one very anxious."

The word is in fact short for "new stories," and the old spelling was "newes," a literal translation from the French *nouvelles*.

NOSE TO THE GRINDSTONE

To focus diligently on the task at hand.

This phrase is thought to have originated with knife grinders. They would sharpen blades by bending over stone, at times lying flat on their stomachs while keeping their faces near the grindstone.

NOT MY BAG

A slang expression for something that is definitely not one's subject or style.

It probably came from the jazz scene, "bag" meaning a personal style of playing; for instance, "playing with a hip-hop band was not his bag."

It shares a meaning with the more common phrase "not my cup of tea," which has been used throughout the twentieth century to denote something that isn't to one's taste.

AS OLD AS METHUSELAH

This means to be very old indeed. Methuselah is the oldest man referred to in the Bible, and it is written in Genesis (5:27) that he died at the impossibly great age of 969 years.

"As old as the hills" is another simile with a similar meaning as hills are indeed extremely ancient features of the landscape.

ONCE BITTEN, TWICE SHY

A phrase meaning that one learns from previous experience. Having been caught out once, one is wary or cautious the next time—and you should therefore learn from your mistakes.

"He that stumbles twice at the same stone deserves to have his shins broke" appears in R. Taverner's list of *Proverbs and Adages* of 1539, while the humorist Josh Billings said that "nobody but a fool gets bit twice by the same dog."

The idea behind the phrase is often attributed to one of Aesop's fables, which includes the line (as translated by William Caxton): "He that hath ben ones begyled by some other ought to kepe hym wel from the same."

ONE MAN'S MEAT IS ANOTHER MAN'S POISON

This is a very old adage that simply means that what is palatable or beneficial to one person is distasteful or harmful to another.

In ancient times, meat and bread were generic terms for food.

The phrase "different strokes for different folks" pretty well sums up the meaning. The rhythm and phrasing of this expression in particular have given rise to an endless stream of imitations. To an adulterer, perhaps, "One man's mate is another man's passion," or even "One man's Jill is another man's thrill."

The proverb's meaning in general has also inspired spin-offs. "One man's floor is another man's ceiling" is attributed to D. Bloodworth, while a contemporary version has a more political ring—"one man's terrorist is another man's freedom fighter."

OUT FOR THE COUNT

Said of someone who is fast asleep, dead drunk or completely demoralized.

It is a boxing and wrestling term describing defeat by being counted out by the referee. If a fighter is floored and does not find his feet within ten seconds counted out loud, he has lost the bout.

To say "count me out," on the other hand, means "do not include me in this."

OVER A BARREL

To be stuck in a helpless position, powerless to get yourself out of it, or to be at someone's mercy.

The phrase is possibly nautical in origin and is said to derive from the practice of draping over a barrel someone who has been rescued from the water when close to drowning, so encouraging the ejection of water from the lungs.

A more likely derivation, however, may be a form of punishment or torture in which the victim is bent over a barrel and beaten.

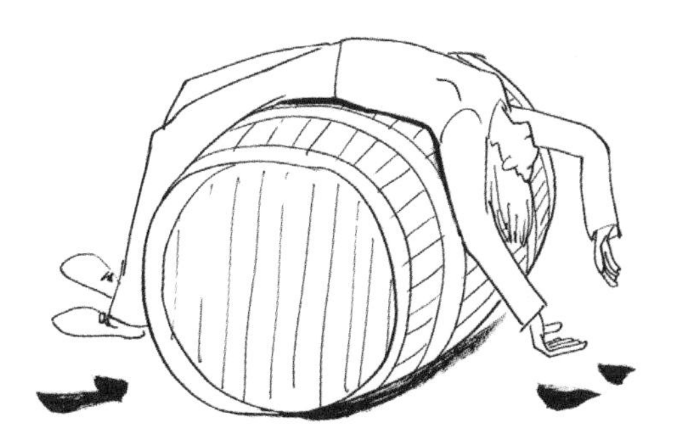

OVER THE TOP

An expression that describes something that goes way beyond the bounds of good taste or good sense, or which is outrageously inappropriate.

It came from the trenches of the First World War, when soldiers were described as going "over the top" when they scrambled out of the trenches to attack the enemy.

P

PAINT THE TOWN RED

To go out and party, to let your hair down and enjoy an uninhibited celebration, perhaps even to cause some disturbance in town.

This phrase, thought to have originated in the 1880s, may be an allusion to a town's red-light district; that is, the area where prostitutes ply their trade, advertising with red lights in the windows of their brothels, and where rogues might begin the evening before later extending the party to the rest of town.

Alternatively, it may have been a euphemism for a rowdy night in which blood would be spilled.

PANDORA'S BOX

This is a troublesome "can of worms"—a gift that seems of great value but is actually a curse, generating all sorts of unmanageable problems.

In Greek mythology, Pandora was the first woman, sent by Zeus as a gift to Epimetheus, who married her, against the advice of his brother Prometheus. As a wedding present, Zeus gave Pandora a beautiful box but instructed her that she must never open it. Over time, Pandora was tempted to defy this condition...but when she finally opened the box, all the evils of the world escaped, ever after to afflict mankind.

According to some, hope was the last thing that flew out; others believe that hope alone remained in the box.

The more modern phrase "to open a can of worms" is a graphic metaphor for a tangled, squirming, unpleasant or uncontrollable situation that had not been apparent beforehand.

PASS THE ACID TEST

Said of someone or something that has been subjected to a conclusive or severe test.

The phrase was used literally during the gold rush, when prospectors needed a sure-fire way of telling gold from valueless metals. Gold is not attacked by most acids, but reacts to nitric acid, also known as *aqua fortis,* which is therefore the acid used in the "acid test" for gold.

To "put on the acid" is probably derived from "to pass the acid test" and is Australian slang meaning to exert pressure on someone when asking for a favor or a loan.

PASS THE BUCK

(see also **the buck stops here**, page 207)

To evade blame or responsibility and shift all criticism elsewhere. A phrase from the game of poker, the "buck" being the token object that is passed to the person whose turn it is to deal the next hand.

Originally, the token was a buckhorn knife, so called because its handle was made from the horn of a buck, or male deer (although some sources argue that the buck was either a piece of buckshot or a buck's tail, which early hunters carried as a talisman).

The earliest recorded use of the phrase is by Mark Twain in 1872, in the first decade after the end of the Civil War (1861–65), when poker or "stud poker"—the stake was probably originally a stud horse—were played in bars by lumberjacks, miners and hunters, those being the days before it became known as a "gentleman's" game.

PASS MUSTER

To come up to an adequate standard, to pass inspection or to get by. Originally, "muster" was a military term for the gathering of soldiers for roll call and inspection.

To "muster in" means to enroll, and to "muster out" means that the group disperses or falls out.

PAST THE SELL-BY DATE

This term comes from the supermarket and is applied to perishable foods. The dates before which, for safety reasons, the goods should be sold and consumed are indicated on the packaging.

The expression is widely applied metaphorically to almost any short-lived or disposable area of life that may lose its freshness or appeal, such as ideas, fashion, relationships; it is sometimes also used of people, especially those in high-profile jobs, such as actors or models.

PEANUT GALLERY

An audience that gives a performer a difficult time with interruption and jeering.

This term has its origin in the days when vaudeville theater was popular. The cheapest seats in such theaters at the time came to be known as the peanut gallery, and this where the crowd was often loudest and most rowdy.

FOR PETE'S SAKE

An exclamation of annoyance or impatience. Just who Pete is exactly remains a mystery.

The expression is perhaps an oath in the name of St. Peter, the guardian of the Gates of Heaven. Saying "for Pete's sake" might be an entreaty to the person you're saying it to; that is, they should consider the fact that St. Peter might judge them for their actions. Alternatively, it may have evolved from "for pity's sake."

Nowadays, this particular expression of exasperation is not so frequently heard because the threshold of acceptability for more blasphemous expletives is far lower.

A PIG IN A POKE

To buy a pig in a poke is to purchase something before you have seen it and verified its worth.

The phrase derives from an ancient form of trickery when animals were traded at market and a small suckling pig was taken for sale in a "poke"—a word shortened from the word "pocket," which was a stout sack.

Sales had to be agreed without opening the poke, supposedly for fear of the lively piglet escaping. Rather, people used the sealed sacks to try to palm off the runts of the litter to unsuspecting buyers, and sometimes even cats were substituted for pigs.

If the less gullible purchaser insisted on seeing the contents of the poke, the salesman might literally have to "let the cat out of the bag" (therefore, that other well-known expression), and the game was up.

This form of suspicious market trading has been around for hundreds of years and is referred to in Thomas Tusser's *Five Hundred Good Pointes of Husbandrie* (1580).

The practice was obviously widespread because other languages have similar expressions—such as the French chat en poche*—which also refer to the folly of buying something without seeing it first. The Latin proverb* caveat emptor*—"let the buyer beware"—warns against such underhand techniques.*

A PINCH OF SALT

To take something with "a pinch of salt" is to treat information or explanations with great reservation, qualification, scepticism, doubt or disbelief.

A version of this phrase, "take with a grain of salt," was in use from the seventeenth century, and is thought to stem from the popular notion that taking a small amount of salt with other ingredients was a good antidote for poison.

PLEASED AS PUNCH

In the traditional comic puppet show *Punch and Judy*, the pompous Mr. Punch gloats smugly at the success of his evil actions and superiority over his shrewish wife, Judy, and it is from this scenario that the phrase originates. Punch had a lot to be pleased about; his quick wit was triumphant even over the Devil.

The present Punch and Judy *scenario is similar to the original by the Italian comedian Silvio Fiorello, dating from about 1600. Although the basic plot varies, it usually involves Punch's enraged bludgeoning of his wife, Judy, their child, and several lesser characters, followed by his imprisonment...and escape, thus him being "pleased as Punch."*

The violence of the storylines is counteracted by slapstick action and comic dialogue.

POUR OIL ON TROUBLED WATERS

A well-known metaphor meaning to mollify or soothe with gentle words, or to use tact and diplomacy to restore calm after an angry or bitter argument.

It has been a well-known scientific fact since the first century AD that rough waves are calmed when oil is poured upon them. According to the Venerable Bede's *History of the English Church and People* (AD 731), St. Aidan, an Irish monk of Iona, knew of this "miracle" and gave a young priest a vessel of holy oil to pour on the sea when the waves became stormy. (The priest was on an important voyage to fetch a maiden destined to be the bride of King Oswy.)

Moreover, on his many Atlantic crossings between Pennsylvania and Portsmouth in the eighteenth century, the ever-curious Benjamin Franklin observed not only the Gulf Stream, but also the calming effect of oil on the waves.

PRETTY PLEASE

An emphatic way of asking for something often used by young children trying to be extra cute.

How can the word please be pretty you ask? Actually the word pretty has historically been used to mean more than just attractive, as in the phrase "pretty penny."

PRIDE GOES BEFORE A FALL

An ancient warning for the arrogant to avoid conceit; do not be too cocksure or big-headed because events may conspire to bring you down. The phrase is shortened from the passage in Proverbs (16:18):

> Pride goeth before destruction, and an haughty spirit before a fall.

"Pride goes before, and shame comes after" is another form of the proverb as it was used in the sixteenth and seventeenth centuries. It has also been said that "he who gets too big for his britches gets exposed in the end."

PROOF IS IN THE PUDDING

To test the limits of something by trying it yourself.

This phrase actually derives from a longer phrase, "the proof of the pudding is in the eating." Now the phrase is often used in respect to flying aircrafts and taking them to the limits of their designated altitude and speed limits.

PUSHING THE ENVELOPE

To go beyond the standard and commonly accepted boundaries; to innovate.

This phrase actually does not refer to stationery, but to mathematics. In mathematics, the term envelope is defined as "the locus of the ultimate intersections of consecutive curves." As such it came to be used the upper and lower limits of flight patterns. To push the envelope was to test these limits while in flight.

PUT A SOCK IN IT!

A plea to be quiet, to shut up, to make less noise.

It comes from the end of the nineteenth and beginning of the twentieth centuries, when the early gramophones, or "phonographs," had large horns through which the sound was

amplified. These mechanical contraptions had no volume controls, and so a convenient method of reducing the volume was to stuff a woolen sock inside the horn.

PUT LIPSTICK ON A PIG

A term used to describe a weak attempt to deceive people by trying to make an ugly person or thing appear attractive.

This term, often used by politicians, derives from proverbs about attempting to make an ugly thing pretty. Similar phrases from the eighteenth century include, "a hog in armor is still but a hog."

PUT ON THE BACK BURNER

To put off or postpone. A very useful expression in business if a decision cannot be made immediately, meaning that an idea, proposition, course of action or project can be put aside and kept in reserve for use when necessary, or when circumstances are more propitious.

It stems of course from the back burners, or rings, of a stove, which are used for simmering, while the front burners are usually the hottest and used for fast cooking.

There is now even a verb form gaining increasing usage in office jargonese, with people talking of "back-burnering" something.

An almost diametrically opposed metaphor is also used: an idea or project can be "put on ice," to be figuratively defrosted at a later date.

PUT ONE'S FOOT IN IT

To make an inadvertent blunder, particularly to say the wrong thing and to embarrass oneself. To make a *faux pas,* which literally means "a false step."

The full phrase, from which this shortened version comes, is "to put your foot in your mouth," and several sources suggest that this was first used in reference to eighteenth-century Irish parliamentarian Sir Boyle Roche.

He famously delivered lines such as: "All along the untrodden paths of the future, I can see the footprints of an unseen hand." A contemporary is believed to have said of him, "Every time he opens his mouth, he puts his foot in it," and the phrase took off.

Prince Philip, who has something of a reputation for saying the wrong thing at the wrong time, calls the affliction "dentopedalogy."

R

READ THE RIOT ACT

Figuratively, "to read the riot act" is to attempt to quell chattering and general commotion or misbehavior, particularly in a group of children, by vigorous and forceful pleas coupled with threats of the consequences if order is not resumed.

The original Riot Act became British law in 1715, and stated that when twelve or more people were gathered with the intention of rioting, it was the duty of the magistrates to command them to disperse, and that anyone who continued to riot for one hour afterward was guilty of a serious criminal offense. It was not superseded until 1986 when the Public Order Act was introduced.

"To run riot" was originally said of hounds that had lost the scent and was later applied to any group that behaved in a disorderly or unrestrained way.

THE REAL McCOY

This is a common expression that originated in Scotland as "the real Mackay," meaning "the real thing."

Mackay was the name of an old family descended from the Scottish people known as the Picts; the term appeared in the *Scottish National Dictionary* in 1856 as part of the phrase "a drappie (drop) of the real Mackay."

In the 1880s, the expression was adopted as an advertising slogan for Mackay whisky, which was exported to the United States and Canada, where people of Scottish origin drank it and kept the phrase alive.

In the 1890s, it was applied to a famous boxer, the prize fighter Kid "the Real" McCoy, and this is the spelling that has remained in use.

Coca-Cola, probably the most advertised product in the world, adapted the phrase in the 1970s by describing their product as "the real thing" in comparison with any rival products.

REVENGE IS A DISH BEST SERVED COLD

Be patient, vengeance will be all the more satisfying if you take your time in getting back at someone.

There is an old proverb from 1578 that advises, "Living well is the best revenge," and according to Euripides (480–406 BC), "There's nothing like the sight of an old enemy down on his luck."

The modern wording of this phrase is often thought to come from the eighteenth-century French novel Les Liaisons Dangereuses by Pierre Ambroise François Choderlos de Laclos, as *la vengeance est un plat qui se mange froid.*

In fact, the phrase does not appear in the original novel and appears only in later adaptations.

The theme of revenge has featured in art since the early Greek dramas; the most famous example in English is perhaps Shakespeare's Hamlet *(1600).*

This particular phrase was revived in 2003 as a tagline for Quentin Tarantino's revenge film Kill Bill.

RING THE CHANGES

This phrase comes from the world of bell ringing, which became popular in the seventeenth century and remains so to this day. It means to make variations in the way you do something.

A "change," you see, is the order in which a series of bells is rung. Thus with a series of four bells, as in many parish churches, it is possible to ring twenty-four changes without once repeating the order in which the bells are struck ($4 \times 3 \times 2 \times 1 = 24$).

In the nineteenth century, the phrase took on a new meaning and was used to imply that someone had been paid back for a wrongdoing or practical joke, usually by being given a taste of his own medicine.

We now most commonly use the phrase to mean simply "to make changes" or "to try several changes."

The greatest number of changes ever actually rung on bells is reported to have been 40,320 changes on eight bells ($8 \times 7 \times 6 \times 5 \times 4 \times 3 \times 2 \times 1 = 40{,}320$), which took about eighteen hours.

ROME WASN'T BUILT IN A DAY

Great achievements, worthwhile tasks and the like are not accomplished without patient perseverance and a considerable passage of time.

This was originally a Latin proverb and has been quoted ever since, as in *A dialogue conteinyng the nomber in effect of all the prouerbes in the englishe tongue* (1546) by John Heywood:

> Rome was not bylt on a daie (quoth he) and yet stood
> Tyll it was fynysht.

Rome was the greatest city in the ancient world and, according to legend, was founded in 753 BC by Romulus (therefore, the city's name) and his twin brother, Remus. However, it is most likely to have been named from the Greek *rhoma* meaning "strength"; its other Latin name is Valentia, from *valens* meaning "strong."

As an indication of its importance in the world, Rome features in numerous old sayings such as "When in Rome, do as the Romans do" and "All roads lead to Rome" (or "All roads lead to rum," as W. C. Fields put it).

ROUND ROBIN

A petition or protest signed in a circular form on the page so that no one name heads the list. The device is believed to have originated in seventeenth-century France, and the term could be a corruption of rond and ruban—round ribbon.

The round-robin letter is believed to have been adopted by British sailors in the seventeenth or early eighteenth centuries, for use when presenting a grievance to the ship's captain. To avoid punishment, the ringleader would arrange for the signatures to be inscribed in a circular fashion around the page—although if the ship's captain was particularly vindictive, he would punish all the signatories for insurrection.

Today we use the phrase to mean the opposite of its original meaning—it is rather a letter or email from a single author that is sent to numerous recipients.

A round-robin tournament is a friendly sporting contest, such as tennis, in which all participants change partners so that everyone competes against everyone else.

ROUND UP THE USUAL SUSPECTS

Since the film *The Usual Suspects* was released in 1994, this phrase has returned to regular use and is employed as a jocular instruction to gather a group of people together.

It is thought that the line was first spoken in the film *Casablanca* (1943), directed by Hal B. Wallis and starring Humphrey Bogart and Ingrid Bergman. Claude Rains, playing the French Captain Renault, chief of police in wartime Casablanca, delivers this classic line in a scene near the end of the movie: "Major Strasser has been shot. Round up the usual suspects."

When shooting began on Casablanca, *the script was not finished. Toward the end of filming, the dialogue was written on demand and literally rushed to the set.*

According to the film chronicler Leslie Halliwell, the film "just fell together impeccably into one of the outstanding entertainment experiences in cinema history."

THE ROYAL "WE"

The somewhat superior choice of the collective pronoun "we" in place of the individual "I" by a single person.

Legend has it that King Henry II was the first to employ the royal "we" in 1169 when justifying a decision to his barons; he argued that since kings were ordained by God, his choices were God's choices too, and so used "we" rather than "I" when issuing his orders.

The current Queen of England, Elizabeth II, often uses this style in referring to herself, for instance during her Christmas Day broadcasts, while the frosty comment "We are not amused" was attributed to Queen Victoria in 1900.

In March 1989, the then Prime Minister, Margaret Thatcher, announced to the world in a famously regal tone:

We have become a grandmother.

RUB SALT INTO THE WOUND

To increase someone's pain or shame.

The phrase alludes to an ancient nautical punishment for misbehavior by members of a ship's crew. Errant sailors were flogged on the bare back, and afterward salt was rubbed into the wounds. Salt is a well-known antiseptic, so it helped to heal the lacerations, but it also made them much more painful.

An extension of this phrase is the saying "Don't rub it in," an admission that one may have made a fool of oneself, but people should not carry on reminding one.

RULE OF THUMB

A rough guesswork measure, a calculation based on generally held experience in a certain field. This rule is distinct from any proven theory.

It refers to the use of the thumb to make rough measurements. The first joint of the average adult thumb measures 1 inch or 25 mm, so could be used to measure objects quickly that were close at hand; while raising the thumb and aligning it with distant objects was a common way of estimating how far off they were.

RUN THE GAUNTLET

To be attacked on all sides or, in modern use, to be severely criticized or to try to extricate oneself from a situation while under attack on all sides.

The expression appeared in English at the time of the Thirty Years War as "gantlope," meaning the passage between two files of soldiers. It is an amalgamation of the Swedish words *galop* (passageway), *gata* (way), and *lop* (course).

"Running the gauntlet" was a form of punishment said to have originated in Sweden among soldiers and sailors. The company or crew, armed with whips, thongs or rods, were assembled in two facing rows, and the miscreant had to run the course between them, while each man dealt him as severe a blow as he thought befitted the misdemeanor.

Native Americans also had a similar, more brutal, form of retribution, because here the victim was not intended to survive the blows he suffered during his run.

S

SAIL CLOSE TO THE WIND

This is another of the many proverbs that come from life on the high seas. It is a figurative term, still in use today, meaning to take a chance, to emerge from an escapade just within the letter of the rule book, or, more riskily, to push the limits of what decency or propriety allows.

The nautical expression refers to the practice of steering a ship as near as possible to the point from which the wind is blowing, while keeping the sails filled.

To "sail against the wind" is to go against the trend, in opposition to current thinking, practice or fashion. And to "sail before the wind" is to prosper, to meet with great success, just as a ship sails smoothly and rapidly with a following wind.

Similarly, to "sail into the wind" is to tackle a difficult task with great vigor and directness.

THE SANDS ARE RUNNING OUT

A metaphor to remind us that time is short; there will be less time to do what you have to do unless you act now. The phrase is frequently used with reference to someone who has not much longer to live.

The allusion is to the sand in an hourglass. The original version of the phrase is "the sands of time are running out," the first part of which appears in the poem "A Psalm of Life" (1838) by Henry Wadsworth Longfellow:

> Lives of great men all around us,
> We can make our lives sublime,
> And, departing, leave behind us
> Footprints on the sands of time.

Or as Robert Burns wrote in "Tam o" Shanter" in 1791:

> Nae man can tether time or tide.

This is a variant of the old (c. thirteenth-century) English proverb "Time and tide wait for no man."

SAVE ONE'S BACON

To have a narrow escape, to be rescued from some dire situation without injury or loss.

This expression dates from the late seventeenth or early eighteenth century when bacon was a significant part of the diet.

According to Nathan Bailey's *Universal Etymological English Dictionary* of 1720, "bacon" was also a slang term to describe booty of any kind that fell to beggars, petty thieves, highwaymen and the like in their enterprises. As such bacon became synonymous with livelihood, so "to save someone's bacon" therefore took the meaning "to save a person."

"To bring home the bacon," meaning to earn the money to maintain the household, describes the custom at country fairs of greasing a live pig and letting it loose among a group of blindfolded contestants. Whoever successfully caught the greased pig could keep it and so "bring home the bacon."

SAVED BY THE BELL

This is a boxing term thought to date from the late nineteenth century. A floored contestant being counted out (see **out for the count**, page 272) might be saved by the ringing of the bell marking the end of the round, giving him the three-minute break between rounds to recover.

However, there is another, albeit unsubstantiated, and rather gruesome theory to explain this phrase. When graveyards became overcrowded in the eighteenth century, coffins were dug up, the bones taken away and the graves reused.

In reopening the coffins, one out of twenty-five was found to have scratch marks on the inside, meaning that its occupant must have been buried alive.

To guard against this most unfortunate occurrence in the future, a string was tied to the wrist of the corpse, which led from the coffin and up through the ground, where it was tied to a bell. Someone would have to sit in the graveyard all night to listen for the bell—hence the phrase "saved by the bell."

From the same derivation, we have night workers on the "graveyard shift" and sailors on the "graveyard watch" between midnight and dawn.

SEE A MAN ABOUT A DOG

This is a very shifty turn of phrase and suggests a desire to cover up one's real actions. It is the excuse offered if one wishes to be discreet and avoid giving the true reason for leaving the room, the meeting or whatever social gathering.

The phrase is sometimes used as a euphemism for some unmentionable activity such as going to the lavatory—or worse, going to do something or meet someone one shouldn't.

The phrase originally referred to betting on dog racing.

SEE RED

To give way to excessive passion or anger, or to be violently moved; to indulge in physical violence while in a state of frenzy.

The reference is to the Spanish spectacle of bullfighting and the art of taunting the bull. The phrase "like a red rag to a bull" is said of anything that is calculated to excite rage. Toreadors" capes are lined with red (although there is actually no evidence to suggest that the color itself incenses the bulls).

The phrase may also have blended with term in use in the early 1900s, "to see things red," which describes the feeling of anger when the blood rises, or the "red mist" descends.

SEE THROUGH ROSE-TINTED GLASSES

To look at life or to regard circumstances with unjustified optimism, always looking on the bright side of life, as though it were suffused with a gentle pink light. Eyeglasses of such a hue would show the world "in the pink"—but it would be misleadingly rosy, bright and hopeful.

The French equivalent is *voir la vie en rose*—again, to see life "in the pink," which in turn means to be in excellent health (abbreviated from the phrase "in the pink of health" or "in the pink of condition," a definition derived from a flower in its best state).

SELL SOMEONE DOWN THE RIVER

This expression means to deceive or to betray. The phrase probably originated in the first few years of the nineteenth century in the South.

Since by then it was illegal to import slaves, there was an internal trade and they were brought down the Mississippi to the slave markets of Natchez or New Orleans. Therefore if a slave was "sold down the river," he lost his home and family.

The saying particularly alludes to the practice of selling unruly slaves to owners of plantations on the lower river, where conditions were harsher than in the more northerly slave states.

To "sell" is old slang for "swindle" or "hoax," and a person who has been tricked is said to have been "sold."

SELL OFF THE FAMILY SILVER

To dispose of long-held and valuable assets for immediate short-term gain. This phrase comes from a speech made by former British Conservative Prime Minister Sir Harold Macmillan to the Tory Reform Group in 1985.

Though in favor of privatization in principle, he objected to methods used by Margaret Thatcher's government and to the use of the profits of the sales of Britain's big industries as if they were income.

"First of all the Georgian silver goes, and then all that nice furniture that used to be in the saloon. Then the Canalettos go," he said, likening the process to the selling off of prized heirlooms by aristocratic families desperate for a quick injection of cash.

The term is now common shorthand for the selling of state-owned resources to private companies.

SEND IN THE CLOWNS

A last ditch effort to salvage a performance by trying to make the crowd laugh.

Having nothing to do with circus clowns, the phrase came into use when a song titled as such by Stephen Sondheim became popular in 1973. The song was written for the musical *A Little Night Music.* A character from the play sings the song as she reflects back on her life and thinks of how her choices in love were foolish. It is a song of regret.

SEPARATE THE SHEEP FROM THE GOATS

To divide the worthy from the unworthy, the favored from the disfavored, the good from the bad. The phrase comes from the Bible, where sheep represent the flock of Christ, while goats symbolize virility, lust, cunning and destructiveness, and, often, the Devil.

> And before him shall be gathered all nations; and he shall separate them one from another, as a shepherd divideth his sheep from the goats.
>
> Matthew 25:32

A similar expression, also from the Bible, is "to separate the wheat from the chaff," meaning to distinguish good from bad. A more modern version is "to separate the men from the boys."

IN SEVENTH HEAVEN

To be supremely happy, in a state of complete ecstasy.

The seventh heaven was defined by the Kabbalists—students of a Jewish mystical system of theology and metaphysics with its roots in ancient Greek teachings, which dates from the eleventh and twelfth centuries, and from which Madonna's famous version of Kabbalah stems.

The Kabbalists interpreted passages from the Old Testament based on the symbolism of numbers, devised and decoded charms and created mystical anagrams and the like. They maintained that there were seven heavens each rising above the other; the seventh being the home of God and the archangels, the highest in the hierarchy of the angels.

Seven is a mystic or sacred number. It is the sum of four and three which, among the Pythagoreans, were, and have been ever since, counted as lucky numbers. Among ancient cultures, there were seven sacred planets.

The Hebrew verb "to swear" means literally to "come under the influence of seven things," while in an Arabic curse, seven stones are smeared with blood. All of which demonstrate the power of seven as a mystical number.

SHAKE A LEG

The summons "shake a leg" is a morning wake-up call. It is a naval phrase and was the traditional alarm call used to rouse the hands from their hammocks.

It comes from the days in the mid-nineteenth century when women were allowed to sleep onboard ship when the navy was in port. At the cry of "Shake a leg," if a woman's limb was shaken out of the hammock, she was allowed to lie in, but if the hairy leg of a rating appeared, he had to get up and get on with his duties.

Later in the nineteenth century, to "shake a leg" came to mean "to hurry up."

AT THE SHARP END

Directly involved with the action, positioned where the competition or danger is greatest. The connection is not with the point of a sword, but with the pointed shape of the bows of a ship, which are the first toward the enemy at the start of any engagement or battle.

The cry of "Look sharp!" or "Sharp's the word!" are both calls to immediate action, whether on the battlefield or in the playground; the expressions also mean to be observant, to "keep your eye on the ball."

Before the days of large supermarkets and closed-circuit TVs, if a shopkeeper suspected a customer of shoplifting, he would give a coded warning to his assistant by saying, "Mr. Sharp has come in."

SHOOT THE MOON

This is an expression meaning to leave without paying one's bills or rent, or to remove swiftly one's household goods under cover of night to avoid their seizure by a landlord or creditor. It's more colloquially known as "to do a moonlight flit" and is often shortened to "do a moonlight" or even "to flit." Another similar expression is "doing a midnight run."

Simply "to moonlight," however, means to take a second—secret—job, supposedly at night, to supplement one's wages from the day job.

References to the moon are often used to denote that something is fanciful: for instance, unrealistic ideas are known as "moonshine"; "to reach for the moon" means to crave what is totally beyond one's reach.

TO SIT ABOVE THE SALT

To sit in a place of distinction at the dinner table.

Formerly, the family "saler" or salt cellar was an ornate silver centrepiece, placed in the middle of the table. Special or honored guests of distinction sat above the saler—that is, between the salt and the head of the table where the host sat—while dependants and not-quite-so-important personages sat below.

THE SIXTY-FOUR-THOUSAND-DOLLAR QUESTION

The ultimate and most difficult question, the nub of a problem.

This widely used phrase comes from the 1940s radio quiz show, *Take It or Leave It*. During the course of the show, contestants were asked increasingly difficult questions for prize money, which also increased as the questions became harder. The final question was worth $64.

Naturally, inflation has affected this expression over the years since it began life as the humble sixty-four-dollar question, growing first to sixty-four thousand dollars and recently to sixty-four billion.

A SKELETON IN THE CLOSET

A domestic source of humiliation or shame that a family or individual conspires to conceal from others. Every family is said to have one, and certainly these days it seems that every public figure does too, whether it is in the form of an ex-mistress or lover, or some ancient but discreditable financial scam.

The expression seems to have been in use from the early 1800s and may have derived from the gothic horror stories popular at the time, in which murders were concealed by hiding the corpse in a cupboard, or bricking it up in a wall. In 1853, it appeared in the figurative sense in *The Newcomes* by William Makepeace Thackeray:

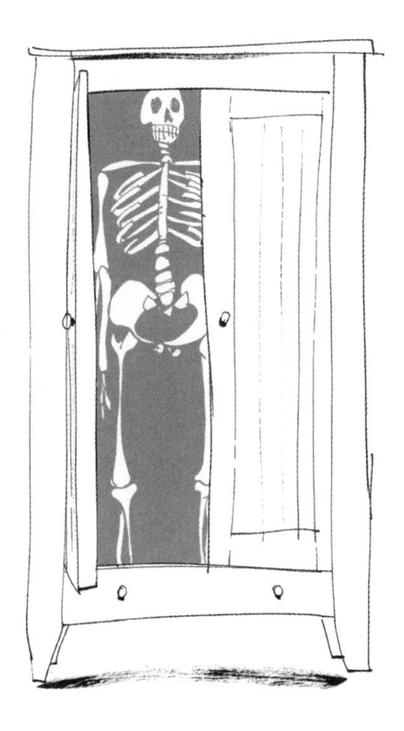

And it is from these that we shall arrive at some particulars regarding the Newcome family, which will show us that they have a skeleton or two in their closets as well as their neighbors.

An apocryphal source of the phrase is a story in which a person without a single care or trouble in the world had to be found. After a long search, a squeaky-clean lady was found, but to the great surprise of all, after she had proved herself on all counts, she went upstairs and opened a closet, which contained a human skeleton.

"I try and keep my trouble to myself, but every night my husband makes me kiss that skeleton," she said. She then explained that the skeleton was that of her husband's rival, killed in a duel over her.

ON SKID ROW

An expression applied to the part of town frequented by vagrants, hobos, alcoholics and down-and-outs. Hence if you are "on the skids," it means that you are on your way to that rather grimy quarter of the city, about to skid off the path of virtue and respectability.

The expression probably comes from the early days of the Seattle timber industry. A "skid row" was a row of logs down which other felled timber was slid or skidded. Tacoma, near

Seattle, became prosperous with the growth of the timber industry, and in due course there were plentiful supplies of liquor and brothels in the town, close at hand for lumberjacks working the skid row.

SLEEP TIGHT

Another way of saying good night and sleep well.

This phrase dates back to when beds were made of rope and straw. It is a shortened form of the expression, "sleep tight and don't let the bed bugs bite." Before going to sleep at night, people would have to pull the ropes tight in order to have a firm bed to sleep on as the ropes would have loosened during the course of the previous night's sleep.

SNUG AS A BUG IN A RUG

A whimsical and comfortable comparison dating from the eighteenth century, although a "snug" is a sixteenth-century word for a parlor in an inn.

The phrase is usually credited to Benjamin Franklin, who wrote it in 1772 as an epitaph for a pet squirrel that had belonged to Georgiana Shipley, the daughter of his friend, the Bishop of St. Asaph.

Franklin's wife had sent the Shipleys the gray squirrel as a gift from Philadelphia, and they named him Skugg, a common nickname for squirrels at the time. Tragically, he escaped from his cage and was killed by a dog. Franklin wrote:

> Here Skugg
> Lies snug
> As a bug
> In a rug.

However, there are earlier uses, as in a celebration of David Garrick's 1769 Shakespeare festival. Seen printed in the *Stratford Jubilee*:

> If she [a rich widow] has the mopus's [money],
> I'll have her, as snug as a bug in a rug.

And there are several similar variations from which the phrase may have sprung. In 1706, Edward Ward wrote in *The Wooden World Dissected*:

> He sits as snug as a bee in a box.

And in Thomas Heywood's 1603 play *A Woman Killed with Kindness*, there is:

> Let us sleep as snug as pigs in pease-straw.

SOUR GRAPES

This is an ancient metaphor used when someone denigrates something that is clearly desirable because they know they can't have it for themselves.

The phrase comes from the well-known fable "The Fox and the Grapes" by Aesop, dated to the sixth century BC:

> One hot day, a thirsty fox spotted some juicy-looking grapes hanging from a vine. The cluster of fruit was just out of reach. However hard he tried, he could not reach the grapes; and the greater the effort he made, the hotter and thirstier he became.
>
> Eventually, the fox gave up and reasoned that as the grapes were beyond reach, they would probably be sour and inedible.

The moral of the story is that we can console ourselves with the fact that, although some things are unattainable, we probably wouldn't like them anyway.

SPEAK OF THE DEVIL

Have you ever mentioned someone's name conversationally and then a few moments later that same person has unexpectedly walked into the room? At this moment you might exclaim, speak of the devil!

This is actually a shortened form of the phrase, "Speak of the devil and he doth appear." This original expression was an English proverb dating back to the Middle Ages. During this period there was a superstition that if you spoke of the Devil, or even of just mentioned evil in general, it may provoke the Devil to appear, bearing with him unfortunate consequences.

SPILL THE BEANS

The expression means "to let on," to tell all—perhaps prematurely—to an eager audience, to give away a secret or "to let the cat out of the bag" (see **a pig in a poke**, page 278).

There are various explanations for the derivation, one of the most colorful being that it may have originated at the turn of the twentieth century as a euphemism for vomiting, because beans represented basic food.

Another possibility is that the phrase comes from ancient Greek voting practices, where black and white beans were used to represent agreement and disagreement with the issue being voted on. Each voter put one bean into a pot or helmet—and the result was revealed by spilling out the beans.

Beans appear in various expressions: "To be full of beans" means to be in high spirits or full of energy, and was originally said of lively horses; beans used to be slang for money or property, so that "I haven't got a bean" means that one is broke.

SPIN DOCTOR

This phrase comes from baseball and refers to the spin put on the ball by a pitcher to disguise its true direction or confuse the batter.

It is an idiom that was first applied in political commentary in the mid 1980s during Ronald Reagan's presidency, describing his public-relations advisers during promotion of the "Star Wars" Strategic Defence Initiative (SDI).

These so-called "spin doctors" were on "spin control," their mission being to give the preferred interpretation of events to the world's media, manipulating public opinion in the desired direction.

STAND IN ANOTHER MAN'S SHOES

"To stand in another man's shoes" is to take the place of another person empathetically.

In a similar vein, the opportunistic phrase "waiting for dead men's shoes" is sometimes thought, if not spoken.

Among the Vikings, when a man adopted a son, the adoptee put on the shoes of his new father.

> Reynard the Fox, *a medieval beast epic (c. 1175–1250), is a satire on contemporary life found in French, Flemish and German literature. Reynard, having turned the tables on the former minister Sir Bruin the Bear, asks the Queen to let him have the shoes of the disgraced bear. As a result, Bruin's shoes are torn off and put on the new hero.*

STEAL SOMEONE ELSE'S THUNDER

To adopt someone else's own special methods or ideas as if they were one's own.

The story behind the origin of this phrase was recounted by the eighteenth-century actor-manager, playwright and Poet Laureate Colley Cibber in his *Lives of the Poets* (1753), and was also mentioned by Alexander Pope in his poem *The Dunciad* (1728).

Legend has it that John Dennis, an actor-manager of the early part of the eighteenth century, had invented a machine to make stage thunder, which he employed in his own play, *Appius and Virginia,* performed at the Drury Lane Theatre in London in 1709.

However, Mr. Dennis, whatever his inventive talents, was not a particularly gifted playwright; the play did not fill the house and was soon taken off in favor of a production of *Macbeth* by another company.

Dennis went to their opening night and was astonished to hear his thunder machine in action. He leaped to his feet and shouted, "That is my thunder, by God; the villains will play my thunder but not my play!"

Since the eighteenth century, the phrase has subsequently been refined to become "to steal one's thunder."

STIFF UPPER LIP

A determined resolve combined with complete suppression of the emotions.

This is supposedly a traditional characteristic of the English, especially military officers during the two world wars. Their upper lips were frequently concealed with a mustache, which perhaps became fashionable because it could conceal any uncontrollable trembling reflexes at the wrong moment. A quivering upper lip is often deemed a sign of emotion.

The phrase appeared well before the First World War in the work of poet Phoebe Cary in "Keep a Stiff Upper Lip":

And though hard be the task,
"Keep a stiff upper lip."

STILL WATERS RUN DEEP

However quiet or calm someone may seem on the surface, do not be deceived: there is probably great depth of knowledge, personality or a hot temper lurking below.

This is a Latin proverb, thought to come from Cato's Morals. The version we use today was first printed in an anonymously authored Middle English verse work "Cursor Mundi" ("Runner of the World"; c.1300), which includes the line: "There the flode is deppist the water standis stillist."

The Malayan proverb, "Don't think there are no crocodiles because the water is calm," means much the same.

It is never a good idea to show off or talk too much, because as everyone knows, empty vessels make the most noise. Speech is silver, but silence is golden.

STRAIGHT FROM THE HORSE'S MOUTH

(see also **don't look a gift horse in the mouth,** page 230)

Some knowledge received direct from the highest authority, from the person whose word need not be doubted.

The expression comes from horse racing, where the tips to be trusted came from those closest to the breeders and trainers. The phrase implies that you've heard something from the best possible source—in this case, the horse itself.

A variation on this as a source is the idea that the true age of a horse can be ascertained by an examination of its mouth. The first permanent horse teeth appear in the center of the jaw at the age of two and a half. A year later, a second pair appears, and at between four and five years, the third pair appears.

So, no matter what an owner may say about a horse's age, the evidence is in the horse's mouth.

STRIKE WHILE THE IRON'S HOT

To act immediately when the opportunity arises. This is a metaphor from the blacksmith's shop, since iron cannot be easily worked once it has cooled down.

The phrase has been attributed to Geoffrey Chaucer, although there are many ancient sayings that encourage action today rather than waiting for tomorrow. Pittacus said, "Know thy opportunity," while **make hay while the sun**

shines (see page 265) appears in an early sixteenth-century book of proverbs.

More up to date, a women's-lib slogan neatly inverts the proverb in a warning against inaction: "Don't iron while the strike is hot."

THE SWORD OF DAMOCLES

Impending danger or disaster in the midst of great prosperity or good fortune.

In the fourth century BC, Damocles, who was a toadying sycophant of Dionysus the Elder of Syracuse (see **the walls have ears**, page 327), was invited by the tyrant to test his self-proclaimed charm and wit. Damocles accepted and was treated to a sumptuous banquet, but over his head a sword was suspended by a mere hair, intended by Dionysus as a symbolic indicator of the fragility of wealth and power, his own included.

This quite naturally inhibited Damocles's performance at the banquet because he was too frightened to move.

TO A T

A way of describing that something is just right.

The origin of this phrase is debated. An early-recorded use comes from James Wright's satire *The Humours and Conversations of the Town* (1693):

> All the under Villages and Towns-men come to him for Redress; which he does to a T.

This early reference may referred to a t-square used to make precise measurements.

TAKE A RAIN CHECK

A rain check is the receipt of a baseball ticket that can be used at a later date if a game has been interrupted by rain.

The phrase is now often used figuratively, to put an invitation on hold and defer it until a later date. It is, in fact, a polite way of postponing something indefinitely, with only a minor commitment to rearrange.

TAKEN FOR A RIDE

This colloquial phrase can be interpreted in one of two ways. It refers either to the victim of a light-hearted joke, prank or con, or—in its sinister and probably original meaning, a completely genuine use of the phrase—to someone who is taken for a ride somewhere and does not come back in one piece, if at all.

The rival underworld gangs of major cities in the 1920s and 1930s were virtually at war with each other, and any unfortunate who was unlucky enough to tempt the wrath of the gang leader, or Don in the case of the Mafia, would be literally taken for a ride in a limousine, ostensibly to discuss certain matters or sort out some misunderstanding. He would be very unlikely to return alive, however—or, indeed, to return at all.

TALK TURKEY

To discuss some subject frankly or seriously.

The origin of the expression is uncertain, but it is thought to date back to the nineteenth century and may have arisen from the efforts of turkey hunters to attract their prey by making gobbling noises. The birds would then either emerge from their cover or return the call, so revealing their whereabouts.

At the turn of the last century, the turkey was considered an amusing bird, and conversations in which one "talked turkey" were convivial. A young suitor's chat-up lines would also be called "talking turkey," perhaps because in a fit of nerves he might become tongue-tied and his words would come out like gobbling noises.

Later, the meaning became more serious and related to stern admonitions.

Incidentally, turkeys do not come from Turkey, but from North America, and were brought to Spain from Mexico. Benjamin Franklin suggested the turkey should be the national emblem; however, the bald eagle was chosen instead.

THICK AS THIEVES

To be intimate with some person or group, to be in collusion with them. "Thick" is used in this context to mean "closely knit."

Thieves notoriously conspire and plot together and devise secret languages so that they can discuss their business in a code that will not be understood by others—a slang or jargon that used to be known as "thieves Latin." Cockney rhyming slang itself was originally a closed language to the uninitiated and was created by crafty East Londoners to outwit authority and eavesdroppers.

"As thick as thieves" was already a common saying by the time it was first used in print in the 1800s, and we now use it primarily to describe people who are close friends.

THREE SHEETS TO THE WIND

To be very drunk.

This phrase was originally a seafaring expression. The sheets refer to ropes or chains fixed to the lower corners of sails in order to hold them in place. If three sheets are loose and blowing in the wind, the sails will flap, causing the boat to stagger about like a drunken sailor.

THROW IN THE TOWEL

To throw in, or throw up, the towel means to give up, to admit defeat. The metaphor is from prize-fighting, which predated modern boxing, and refers to a second from the boxer's corner tossing a towel, used to refresh his contestant in between rounds, toward the center of the ring, to signify that his man is beaten.

"To throw in the towel" also means to concede defeat in boxing, for a second might also literally throw a towel into the ring to show that the game is up.

THROW ONE'S HAT INTO THE RING

To enter a contest or to become a candidate for office.

This expression relates to the early nineteenth-century custom of throwing one's hat into the boxing ring to indicate that you wanted to take on the pugilist.

By the early twentieth century, the term was regularly used in professional boxing and in 1912 it became firmly linked to political ambition when Theodore Roosevelt announced his intention to run for the presidency by telling a reporter: "My hat's in the ring, the fight is on, and I'm stripped to the buff."

TOO MANY COOKS SPOIL THE BROTH

A well-known proverb meaning that too many opinions on a matter become self-defeating. The adage has been in use since the sixteenth century, if not before.

For almost every proverb or nugget of wisdom, however, there is usually another that means precisely the opposite: The usual riposte for "too many cooks spoil the broth" is "many hands make light work."

Groucho Marx once commented: "I'm going to stop asking my cooks to prepare broth for me. Over the years, I've found that too many broths spoil the cook."

TURN THE TABLES

To reverse a situation and put one's opponent in the predicament that one has been suffering. The saying was recorded in the early seventeenth century and was applied to the game of backgammon, the table or board on which it was played being known as "the tables."

The phrase may come from the old rumored custom of reversing the table, or board, in games of chess or draughts, so that the opponents' relative positions are altogether changed—but even then it had a figurative meaning, too.

In a sermon published in 1632, an English deacon called Robert Sanderson, who later became the Bishop of Lincoln, said:

> Whosover thou art that dost another wrong, do but turn the tables: imagine thy neighbor were now playing thy game, and thou his.

UNDER THE TABLE

This phrase originated during the Second World War, and describes a—then very common—practice among businessmen.

From the outbreak of the war, many items, ranging from the basics like eggs, butter, meat and jam to "luxuries" such as gas, silk stockings and chocolate, were rationed. Dishonest businessmen would keep articles and foodstuffs that were in short supply out of sight or "under the table," for sale to favored customers, usually at inflated prices.

This form of trading was part of the thriving wartime black market, and the term is still used today to describe any illicit trading.

WALK THE PLANK

To be put to the supreme test or, worse, to be about to die.

"Walking the plank" is a nautical term for a punishment involving being made to walk blindfold and with bound hands along a plank suspended over the ship's side—one eventually lands up in the drink as shark food, if not drowned first. It was a pirate custom of disposing of prisoners at sea in the seventeenth century.

The practice is probably more familiar in fiction than in fact, however, since pirates would have been unlikely to kill off captives, who could have been sold as slaves or ransomed.

In R. L. Stevenson's novel The Master of Ballantrae *(1889), James Durie and Colonel Francis Burke enlist with the pirates who capture their ship, but the brigands make their other prisoners walk the plank.*

The infamous Captain Hook, in J. M. Barrie's Peter Pan and Wendy *(1912), meanwhile, threatened to flog Wendy and the Lost Boys with a cat-o'-nine-tails...and then make them walk the plank.*

THE WALLS HAVE EARS

This is a warning to watch what you say, or what secrets you divulge, wherever you are, because someone might be listening.

In the time of Catherine de'Medici, wife of Henry II of France, certain rooms in the Louvre Palace, Paris, were said to be constructed to conceal a network of listening tubes called *auriculaires,* so that what was said in one room could be clearly heard in another. This was how the suspicious queen discovered state secrets and plots.

The legend of Dionysus's ear may also have been the inspiration for the phrase. Dionysus was a tyrant of Syracuse (see **the sword of Damocles**, page 318) in 431–367 BC, and his so-called "ear" was a large ear-shaped underground cave cut into rock. It was connected to another chamber in such a way that he could overhear the conversations of his prisoners.

WASH ONE'S HANDS OF SOMETHING

To abandon something, to have nothing to do with some matter or person, or to refuse to take responsibility.

The allusion is to Pontius Pilate's washing of his hands after the trial of Jesus. Pilate was the Roman Governor of Judaea who tried Jesus. Although he found Christ not guilty, he washed his hands of the matter by bowing to the pressure of Jewish religious leaders and letting them decide Christ's fate:

> When Pilate saw that he could prevail nothing, but that rather a tumult was made, he took water, and washed his hands before the multitude, saying, I am innocent of the blood of this just person: see ye to it.
>
> Matthew 27:24

WHAT THE DICKENS?

An exclamation of surprise or disbelief, akin to "What the devil?" The phrase is often shortened to "What the...?"

"Dickens" here is probably a euphemism—one possibly in use since the sixteenth century—for the Devil, otherwise known as Satan or the Prince of Evil, and has nothing to do with the novelist Charles Dickens.

In Low German, its equivalent is "De duks," which may have become altered in English to "dickens."

The phrase was already in use by the time Shakespeare was writing:

> I cannot tell what the dickens his name is.
>
> *The Merry Wives of Windsor* (1600; 3:2)

"To play the dickens" is an old-fashioned expression meaning to be naughty, or act like a devil.

WHAT IS GOOD FOR THE GOOSE IS GOOD FOR THE GANDER

This old phrase seems to promote sexual equality long before it was fashionable. It suggests that the same rules apply in both cases—what is fitting for the husband should also be fitting for the wife—though it is more likely that the phrase was used more generally to mean what is good enough for one person is good enough for another.

WHERE'S THE BEEF?

Advertising slogan meets political catchphrase. The Wendy hamburger chain's 1984 television commercial showed a group of elderly women looking at the small hamburger of a competitor on a huge bun—they all admired the bun, but the unimpressed third woman asked, "Where's the beef?"

Later in 1984, when Walter Mondale was seeking the Democratic presidential nomination, he famously quoted the slogan to describe what he thought was a lack of substance in the policies of his rival, Gary Hart.

The phrase is also used to mean "where's the problem?"

WHITE ELEPHANT

A useless and costly possession that cannot be disposed of because of some sort of value associated with it.

This term comes from Southeast Asia where white elephants are considered sacred. A gift of a white elephant is a sign of peace and prosperity, and the elephants are protected by laws. Receiving a gift of a white elephant could be both a blessing and curse as the animals cannot be put to practical use and are costly to care for.

WIN HANDS DOWN

To win easily, with little effort.

This phrase comes to us from the sport of horse racing. During competition a jockey has to hold the reins of the horse tight in order to encourage it run quickly. If a jockey has such a lead that he can lower his hands, and the reins of the horse, he is winning the race with great ease.

ON A WING AND A PRAYER

To chance it, to hope for the best and have faith, with perhaps only small chance of success.

The phrase comes from a Second World War song by Harold Adamson. He based his lyrics on the actual words spoken by the pilot of a damaged aircraft, who radioed the control tower as he prepared to come in to land. The 1943 song runs:

> Tho' there's one motor gone, we can still carry on,
> Comin' in on a wing and a pray'r.

Even in his moment of panic, the pilot might have been inspired by words from Psalm 104 (v.3):

> Who layeth the beams of his chambers in the waters:
> and maketh the clouds his chariot, and walketh upon the wings of the wind.

A WOLF IN SHEEP'S CLOTHING

Used to describe a malicious or dangerous person who uses a facade of innocence to fool others as to his or her true character.

The idea of such dissemblance has long been in circulation. One of the earliest phrases linking wolves and sheep comes from the Bible:

> Beware of false prophets, which come to you in sheep's clothing, but inwardly they are ravening wolves.
>
> Matthew 7:15

The original source of the phrase, however, is thought to be Aesop's fables, written in the sixth century BC. In the story, a wolf who is hunting sheep realizes that he can get close to the flock by disguising himself with a sheep's skin. But once he is among them, the shepherd—looking for a sheep to kill for his supper—mistakes the wolf for a suitable sheep and cuts its throat.

The moral of the story is that the wrongdoer will be punished by his own deceit.

WORTH ONE'S SALT

"Salt" is a significant euphemism, from the early nineteenth century onward, for one's financial worth, as a play on the word "salary," or the amount one earned.

In Roman times, a soldier received part of his pay in the form of a *salarium,* or salary, which was actually an allowance for the purchase of salt (the Latin for "salt" is *sal*). Salt was not easily obtainable then, and a soldier was not "worth his salt" if he did not **come up to scratch** (see page 223)—that is, did not deserve his *salarium*.

Consequently, to be "true to one's salt" is to be loyal to your employers, those who pay your salary, or to maintain or stand by one's personal honor.

THE WRITING ON THE WALL

This is not graffiti, but a bad sign, a portent, often foreshadowing trouble or disaster.

The metaphor is biblical in origin and comes from Daniel 5:5–31, where King Belshazzar, while he was feasting, found out about the forthcoming destruction of the Babylonian Empire through the mysterious appearance of handwriting on a wall.

The words read in Aramaic, *mene, mene, tekel, upharsin*: literally, "counted, weighed, divided." Daniel interpreted these words as, "You have been weighed in the balance and found wanting," thereby predicting the King's downfall and that of his empire.

Indeed, Belshazzar was killed that night, and his kingdom was conquered.

YOU ARE WHAT YOU EAT

An informal slogan with "alternative-lifestyle" overtones that dates back to the 1960s. Today, the phrase is often associated with nutrition adviser Gillian McKeith's former popular TV show of the same name.

The idea behind the phrase, however, is far from new. In *Psychologie du Goût* (1825), the great philosopher of French cooking Anthelme Brillat-Savarin wrote, "Tell me what you eat and I will tell you what you are," while in 1945, the diarist Sir Henry "Chips" Channon fondly commented on the death of Sir Harcourt Johnstone, Liberal MP, bon vivant and Minister for Overseas Trade:

> He dug his grave with his teeth.

YOU CAN'T MAKE A SILK PURSE OUT OF A SOW'S EAR

Don't attempt to make something good or of great value from what is naturally bad or inferior in quality. A similar old proverb is "you cannot make a horn out of a pig's ear."

To make a pig's ear of something is to botch it; the ear of a slaughtered pig being its most worthless part, no good for anything.

This ancient phrase was already a proverb by the mid 1500s and over time has inspired similar slang expressions, thought to have been instigated in the 1920s, such as "to make a dog's breakfast" or "dog's dinner" out of something.

YOU REAP WHAT YOU SOW

You cannot escape the consequences of your actions.

This agricultural metaphor expresses the idea that as a farmer reaps the harvest of the seeds he has sown in the earlier season, you face the repercussions of the actions you have taken. In other words, you get what you deserve. This maxim originates in the Biblical New Testament, in Paul's letters to the Galatians 6: 7-9:

> Be not deceived; God is not mocked: for whatsoever a man soweth, that shall he also reap. 8: For he that soweth to his flesh shall of the flesh reap corruption; but he that soweth to the Spirit shall of the Spirit reap life everlasting. 9: And let us not be weary in well doing: for in due season we shall reap, if we faint not.

ZIP IT!

Be quiet!

This phrase is often used in exasperation when one is frustrated with what someone else is saying or perhaps complaining about. As you would close a bag by zipping it shut, you wish the whiny person would close his mouth and stop talking. This is similarly often expressed as, "Zip your lips!"

ZIGGED BEFORE YOU ZAGGED

You did things in the wrong order.

Perhaps used more for its assonance than any other reason, this playful phrase rolls off the tongue expressing that the actions you have taken may have been correct, but they were not in the correct order.

INDEX

Centrifugal Force • Electricity

ergy • Inertia • Quantum Mech

Newton's Laws • Ohm's Law

Radioactivity • Levers • Theory

Dynamics • Acceleration • Cu

Velocity • Vector • Gravity • A

Amplitude • Alternating Curren

of Reflection • Atom • Atomic

Cathode Rays • Centrifugal F

Convection • Decibel Scale • I

nagnetic Force • Electrostat

$E=MC^2$

Simple Physics

Why Ballons Rise, Apples Fall, and Golf Balls Go Awry

JEFF STEWART

1

A Brief History of Physics

What exactly *is* physics?

Well, in a way, it's everything.

Physics aims to tell us about a big bang that created the universe long ago, to explain how people got here from there (and why we won't be going anywhere else in a hurry), and to show how and why everything around us works as it does.

It tells us how the first bits of matter appeared, how the first stars were born, and how, over billions of years, the universe came to be the vast and violent place we know, with our planet an insignificant speck on the edge of one galaxy in 125 billion.

It explains almost everything that happens in the world around us: energy and movement, sound and light, electricity and matter. And its laws form the basis of chemistry and biology.

Physics also suggests exciting new ideas. For example, it says that time travel may be possible. Unfortunately, it also says that we're probably too big to try it.

In short, modern physics gives us a fascinating, awe-inspiring, and sometimes downright weird view of the universe and our place in it.

Falling apples, rising balloons, and errant golf balls are just the start.

It's the law

Physicists—a mixture of mathematical thinkers and more practical types who enjoy doing experiments, such as smashing tiny bits of stuff into even tinier bits—think that they can explain all this because everything happens according to the laws of nature.

These laws show that, if this thing happens, then so will that. If I hang a weight (me, for example) from a spring, the amount it stretches will be proportional to my weight: double the weight, double the stretch. (This particular law is known as Hooke's Law because it was discovered by the 17th-century British physicist Robert Hooke.)

The laws of physics are useful to us because physics is a practical science. What we've learned has helped us build everything from bathroom scales (that spring again) to a billion shiny gadgets, from the bulbs that light up our cities to the airplanes we take to fly between those cities.

Of course, it has also brought us enough nuclear warheads to blow all of this—and us, and life as we know it—to pieces.

How we found physics

People have always tried to explain and predict the world around them. It seems to be an essential part of what makes us human. But it wasn't until we got past blaming everything from lightning to earthquakes on a bunch of irritable gods that we started getting anything useful out of our explanations.

So that's what physics is. But a quick run through 2,500 years of scientific progress will give us a better idea of how it got us here. And, hopefully, prove to anyone still frightened by the subject that it doesn't bite—even if it does bang.

It's all Greek

Almost 2,500 years ago, the ancient Greeks did a lot of thinking about science. Besides running around naked at the first Olympic games, writing tall tales about gods, cunning heroes and many-headed monsters, and building wonderful temples, they came up with plenty of interesting theories.

For example, Thales supposed that all the earth floated on water, so that earthquakes were caused by waves. Aristotle, whose *Physica* is the first work on physics to use the word in the title, believed that everything in the world was made up of earth, air, fire, and water, with the heavens made of a divine substance called ether. Smoke, he thought, rose, because it was mainly made up of air, and air always tended to be above earth.

These were nice simple theories, but the Greeks generally argued that an object does something because it's the kind of object that does that kind of thing. This gets us nowhere: it's a circular argument; a good example of what modern physics isn't. (Today, we try to explain things in terms of other things, which is a nice way of saying we usually like to blame someone else.)

Strictly speaking, the Greeks said that, for example, all circles we see are somehow shadows of the "Form" of roundness. Forms were supposed to be divine, perfect and not of this world, so that the Form of roundness set the perfect example for all other round things. But, it seems, there's no getting around the fact that an object's roundness is still explained by the fact that it is, well, round. Which is, as we noted, circular.

Mind games

Part of the problem was that the ancient Greeks tended to think that you should be able to figure out what happens in the world through the power of thought alone. The world around us was imperfect, so, they thought, there wasn't much point looking at it too closely and expecting it to behave in a regular way.

And even when they did observe what was going on around them, they made some strange mistakes. For example, Aristotle made detailed studies of plants and animals, but thought that as a rule, men have more teeth than women.

Predicting the planets

A few hundred years later, another ancient Greek called Ptolemy (ignore that first "p" when you say his name, or you may be accused of spitting) came up with a fairly accurate mathematical system for predicting the position of the stars and planets.

This was a big step forward for science, except he also thought that the planets (and the sun) revolved around the Earth. This meant that to make his numbers work, he had to predict that the moon would sometimes come twice as close to the Earth as at other times. As a result, he thought that we should regularly see the moon appear to double in size.

Of course the moon never grew, but in the Western world, Greek ideas held sway in physics for 1,500 years. Partly this was because the church supported them: Greek thinking, like Christianity, put man at the center of the universe, and with the stars all fixed to the inside of a huge sphere that contained the universe, it also left plenty of room outside for heaven and hell.

As Greek civilization declined, many of its ideas and writings were saved by Islamic scholars, who refined them and slowly increased the importance of math and observation, particularly in the study of light, the stars and motion. This was a good move because, as it turned out, math and observation turned out to be the key to progress in science.

The scientific revolution

It may seem obvious now, but this new way of thinking revolutionized the way we understand the world. People started to discover that by looking carefully, measuring time and distance and energy, and by putting the numbers together with math and careful thought, we could predict—at least in the laboratory, under carefully controlled conditions—what would happen next and why it would happen. (Actually, it's amazing how far you can get without mathematics, as this book proves. You need math to write your theories neatly and to prove them to other scientists, but usually you can understand the big ideas pretty well without it.)

Astronomy also progressed, with the theory that the Earth revolved around the sun slowly gaining favor, despite the efforts of the Catholic Church. The Bible says that the world is firmly fixed, and this revolutionary new theory was, indeed, revolutionary.

The great Italian physicist Galileo Galilei, who was handy with a telescope and was a dedicated star watcher, offered the first direct evidence for the new theory. For this heresy the church had him placed under house arrest in 1633. He remained there until he died.

Then came Sir Isaac Newton—an English mystic, alchemist, and theologian—a complicated and often very cranky man who was also the greatest mathematician and second greatest physicist ever. In one book, the *Principia Mathematica,* published in 1687, he laid down the law of gravity, as well as three elegant laws of motion that describe how objects move. These were unchallenged for two hundred years and still form the basis of most movement calculations by scientists and engineers.

For example, if you want to know the minimum distance in which you can stop your car when you're doing 80 m.p.h. (130 km/h) on the highway, and you don't want to cause an accident trying it out, all you need is one quick experiment at 20 m.p.h. (32 km/h) on a quiet side street, a copy of Newton's laws of motion, and, for the arithmetically challenged, the ability to multiply and divide on a calculator.

A clockwork universe

After Newton, it seemed that the universe ran according to a hidden clockwork code, and that it was governed by rules that we can discover and understand. This idea changed the course of human history. It led scientists all over the world to use Newton's mathematical tools to build on his ideas and develop science. And so Newton began the rush of scientific discoveries that continues to this day.

We found out why the Earth goes around the sun and how its heat reaches us. We learned about light, sound, electricity, and energy: how it changes, how it moves, and how it doesn't disappear. We found that everything we see is made up of tiny things called atoms, which are made up of tinier things called electrons and protons and neutrons. And that even then there are tinier things in them.

With this information in hand, engineers began building the modern world.

At the speed of light

Throughout the 19th century, scientists began to discover tiny flaws in Newton's laws—and the branch of physics known as classical mechanics, which flowed from them. For example, the orbit of the planet Mercury seemed wrong: Its orbit didn't change exactly as the equations said it should. There were also difficulties with handling the speed of light and the way objects radiate heat.

It took the genius of a German patent clerk named Albert Einstein to begin to solve these riddles. In one year, 1905, he wrote four papers that helped physics take huge steps forward—and all while holding down his job at the office. His new ideas included the theory of special relativity (which showed we could never travel faster than the speed of light) and mass-energy equivalence (the famous $E=mc^2$ equation, which showed we could turn objects into energy, and paved the way for nuclear power and atom bombs).

Einstein's theories agreed very closely with Newton's laws under everyday conditions and showed why Mercury went where it did. They also suggested a whole new direction for physics, now called cosmology, which takes it out to work on the entire universe, to tell how stars and even universes might be born.

A hundred years later, Einstein's physics still points the way in cutting-edge research.

It's neither here nor there

In 1900, German physicist Max Planck solved the radiation of heat problem when he showed that the energy of electromagnetic waves is quantized, so that heat energy is emitted in chunks, which can only get so small and no smaller. In the 1920s his insight led to quantum physics, a whole new branch of the science, which was discovered and fleshed out by a large group of physicists, working at the same time, in different countries, on what often seemed like separate problems. Together, they made quite a mess of the comforting idea of a predictable clockwork universe.

Quantum physics is the science of the very small: of individual light particles, the structure of atoms, and all the things that make them up—not just the electrons and protons that we already knew, but the tinier bits of these bits, such as quarks, all of which have the odd property of being really just waves that are probably here and probably there, though we can never quite be sure.

New questions

And so we reach the present day. The main thrust of physics today is to put together the theories about the big stuff (Einstein's relativity) and the tiny stuff (quantum physics) into one explanation of the whole universe: how it works, why the laws are as they are, its birth in a big bang, and maybe its death, billions of years in the future.

One version of this goal is called a GUT: a Grand Unified Theory. But whatever it's called, at the moment it's got physics pretty well stumped. The bad news is that it may actually be impossible to create such a theory; or possible, but not possible for human brains.

No one's giving up yet, but these are some of the reasons that some physicists are thinking carefully (or possibly staring out the lab window and daydreaming) about what kind of things their laws are, and how they fit into the universe.

Wrong again

Of course, physics—and its laws—aren't nearly as straightforward as this history might suggest.

Apart from the risk of nuclear armageddon, the greenhouse effect, and the time we waste deciding which of the many shiny gadgets that physics has spawned we should buy next, there is also the fact that—as we've seen throughout its history, and despite all the trust we put in it to stop our cars—sometimes physics is wrong.

For example, Aristotle thought that heavier things fall faster, which seems to be what we all see: think of feathers and lead weights. But Galileo and Newton proved him wrong.

Then Newton, with the help of falling apples, used the theory of gravity to explain why things fall, and to predict how quickly they gain speed. That was great, but a few hundred years later, Einstein made everything much more complicated.

His theories of relativity say that weight and speed of falling are linked, but in a strange way: the faster things fall, the heavier they get. You would have to be moving many thousands of times faster than a jet aircraft before you'd really notice the weight you put on, but experiments have shown that the theory is true.

So, Einstein's theory is true—and, on the other hand, sometimes it isn't. In quantum physics, where we look at the motion of tiny and often very light objects (like, for example, bits of light called photons), it doesn't quite work.

It turns out that our current best theories about tiny particles are incompatible with relativity. Somehow, somewhere, we're still a bit wrong.

Solving the problem

Partly, these mistakes are explained away by progress. As we get better at physics, at coming up with clever experiments and measuring the results more and more accurately, our theories slowly get better.

A good theory should always make predictions about things we can see happening (for example, if we double the weight we hang on it, our spring will double in length). If we see a prediction come true, that supports the theory. If we don't, it is disproved, and we have to try again. Every time we see what we expect, our confidence in the theory is increased, but it only takes one counterexample to destroy the theory. At least it does in theory.

Actually, when a physicist—let's call him X—gets a "wrong" result, science has a problem. One way to solve it is to adapt and improve the theory, without changing its basic rules, so that it predicts X's results, too. That way we don't have to throw away whole, useful theories just because that troublemaker X was up to his experiments again.

When it comes to springiness, we say that Hooke's law only holds for certain kinds of material, under certain conditions—to be precise, it holds when springs are springy. Pull your spring too hard and it reaches a point where it turns into a twisted piece of wire. Keep pulling and it will break. But breaking a spring doesn't break Hooke's law, which long ago stopped applying to that spring.

Simply improving a theory, setting limits and exceptions, is pretty hard work. One easy alternative is to accuse X of getting his results wrong and wonder why he gets so much money for his wrongheaded research. There's always plenty to argue about in science—for researchers that's half the fun of it.

Revolting physicists

Sometimes, the little adjustments and strange results begin to mount up, as they did for Newtonian physics in the nineteenth century. Our best theories become a hodgepodge of exceptions and special cases, and arguments rage about unexplained results and experimental error.

At this point it takes a revolution to sort things out, to explain a host of problems, and to give us a whole new way of seeing the universe. The arrival of quantum physics was just such a revolution. Newton's universe was solid and precise and ran like clockwork. Quantum physics says that this is just how it looks to us, but that underneath it is flimsy and never completely predictable.

In the same way, some think that the current struggle to produce a unified theory may be a signal that relativity and quantum physics are missing something important, too. No one knows what the next revolution might look like.

Fundamental physics

The hope of physicists is that these revolutions give us a deeper understanding of our world and how it works. Hooke's law is fine, but we now also have complicated theories (about how atoms move in a piece of metal and the law of conservation of energy) that explain Hooke's law, and what happens to a piece of metal when Hooke's law stops applying, how it stretches permanently and eventually breaks.

So there are laws that explain other laws. And somehow the explaining laws (which should be equally testable in experiments) are more important and deeper than the others. At the bottom of all the layers of explanation, we think that there may be just a few fundamental laws that will prop up all of physics and the universe we know.

Even now, all our best attempts at the deepest laws—which seem to explain almost everything that happens in the universe and to explain all the other laws we know—could be written, in mathematical symbols, on a single sheet of paper.

One goal of physics is to reduce that sheet to a single mathematical sentence that explains everything. Another is to get it exactly right.

Putting it all together

The idea of fundamental laws leads to deep questions about what exactly physics does. Physicists tend to believe that there are real laws to discover, but they find it difficult to answer questions about what these are and how they work.

We'll come back to these debates, and what they may tell us about our place in the universe, at the end of this book, when we've had more of a look at the laws themselves.

For now, we'll note that physics tries to fit together a picture of the whole universe, which means that to understand one part you need to understand another, but to understand that part it helps to grasp the first. So don't give up if you don't get one part. You might understand after reading something else.

Mad (and angry) scientists

It's also worth remembering that physics—like football, fashion, fishing, and even things we do that don't start with "f"—is a human activity. Physicists are people. They argue about their ideas, they make mistakes, and they do what needs to be done to make sure they have money to continue their work next year. Many of them work obsessively on their ideas and get very excited about them. And it's only with a dose of hindsight, when we forget the dead ends and the debates, that the story of physics seems neat and tidy.

Maybe another way to put it is that many physicists are, quite frequently, a bit nutty. Einstein, for example, liked to go sailing when there wasn't any wind ("for the challenge," he said). Newton, though, wasn't so much crazy as just very cranky (possibly because the mercury he worked with got to his brain). He went to extraordinary lengths to get his scientist friends to gang up and belittle some of his rivals.

Nikola Tesla, the gifted Serbian physicist and engineer who made huge advances in the study of electricity, probably had obsessive compulsive disorder. He insisted that the number of his hotel room be divisible by three; he didn't like to touch round things; and he kept saying his physics theories were right after he moved to the United States and ended up fixing roads because no one believed him. The thing is, he was (mostly) right.

The nuttiest of them all

But the best mad physicist was an ancient Greek named Archimedes. It seems unlikely that he actually ran naked down the street shouting "Eureka!" (which means "I have found it!") because he was so excited after noticing that the water level rose when he stepped into his bath. But then again, in doing that he had just discovered the answer to an important question asked by his king, Hiero of Syracuse, and he was then able to prove that a crown the king had been given was a fake.

Archimedes is important because he reminds us that, in physics, we can all enjoy "Eureka!" moments.

We can all appreciate the everyday—but amazing—physics of rainbows, and make a good argument for our belief that the world is round even though it seems flat. And with a little effort (a bit of peace and quiet, accompanied by a stiff drink), we can even think through a thought experiment that demonstrates something as odd as Einstein's theory of relativity.

Read on, and see for yourself. Just remember, at all times, to keep your clothes on and your wits about you.

2

Forces

In this chapter, we'll find out how pushing and pulling change the way things move according to Sir Isaac Newton's three laws of motion; and how sometimes, no matter how hard you try, you won't get anywhere.

OK. So let's get moving.

Four hundred years ago, as the scientific revolution started putting the whole world in a spin, Galileo, Newton, and other early physicists spent much of their time looking at how and why things move. And if forces were a good enough place for Galileo and Newton to start, they should be good enough for us, too.

They're also a good place to start because we intuitively have a feeling for forces and motion. They are part of the physics that we use and control every day: for walking, lifting, carrying, driving, and playing with hammers. And occasionally, forces and motion remind us how big and wild and implacable the laws of the universe are. For example: Don't play with hammers—you may drop one on your toe.

So we know that the faster we drive, the longer it takes to stop; or that when it's just you in the car, it goes like a rocket, but fill it with luggage and your extended family, and it would practically lose a race with a snail.

Sometimes, though, our intuitions about forces and motion mislead us. Let's look at an example.

Float like a feather, fall like a hammer

We all know that something as light as a feather (like, for example, a feather) will fall more slowly than something heavy (like, for example, a hammer). Except, sometimes it won't.

In July 1971, when Dave Scott, commander of NASA's Apollo 15 mission, stood in the desolate moonscape and dropped a hammer and a feather at the same time, they fell together, and hit fine powdery moon dust together. And since it cost the American taxpayer around $150 billion (at today's prices) to get him there, we'd better hope we can learn something from that.

Of course, if you drop the feather on Earth, it doesn't fall straight down, but floats in the breeze. Actually, the breeze is the clue to what's happening. On the moon, there's no air to slow the feather. Taking the air out of the equation by doing the experiment in a near-vacuum on the moon is a great example of the way physics simplifies problems so that we can find out exactly what's happening.

Anyway, our experience with light things like feathers still makes it difficult to get a feel for the physics.

Somehow, even after all of Scott's effort, it still seems as if a 4-lb. (2-kg) weight will fall faster than a 2-lb. (1-kg) weight. Well it won't. And here's how to prove it in your head, using a thought experiment.

For this thought experiment, you'll require the following: three imaginary apples.

Imagine dropping three apples, all at once, from shoulder height to the floor. (It's easy: Just imagine you have three strong arms to hold them. And imagine you're really tall so that they take a long time to fall. See, you can do this physics stuff.)

So, all three apples hit the ground at the same time. Of course they did. Now what if we loosely tie one apple to another with a handy piece of imaginary string, and drop all three again. Again, all three crash down together. Of course they do. How could loosely tying two apples together make them fall faster?

Imagine making that piece of string shorter. Does that change the speed at which the tied apples fall? Of course not. Even shorter? Still no change. In fact, even if we get a whole roll of sticky tape and turn two apples into one big messy apple bundle, it won't suddenly start falling faster than its pristine comrade, even though that messy bundle is now twice as heavy.

So that's it, all proven—heavier things don't fall faster. Enjoy your apples.

And let's head back to the moon.

The gravity of the situation

Have you ever seen videos of Neil Armstrong or any of the other lunar astronauts out on a moonwalk? Have you noticed their strange gait, how they lope around and execute huge two-footed kangaroo hops?

On Earth, heavy things and light things fall at the same speed (if the breeze doesn't get in the way), and the same is true on the moon, but there is an important difference between what happens here and up there. It turns out that the actual rate at which things pick up speed when falling (their *acceleration,* to use the proper physics word for getting faster) is less on the moon than it is on Earth. So even in a vacuum, it isn't how heavy things are that decides how quickly they fall, it's where you are when you do the experiment.

In fact, moon-walking astronauts could jump six times as high as they could on Earth. The reason why has nothing to do with Michael Jackson's famous dance move and everything to do with a force called gravity, which is what sticks us all to the surface of the Earth and makes everything right side up.

But what's a force?

Feel the force

We can't see forces. But we can feel them and see their effects. The force of gravity keeps the Earth traveling around the sun and the moon traveling around the Earth, while other forces inside atoms hold them together and help create the matter that makes up everything around us. Forces make your car go faster and slow it down, push it around corners, and stop it from sinking into the road.

Pushing, pulling, turning, squeezing, and stretching all involve forces; we see objects move differently or change shape because of these forces every day of our lives.

Newton's first law

Isaac Newton summed this up in his first law of motion:

Things stay at rest, or continue moving in a straight line at a steady speed, unless acted upon by a resultant force.

This is a beautifully simple law. But that doesn't mean you don't have to be careful with it.

Direction makes a difference

OK. We're in that car at the start of the chapter. Lugging the family away somewhere nice on vacation. We're doing a steady speed of 67 m.p.h. (30 m/s), on a straight section of the highway, in the outside lane, probably with a long line of people in a hurry behind, all cursing and complaining and wishing we'd move over so they can break the speed limit and get wherever they're going 10 minutes earlier. But, hey, this is an important experiment, so they can wait.

We're traveling at a steady speed, in a straight line. Are there forces acting on our car?

Try rolling down the window and sticking your hand out. Phew! That's windy. So there's a pretty strong force (wind resistance) slowing the car down. But doesn't Newton's law talk about forces making things speed up or slow down?

True. It does. But there is one vital word we haven't examined yet.

*Things stay at rest, or continue moving in a straight line at a steady speed, unless acted upon by a **resultant** force.*

Wind resistance (along with a few other forces, such as friction acting on the wheels) is slowing your car. But the engine is working to overcome that resistance and keep it rolling at a steady 70 m.p.h. (113 km/h). And the result of these forces, one pushing forward, and an equal bunch pushing back, is no overall resultant force acting on your car. They cancel each other out and you keep up a steady speed.

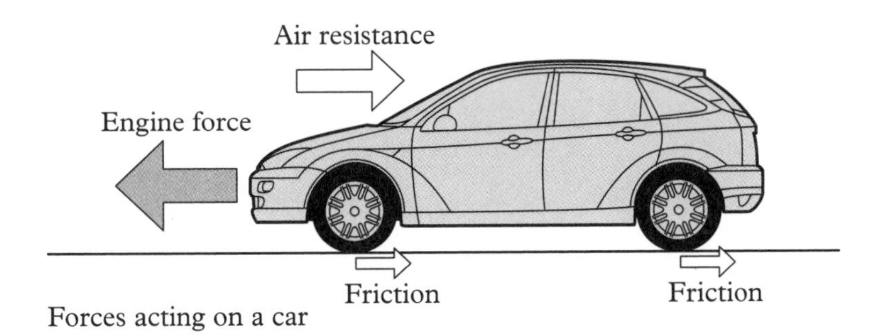

Forces acting on a car

Not only does this tell us how clever Newton was to put the word "resultant" in, it also points to an important aspect of forces: They have direction as well as size, or as physicists like to say, forces are a *vector* quantity.

Scalar quantities, like volume, on the other hand, are one-dimensional. A quart of milk is purely a quart of milk. Add it to another quart of milk in a big jug and you have two quarts of milk; there's nothing else to think about when add those up.

Vectors are more complicated. If I'm pushing a car with a force of 1 Newton (that's right, Sir Isaac was such a genius, they named the unit of force after him), and you're pushing with a force of 1 Newton, neither of us is pushing very hard. And, more importantly, because I haven't told you which way we're pushing, it's not clear whether there is a force of 2 Newtons acting on the car, or none at all.

If we're both pushing in the same direction, you can add our pushing power: there is a 2-Newton force on the car, and if we're lucky, we might move it. But we could be pushing in opposite directions, and the resultant force would be zero. And in between those two extremes we could be pushing more or less in the same direction, or almost in opposite directions, and then we could figure out the exact angles of our pushing and ask a passing physicist to calculate the exact size and angle of the resultant force on the car.

Balancing acts

Remember our floating, blown-around feather? Well, we should now be able to understand why, even though on the moon it falls as quickly as a hammer, on Earth it doesn't.

Feathers are, light, flat, and wide, so wind and air resistance have a large area to push on. This means that, as a feather falls on Earth, air resistance quickly creates a force that is big enough to balance the small force due to gravity that's pulling the feather down. And once those forces are balanced, the feather will float down at a constant, slow speed.

Hammers, on the other hand, have a small surface area relative to their heavy weight. So they can fall much faster before the forces of gravity and air resistance balance out.

Terminal velocity

Once gravity and air resistance have balanced out, there is no resultant force on an object. No resultant force means no acceleration (remember Newton's first law!), and so the object will continue falling at a constant speed. This speed is known as *terminal velocity*; in other words, the final velocity it reaches.

On the moon, of course, there's no air resistance. The feather and hammer fall at the same speed because the force of gravity is all that's acting on them.

You can clearly see the effect of air resistance in action when you watch a video of groups of skydivers chasing each other and joining hands as they plummet toward the ground. They are experts at changing their size and shape, and therefore the air resistance acting on them, so they fall more slowly or quickly. In fact, they can vary their speed from about 125 to 200 m.p.h. (55 to 90 m/s).

When forces balance

Floating and flying are also good examples of balancing acts. An aircraft stays up because the lift that its wings produce is enough to balance the pull of gravity. Similarly, boats float when the upward push of the water—which is due to an effect called buoyancy—equals the pull of gravity.

Archimedes' principle

Archimedes discovered that:

Any object, wholly or partly immersed in a fluid, is buoyed up by a force equal to the weight of the fluid displaced by the object.

So if you gently float a small boat in a tub of water filled to the brim, and catch all the water that flows over the edge when it is displaced by the boat, you'll find that the weight of the boat is the same as the weight of the water you caught. Neat, huh?

Buoyancy is the reason we feel so wonderfully light and maneuverable when we swim. Even a diver with a heavy tank and a weight belt is so buoyed up by the water that she weighs almost nothing as she cruises around the coral reef.

Buoyancy also lifts hot-air and helium balloons in the air. Heated air and helium gas have lower densities than normal cold air. This means they are lighter than air, so a balloon filled with hot air or helium displaces a weight of air greater than its own weight. According to Archimedes' principle, this creates an upward force on the balloon.

This makes it clear why hot-air balloons have to be so big. A rough calculation shows us that, because air weighs only 1.2 kg per cubic meter, you need to displace at least 80 cubic meters of it to make sure that the displaced weight is greater than the weight of your average hot-air

(continued on page 371)

What Archimedes told us about density

Buoyancy is also useful for finding fake crowns, as Archimedes is said to have demonstrated soon after his Eureka-shouting, running-around-naked antics more than 2,000 years ago. All you need is a little understanding of density, to go with what you know about buoyancy.

The density of an object is its mass divided by its volume. It's a measure of how much something weighs per 1 cubic meter lump (or sometimes in pounds per square inch).

Material	Density in kg/m^3
Air around us	1.2
Water	1,000
Lead	11,340
Gold	19,300
Core of the Sun	150,000
Neutron star	1×10^{18}*

**That's 1 with 18 zeros after it. Be careful where you drop that lump of neutron star. It's super heavy. Even a teaspoonful would weigh 10 billion tons on Earth if you could get it here, which you can't.*

Archimedes' task was to find out whether a crown, given to his king, Hiero II of Syracuse, was really made from gold. First, he borrowed a chunk of gold from the king that weighed the same as the crown. Then he hung the gold from one side of a set of scales and the crown from the other, so they balanced. And finally, while it was still hanging there, he dipped the crown and golden chunk into a bath of water.

If the crown, like the chunk, had been gold, the scales would still have balanced, because they would both have displaced the same amount of water (and therefore felt the same upthrust). But, because the crown was a fake, it was less dense. That meant it had to be bigger to weigh the same amount as the gold. And because it was bigger, it displaced more water and was buoyed up more than the gold. So the crown rose and the gold sank (along with, it would seem, the fortunes of the stingy crown-giver).

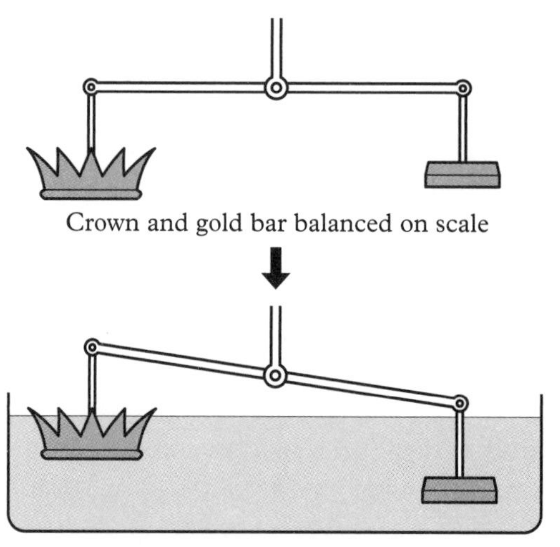

Crown and gold bar balanced on scale

Once in the bath, the gold bar sinks as it is more dense

Checking that a coin is real gold the Archimedes way is smart because, as you can see from the table above, it's more dense even than lead, so it's difficult to fake.

balloonist (who weighs around 80 kg). And to take up 80 cubic meters of space, a cube of air would need to measure 15 ft. (4.5 m) along each side.

Since we displace air, too, buoyancy is also acting on us. In air, we weigh about 0.1 percent less than we would in a vacuum. That is, the atmosphere gives us a weight reduction of almost 3 ounces (about 80 grams) for the average-sized adult! And we don't have to diet to get it.

Speed and velocity

Let's get back into our car, still hurtling down the highway. But now, while we're roaring along at 65 m.p.h. (30 m/s), a side wind hits our car.

This new force isn't balanced by the friction pushing the other way (because you are caught up in the physics of the moment and you've let go of the wheel). So now there is a resultant force on the car, and it changes direction. It accelerates across the lanes of the highway, and a dozen cars have to swerve out the way, their drivers shaking their fists.

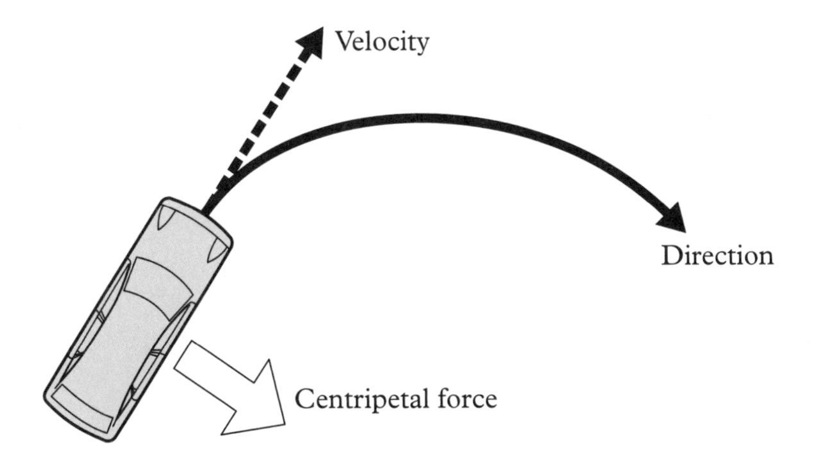

To take account of this, in physics, we talk about velocity rather than speed. Velocity is a vector quantity: Like a force, it has a magnitude* (the speed of the car) and a direction (at this point, veering dangerously across the highway). We tend to think of acceleration as getting faster, but in physics it means any change in velocity, so a change in direction counts as an acceleration.

For an object to move in a circle at a constant speed, you need a centripetal force: one that is continually changing direction so that it is always acting toward the center of that circle. Does that sound complicated? It isn't, actually. Swing a lasso around your head, and the rope is just right to provide a force toward the center of the circle (your hand) and to keep the hoop moving round and around (until you let go and the hoop, with no resultant force acting, flies off to rope in the nearest pedestrian). In a similar way, gravity, which always acts toward the center of an object, keeps the planets going around the sun at a constant speed.

Car seats are pretty good at this, too. The force you and your passengers feel as the car swings across the highway pushes so that instead of continuing straight down the highway at 65 m.p.h. (30 m/s), you all stay in the car and turn with it...

Look out! You're gonna hit that truck!

Thinking time

We're all so used to zipping along highways that we hardly think about how quickly we're really traveling.

*Magnitude is just a fancy physics word for "size."

And highways are designed for fast driving: There are few features to distract us, bends and hills are long and gentle so we can continue quickly and see a long way ahead, and signs give us lots of warning so we're prepared for what's coming up.

Try doing 65 m.p.h. (about 30 m/s) in town and you'll soon get a feel for how fast the highway speed limit is. Or rather, don't. Have a quick look at the table below instead and stay safe.

Speed of light	300,000,000 m/s
Speed of sound	300 m/s
Car on highway	30 m/s
Person jogging	3 m/s
Child crawling	0.3 m/s
Snail	0.03 m/s

Thinking about your car's speed in unfamiliar units helps you come to grips with it. Every second, your car is traveling 98 ft. (30 m). Remember, that's 30 long paces. Every second.

When you look at it like this, it's hardly surprising that even a driver who is concentrating can travel almost 150 ft. (45 m) before slamming on the brakes after they notice that slow truck bumbling along in the inside lane. That's because it can take the human brain 1.5 seconds to realize, hey, that's a slow truck, I'm gonna hit it, to then decide to brake, and finally, actually hit the brake pedal. And that's an alert driver! If you're thinking deeply about physics, you might take even longer.

The upshot? Nothing. We're all in a hurry. But if we were sane we'd be scared witless every time we drive. Especially when you consider that so far we've only thought about distance...

Screeching to a halt

Brakes on? Good. But you aren't slowing down very quickly, are you? There was a reason I told you the car's packed with luggage and your extended family. Didn't you notice when we pulled away from those lights back in town that those snails outpaced us for a bit?

As we started to see earlier, stronger forces cause greater accelerations, for any given object. The relationship is proportional. Double the force, double the acceleration (or, when you apply the brakes, the deceleration). But what if you're using different objects? Well, then you'll find that heavier things accelerate more slowly. Double the mass (mass is a bit like weight—we'll come to it in a moment) and you *halve* the acceleration.

Plugging some numbers into the equation should make it easy to understand the relationship between these three quantities. If our brakes are trying to stop the car with a force of 7,200 Newtons, and our car has a mass of

Newton's second law

This is Newton's second law of motion. Physicists usually sum it up by writing:

Force equals mass times acceleration
or
$F = ma.$

(*ma* has nothing to do with your mom but is instead a short way of writing *m times a*.)

1,200 kilos (typical for an empty car), our deceleration would be 6 m/s every second, because

$$7{,}200\ N = 1{,}200\ kg \times 6\ m/s^2.$$

But if we add in four adults and their luggage (*1,200 kg + 400 kg = 1,600 kg*), we get: $7{,}200\ N = 1{,}600\ kg \times 4.5\ m/s^2$. Our deceleration is now only 4.5 m/s.

Physicists like to work with numbers and mathematical equations like this, but learning equations isn't the same as learning physics. If $F=ma$ is all Greek to you, don't worry. You can still understand forces and how they make things move. You just don't know your a from your Ω.

Everybody's equal (and opposite)

So, where were we? Safely stopped on the shoulder of the road? Good, good. And luckily, there's Newton's third law to keep us that way.

Remember gravity? It's pulling the car toward the center of the Earth. And the equal and opposite force? Well, it's pulling the Earth toward the center of the car! Of course,

Newton's third law

This says:

If a force acts upon a body, then an equal and opposite force (of the same kind) must act upon another body.

When golf balls go awry . . .

Newton's laws of motion apply perfectly to the world of golf. We're all aware that a golf ball moves when it is hit by force. However, there are outside forces that keep a golf ball from moving in its original direction forever. A ball may have a straight path when the club hits it, but then gravity pulls the ball toward Earth and can keep it from going straight. Air resistance—a form of friction—then slows the ball's velocity as it speeds through the air. Once a golf ball connects with the ground again, it slows down even more because a grassy or sandy surface creates more friction with the ball than air.

The reaction of a golf ball when a club hits it is usually predictable. When a force is applied to the back of a ball with a club by swinging—an action—the ball zooms down the fairway—a reaction. But golfers become extremely frustrated when the desired action and reaction doesn't happen. And when a golfer does not hit the ball squarely with his club, things can go awry—a slice, a hook...yes, sometimes, even a broken window.

the mass of the Earth is 5×10^{21} times greater than that of your car, so the effect on the Earth isn't noticeable.

Here's another example of the third law. Remember when we were braking hard as we tried to miss that slow truck? Friction applied a force of 7,200 N to our car that slowed it. And the equal and opposite force? Well, it's 7,200 N acting in the opposite direction on that bit of the surface of the Earth known as the highway. So, although the effect isn't noticeable because the Earth is so massive, our braking does actually affect the way it rotates.

Anyway, enough of these death-defying near-misses. We need to save our energy for something much more important, called—guess what?—energy.

3

Energy and Power

In this chapter we'll talk about all kinds of energy: energy that things have because they're moving, because they're where they are, or even because of what they're like inside. We'll also talk about power, or putting that energy to use. And finally, we'll put it all together and find out how the physics of energy can save us from going out with a bang.

Energy doesn't like to sit around, which is hardly surprising, given that it's so energetic. Energy is always here, there, and everywhere; always doing this and that; always changing into something new. It's like the trendiest party animal in the universe. Besides propelling us down highways and into physics experiments, energy keeps us warm, grows our food, and helps us see. It even gets us up in the morning and makes the toast.

All our energy comes, initially, from the sun. The sun is one great big long-lasting nuclear explosion, and it's chucking solar energy at us at a fantastic rate. A third of what comes our way is bounced straight back off the Earth's atmosphere and the clouds and goes back into space, yet our planet still absorbs more energy from the sun in *1 hour* than humans burn in *10 months*.

So the sun warms us and the planet (the energy that it sends becomes thermal energy). It makes the plants grow, turning solar energy into chemical energy through photosynthesis. We eat some plants, turning their chemical energy into all kinds of other energy, such as kinetic energy (energy you have because you're moving), as we bounce out of bed, and sound energy as we shout at whoever's in the bathroom to get a move on. The sun's energy also evaporates water from the sea and turns it into clouds, and generates the air currents that turn into wind.

Some plants nourished by the sun millions of years ago have been turned into coal and oil. We dig and burn them; they warm us and light our way when the sun's hiding behind clouds or on the other side of the planet. Or we burn them and they shoot us off on vacation, fueling our airliner as we head someplace where the sun's still shining.

Counting the calories

If you're on a diet, you count calories*, but if you're a physicist, you measure energy in Joules.

1 calorie = 4.2 Joules.

*The calories you count are kilogram calories (or kcals), but in most other contexts, we are actually talking about gram calories. A calorie is the amount of energy needed to heat some water by 1°C, and the "gram" or "kilogram" refers to exactly how much water, so a kilogram calorie is 1,000 gram calories. (There is also the rarely used pound calorie.)

Joules are named after James Joule, a wealthy brewer from Manchester, England, who was fascinated by electricity. As a child, he experimented by giving his brother and some of his servants electric shocks. But in the 1840s, when he'd grown up, he made himself useful by looking at how he could use the newly invented electric motor instead of steam engines in his brewery. From there, he discovered lots of interesting things about how electrical and mechanical energy is converted into heat.

Eventually it was decided that 1 Joule would be the amount of energy expended by a force of 1 Newton if it moved an object 1 meter. (They try to keep it simple, don't they?)

So in real life, a Joule is the energy it takes to lift a small apple 1 meter straight up. Or the kinetic energy of a tennis ball lobbed gently over the net. But there are around 720,000 Joules of food energy (carbohydrates and alcohol) in a pint (500 ml) of beer, which is probably why you're going to have to try something more strenuous than the apple-lifting workout if you want to get rid of that beer belly.

What a waste

However, converting energy is rarely straightforward. Modern experiments on rowers show that for every 5 Joules of energy they burn, only around 1 Joule is actually used to move their oars. The rest goes in heat, in sweating and swearing and making pained expressions for the camera.

Energy conservation

Joule's work on energy conversion led to the discovery of the law of conservation of energy, one of the most basic and important in all physics. Once you know that energy is converted from one kind to another, careful measurement can show that all of it is always converted, that energy is never created or destroyed. Then you have a very important law: the first law of thermodynamics.

It says:

The total amount of energy in a closed system remains constant.

So our universe, the biggest closed system we know, is just as energetic now as it was when it first exploded into existence. And when Mr. Joule gives an apple 1 Joule of potential (height) energy by lifting it up, all that energy becomes kinetic energy as it falls, and then heat and sound (splat!) energy when it hits the floor.

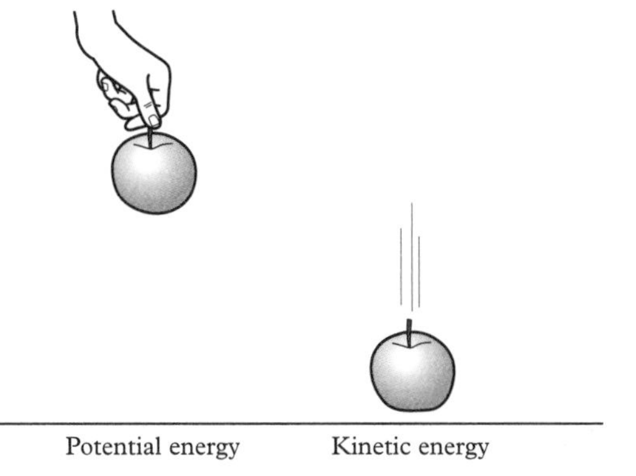

And it's not just Olympic gold medal winners who waste energy. Something similar is true of all us when we burn food energy. As a Victorian gentleman, Mr. Joule can surely lift an apple without swearing, but he still wastes 4 Joules of energy doing it.

Most energy conversions are, like Mr. Joule's, very inefficient. Even modern low-energy lightbulbs only turn half the electrical energy they consume into light. The rest is, again, wasted as heat.

In old-fashioned, conventional lightbulbs, only 10 percent of the energy is turned into light, with the rest warming the room. But even that looks efficient compared to some other energy conversions.

It has been calculated, for example, that for every Joule of energy available in Mr. Joule's pint of beer, at least 10,000 Joules of energy have been used in making that beer. That energy is applied mainly in the form of sunlight

The definition of work

When Mr. Joule picked up that apple, he did some work. Not much work, agreed, but certainly a physicist would call what he did work. That's mainly because, in physics, work is defined as "energy transferred during a process".

When that apple is lifted, it gains 1 Joule of energy. We know that because it has a weight of 1 Newton (so it took 1 Newton of force to lift it) and because we know it moved 1 meter, and *work done (or energy gained) is force times distance moved in the direction of that force*.

If we drop the apple, that energy is transferred again; gravity does the work to speed it on its way to the ground.

growing the hops and barley, and in the heating required at various stages as the beer is brewed.

Watts and work

It isn't very exciting that Mr. Joule can lift an apple to the not-very-high height of 1 meter. But what if he can lift that apple quickly? What if every second, he lifts an apple a meter, so he's lifting 60 apples a minute, and 3,600 an hour? Well, then he'd be doing 1 Joule of work per second, which means his power output is 1 watt, for no other reason than that is what a watt is defined to be.

The watt (W), which is the unit we use to measure power, or how quickly something does work, is named after James Watt, a Scottish inventor whose redesign of the steam engine in the 1700s gave it the power to be the workhorse of the industrial revolution.

You have more energy upstairs

As you will have realized from all that apple lifting, the higher something is, the more gravitational potential energy it has. That applies to you, too. The higher you go, the greater your potential energy is. In fact, your potential energy is directly proportional to your height off the ground. If you're eight stories high in a hot-air balloon, you have 8 times more energy than when you were only upstairs at home.

The amount of potential energy is also dependent on your weight. If you're heavier, you don't fall faster, but you will make a bigger splat when you hit the ground.

You can do the thought experiment. We already know that if you irresponsibly drop from your balloon two apples joined by a loose piece of string, they don't fall faster than one apple. But, compared to one apple, those two do make double the mess and double the bang when their potential energy, after becoming movement (kinetic) energy as they fall, turns into splat energy as they hit the pavement and explode, lightly coating surprised passers-by with apple juice. The law of conservation of energy says that splat energy had to come from somewhere, so it must have come from their potential energy, which became kinetic energy.

So it's clear that an object's gravitational potential energy is directly proportional to its weight (eight apples have 8 times as much potential energy as one, which will be released as 8 times as much splat energy when they hit the pavement).

It is weight that is important here, not mass. On the moon, in one-sixth Earth's gravity, those apples would fall more slowly and splat much less. How much less, we don't know, unfortunately. Thought experiments only get you so far, and no Apollo astronauts threw apples out the window of the lunar lander.

The law of conservation of energy applies in this experiment because our falling apples are very close to being a closed system. Only a tiny amount of energy is lost to air resistance. At a point when the falling apples are just a fraction of an inch (a few millimeters) above the pavement, and just before they splat, they have lost all their potential energy: It has all been turned into kinetic energy. A millisecond later and all that kinetic energy has become splat energy.

Frankly, though, finding the kinetic energy of falling apples is not that useful. What about the kinetic energy of a speeding car?

Car crash equations

When you're driving down the highway and brake hard to avoid a slow truck or bus, your brakes do work (in the physics sense) to slow you down.

Of course, if your brain was working, you'd have remembered all those stopping distances you learned in order to pass your driving test, you would have left a bigger gap between you and the car in front, and you wouldn't have had to brake so hard in the first place. But then again, I'm sure you forgot those facts about stopping distances as soon as you had your shiny new licence and 15 friends in the back of your parents' station wagon for

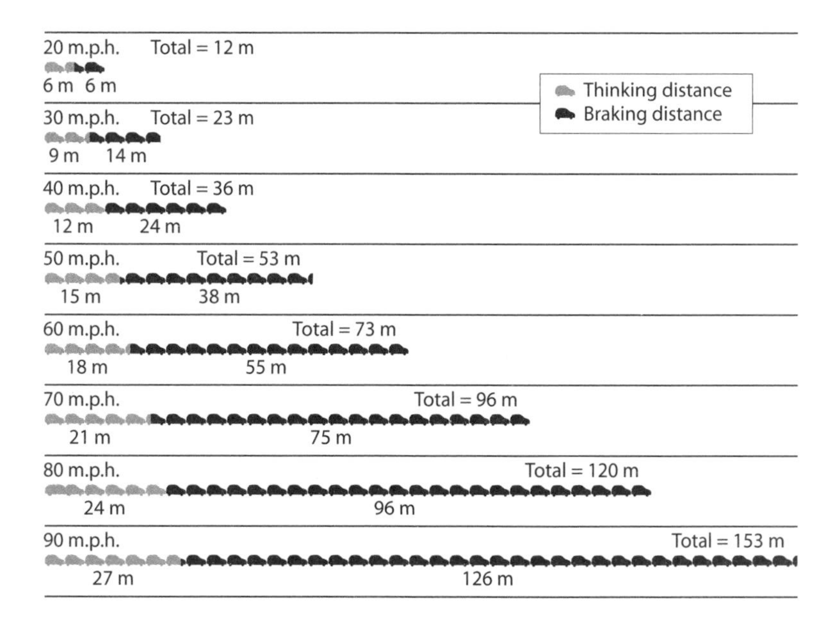

a celebratory drive around town. Of course, you are now mature and fascinated by physics, so stopping distances are worth a closer look.

If you double your speed, from say 20 m.p.h. to 40 m.p.h., your stopping distance is quadrupled (from 20 ft. up to 80 ft., or from 6 m to 24 m). Double your speed and you quadruple your stopping distance. Triple it (from 30 m.p.h. to 90 m.p.h.) and your stopping distance increases *ninefold.* This is obviously one factor that makes speed so dangerous. But why does it happen?

Well, kinetic energy has the answer, but only if we know a bit more about friction, the force that makes your brakes work. (And it's just as well they do work. Imagine if you ran head on into a slow truck, or worse, a brick wall. Well the good news is, you don't have to imagine it: we'll get to that, too.)

Get a grip

Friction is a force caused by the resistance of surfaces as they slide over each other. Without it, we'd all be slipping around like non-skaters on an ice rink.

Scientists used to think friction was caused by the bumps and lumps of the surfaces as they knock together. But it seems friction is actually mostly caused by chemical bonding between the moving surfaces: It's more like sticky tape being dragged along a surface, rather than sandpaper.

Anyway, friction causes motion energy to be transferred into heat and screeching sound energy. Or, as a physicist might say, the heat and sound cause the frictional force (because the transfer of energy away from motion is what causes the force to be felt). Confused? Don't worry—so are scientists. There's still a lot to learn about friction. But we can all agree that friction is greater the harder you push the rubbing surfaces together, so heavier things feel greater friction: It's easier to slide a single armchair around the living room than a great big sofa full of couch potatoes.

Friction also depends on the kinds of surface involved. It's not just fashion that encourages us to wear rubber-soled tennis shoes rather than leather-soled loafers on the tennis court: we wear tennis shoes because they grip better.

Anything that comes between surfaces can affect friction. For example, fluids, such as oil and water, reduce it by keeping the surfaces apart. This is useful inside your car's engine (it stops energy from being wasted as your crankshaft turns), but it's dangerous outside when the road gets wet or oily.

The work the brakes do, according to the law of conservation of energy, converts all the kinetic energy of the car into heat, through the friction of the brake pads on the brake discs.

For a car braking hard from highway speeds, that's a lot of energy to convert. During hard braking, each brake heats up with the power of a small electric fire, and if you hit the pedal hard a few times in a row, that heat can build and build until your brakes stop working properly (which is why signs are sometimes placed at the top of steep hills encourage you to select a low gear and use your engine to slow you).

Now, here's the clever part. We know that all our car's kinetic energy has been converted into heat as the brakes did work to slow it. We also know, from the "work" equation we looked at earlier, how much energy that is: It is

Slip-sliding away

There are two kinds of friction: static and dynamic. Static friction is the force you feel when you're walking carefully on an icy pavement. There's quite a lot of grip there: So long as you move gently, your feet don't slip. But as soon as they start to slide, and the much lower force of dynamic friction takes over, you're on your backside. This is one reason why cars have anti-lock (or ABS) brakes. They are designed to release before your wheels slide on the road, and lower, dynamic friction takes over.

given by the braking force multiplied by the distance moved. And we know something odd about that braking distance, namely that it quadruples if our car goes twice as fast. Therefore, the kinetic energy of our car must also quadruple if we go twice as fast. So, kinetic energy must be proportional to the speed of our car squared.

See how v, the speed (or velocity) of the object, is squared, so that if we double the speed we get 4 times the energy ? And if you're really good at math, you can actually derive this formula from the work equation (*F times d*). That's interesting, isn't it? There's something about our math, and the way the universe works, so that when we do clever mathematical things to our work equation (*force times distance*), we get our kinetic energy equation. That's the start of how mathematics and physics go hand in hand.

Even better: Now that we have the equation, you don't need to look at government figures to figure out your stopping times. All you need to do is one experiment, in a deserted parking lot. Measure how quickly you can stop from 20 m.p.h. (32 km/h).Then you can quickly fill in your own table. If you doubled your speed, to 40 m.p.h. (64 km/h), your stopping distance would quadruple. If you multiplied it by 3.5, to get 70 m.p.h. (113 km/h), your stopping distance should increase by $3.5^2 = 12.25$ times.

Watch that child

Government figures also tell us that, four times out of five, a child hit by a car traveling at 40 m.p.h. (64 km/h) will die. But if the car that hits a child is traveling at 30 m.p.h. (48 km/h), four times out of five the child will survive.

Drivers who don't like speed cameras or speed bumps take issue with these figures. How do we know, they ask, the exact speed of a car when it hits a child who has run out into the street? It certainly seems unlikely that anybody has been throwing children in front of cars traveling at various speeds to see how many survive.

Well, even if you don't believe government figures, and skid mark data, and experiments that were done on dead bodies and animals, and the stories told by the kinds of injuries children receive when tossed into the air by a carelessly driven car, physics might convince you to slow down. Firstly, there are those thinking and stopping distance figures we've already looked at. At 30 m.p.h., if a child stepped out 82 ft. (25 m) ahead of you, you'd hit him or her at 19 m.p.h. (31 km/h). At 40 m.p.h., you'd hit them twice as fast—at 38 m.p.h. (61 km/h).

You can also look at the forces on the child's body. Let's say a child is struck by a car, and carried down the road

Crash test hero

Crashing into children is horrible; but crashing into other cars is—apart from being dangerous, noisy, and expensive—quite exciting. That's why we like bumper car rides at amusement parks—and why some people have an unhealthy interest in accidents.

Starting in the 1940s, Dr. John Stapp, a U.S. Air Force officer, did lots of research into the forces that human bodies can survive, by appointing himself crash test dummy and driving a rocket-powered sled into what was, basically, a wall. In this way, he proved that the human body can survive accelerations 40 times stronger than gravity—so long as they act for just a short fraction (0.05) of a second.

Stapp played the dummy, but he was sensible enough to wear a seatbelt. And, although his crashes broke numerous bones and caused permanent damage to his eyesight (because his retinas became detached), he survived to discover a lot of useful information that helped others design aircraft ejector seats and car seat belts.

Later, his campaigning was a major factor in making seat belts a compulsory feature on U.S. cars. (He also came up with Stapp's law: "The universal aptitude for ineptitude makes any human accomplishment an incredible miracle." It explains why so many people didn't and still don't bother using those belts he worked so hard to put in their cars.)

by it. That means they have been accelerated very quickly to the same speed as the car (because hitting a 40-pound child with a 2,600-pound car won't slow the car down much). But we know from the kinetic energy equation that the force involved in accelerating something is proportional to the square of the speed. So, although our 40 m.p.h. car is traveling twice as fast when it hits the child, the force that acts on the child's body is 4 times greater. And human bodies are very soft compared to cars.

Smashing fun

So we've looked at stopping times and seat belts. But what else can physics tells us about how to make cars safer for humans hell-bent into crashing them in thought experiments?

Let's say we build a really strong little car. You can smash it, head on, into a brick wall, and it'll hardly get a dent. However, if we think of the work equation and kinetic energy again, it's clear that, when you hit that wall, the fact that your car stops very quickly means that the force required to stop it—and you—is very large.

Let's do the math.

From the kinetic energy equation, a 175-lb. (80-kg) imaginary person named Bob, who has for some unknown reason volunteered to be in our little car, is driving it at 60 m.p.h. (27 m/s). As a result, he has:

$$\frac{1}{2} mv^2 = \frac{1}{2} \times 80 \times 27^2 = 29{,}000 \text{ Joules of kinetic energy.}$$

Now, let's say, as Bob drives head-on into a wall, that his seatbelt stretches enough to let him move 4 inches forward (that's 10 cm, or 0.1 m) as it stops him from crushing his skull on that hard little steering wheel. Then the force required to take away all his kinetic energy is given by:

KE (29,000 Joules, in this case) =
F x d (force times distance) = F x 0.1
So F is 290,000 N.

For an 175-lb. man, this is an acceleration 360 times bigger than gravity.

Well, that's no good. Bob's little car might still work, and his body might still be strapped in, but after experiencing a force like that, his brain has been squished into soup as it was stopped by the inside of his skull. Stapp was pretty much OK after acceleration 40 times stronger than gravity; a racing driver named David Purley almost lived after he crashed and experienced 180 G. But at 360 G (in other words, 360 times the force of gravity), you've got no chance.

To survive, you need to take longer to stop. So what modern car engineering has done is to slow things down by adding, to the front of our car, a 3-ft.-long (1 m) crumple zone: an area that is strong enough to take some of the sting out of an accident by crumpling. This converts some of the energy of the collision into heat and sound, and making it take longer for the car to slow, so that the force on you is reduced.

Add this to our seat belt stretch, and you now have 10 times as long to stop as Bob did (up from 0.1 m to 1 m, because the crumple zone shrinks from 100 cm to 10 cm in the accident).

Now, when the car stops, the 10 times the distance to stop means the force on you is reduced to a tenth; which means the acceleration is a tenth, which means it is only 36 times the force of gravity. And Colonel Stapp proved you could survive that.

Hooray. The numbers work. So, in you go, but do drive carefully. Oh, and do buckle up. Steering wheels and dashboards are very efficient stoppers. They'll bring you to halt in about ½ inch (1 cm). That's 10 times quicker than a seatbelt: enough to make even a 30 m.p.h. crash fatal. And enough to make it unlikely you'd ever come to grips with the momentous stuff we've got coming up next.

4

Momentum

In this chapter we'll find out about momentum and inertia, and how physics shows us that, once something starts moving, that movement never stops. Then we'll go around in circles, and discover how spinning tops and gyroscopes rely on similar principles. To finish up, we'll talk a bit about torque, the force that makes big engines fun.

In the martial arts movie *Crouching Tiger, Hidden Dragon,* the heroes can break the laws of physics, which makes for all kinds of spectacular floating and flying as they fight. At one point the rebellious young heroine, Jen Yu, is attacked as she's having lunch. A young tough guy runs at her, but, without standing or bracing herself, she blocks him with her left hand, and he bounces off her. All the while, she holds her cup of tea in her right hand and doesn't spill a drop.

Her move, though handy, is obviously impossible. But why? Her attacker has just as much kinetic energy after she blocks him as before. He rebounds, so energy is conserved, just as it should be. Yet some law of physics must have been broken—otherwise a smart flyweight boxer would by now have taken a few classes in Jen Yu self-defense and become heavyweight champion of the world.

It's clear, then, that the laws of energy alone cannot show why Jen's heroics are impossible. For a start, energy lacks a sense of direction—it is a scalar quantity, like mass and volume. It has size and nothing else, so it can't explain why it's odd that Jen wasn't knocked backwards (and into next week).

But lack of direction isn't energy's only failing when it tries to describe motion. To discover more, let's try a thought experiment on a glacier: Let's try to stop it.

Hold the ice

A glacier is a massive, slow-moving river of ice, so it won't mind us giving it a shove back the way it came. Come on, push as hard as you can. Any luck? How about if you bring in a fleet of tow trucks? Well, it's still hopeless. Even hills and rocks can't stop a glacier: It plows right on through whatever is in its way, slowly carving out massive U-shaped valleys as it goes. The forces involved are tremendous.

But what if we string a giant waterwheel-kind-of-thing over a glacier, and try to convert its kinetic energy into electricity, as we could with a river. Can we solve the energy crisis using glaciers?

Well, let's continue with our thought experiment and find out. Let's say our glacier is a 1 cubic-kilometer (0.6

miles cubed) block of ice. Its mass is roughly 10^{12} kg (1 followed by 12 zeros) because water weighs 1 kg per cubic meter. And let's say it moves, like the Byrd Glacier in Antarctica (the biggest in the world), at a speed of around 0.00001 m/s. Then its kinetic energy is a not-so-whopping 50 Joules. Convert that all to electricity and you get a low-energy bulb lit for a few seconds.

Again, energy isn't giving us the full picture. Glaciers are unstoppable—but they have about as much energy as a student physicist after a night's overindulgence on Mr. Joule's brew (see chapter 3).

What we need is something that describes unstoppable glaciers and lunging bad guys. That something is called *momentum*.

Don't stop now

Momentum is something we all intuitively understand: It's why you can't stop a car by giving it a shove; it's what makes pool and billiard games worth playing; and, as you'll have guessed by now, it comes up in a law of the universe that makes Jen Yu self-defense impossible.

The idea of there being something in a moving object that keeps it moving has been around since Roman times. But it wasn't until Newton came along that it was properly, mathematically useful. This is hardly surprising, as momentum is intimately tied up with Newton's laws of motion, especially the third law, as we'll see when we discover that flaw in Jen Yu self-defense.

The momentum equation

Momentum is calculated by multiplying mass by velocity, and so is given by the formula:

$P = mv.$

So our glacier from earlier can have huge momentum even though it is moving slowly. (Its momentum, 10,000,000 kg m/s, is big: about the same as that of a giant car transporter carrying 300 cars quickly down the highway.)

Momentum is why oil tankers take 20 miles (32 km) to stop. It's a measure of the "quantity of motion," so it is proportional both to the mass of an object and to its speed.

A load of balls

As physicists, we like to simplify things to find out what's really happening. So instead of trying to find a Jen Yu martial artist and a cooperative thug, we can recreate the scene with pool balls. But if we're going to do experiments on a pool table, we want to carry them out on a physicist's *ideal* pool table: one that's perfectly smooth, not bumpy or beer-stained. Then again, ideal pool tables are in short supply. So you may as well find a friendly bar or pool hall, get yourself a drink, and settle down for some physics.

First up—to play the part of a relaxed and lunching Jen Yu—choose a ball that's blue. Then, entering from stage left, playing the thug, a gently rolling red. (We won't use the white ball because, on most pool tables, it's a different size and weight than the others, and that makes everything less ideal.)

Now, red hits blue, full ball, right in the middle. What happens? Well, unless you muck things up by putting spin on the shot, the red stops and blue keeps going—and it keeps going at exactly the same speed, and in the same direction, left to right, that red was moving.

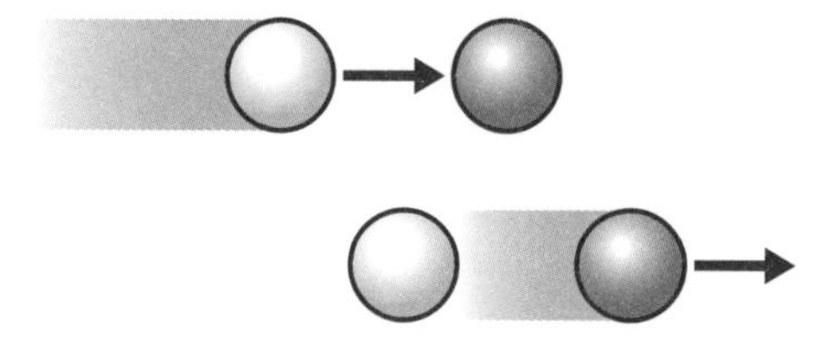

How momentum works on pool balls

Try it again. And again. Try it in a different pool hall. And another. The result will always be the same (so long as you get the collision smack dab in the middle of the blue ball).

Now that makes sense. Again, energy is conserved, but now our new quantity, momentum, is, too. All the energy and all the momentum on our pool table has been transferred from red to blue.

Newton's third law—the one about equal and opposite forces—has been obeyed, too. As the balls collided, the amount that red pushed blue equalled the amount that blue pushed red, and that amount was enough to stop red and send blue on its way.

The amazing thing is that what you have discovered about momentum, right there in front of you on the pool table, is one of the most basic laws of the universe.

Exactly right

Energy and momentum are so important that they are mentioned in a bunch of laws that physicists are pretty much absolutely, completely, honest-we-haven't-got-these-wrong sure about. As far as we know, these laws have never been broken. They applied in the beginning, right after the big bang. And they will apply forever, until the end of time.

They are called the exact laws.

The exact laws are all conservation laws. They say that the total amounts of certain properties in the universe are always conserved, so that these properties can be neither created nor destroyed. (More usefully for those of us who aren't gods, they also apply to small closed systems like our pool table, if we're careful.)

We've already seen the law of conservation of energy. Now that you've done the experiment with the pool balls, you have discovered the momentum version for yourself. It says:

The total momentum in a closed system remains constant. It cannot be created or destroyed.

Energy and momentum are always conserved in our universe simply because of its underlying shape, which is the same whichever way you go, and because time ticks on constantly, without changing the laws of the universe.

(The other exact laws describe the conservation of slightly more complex properties, such as electric charge, and much more complex properties, such as color charge (nothing to do with the price of red paint), weak isospin (nothing to do with a gentle wool wash) and—unluckily for gamblers—probability.)

So conservation of momentum is there for racing drivers who want to slingshot out of corners, and for football players who need to flatten their opponents. It's there for pool players and for people who like to poke holes in martial arts movie fight scenes.

What's more, and like we saw in the last chapter with energy, momentum can be simply and beautifully useful in everyday physics, because it is easier to use the fact that momentum is never created or destroyed than it is to get involved with Newton's laws of motion, and all those tricky forces and accelerations.

Using your momentum

As you noticed when you were diligently rolling that thuggish red ball into poor Jen Yu blue, it was difficult to get the collision quite straight, so that red stopped and blue escaped.

Often, red, coming in left to right, would kiss blue at an angle—and our nice little experiment would be ruined. Instead of red stopping, it would keep going one way, maybe slightly up the table as well as left to right, with blue going off at different angle, slightly down, as well as left to right.

When you think about it carefully, what's happening is quite simple.* After all, even average pool players know this behavior well, and of course it is all another result of the conservation of momentum. Let's look at this more closely—but first, time for a bet.

If you can gently mark on the table a straight left-right line that red is rolling along, I bet you that, whatever distance from that line (measured at a right angle from it) blue finishes, red will finish the same distance away, but on the opposite side.

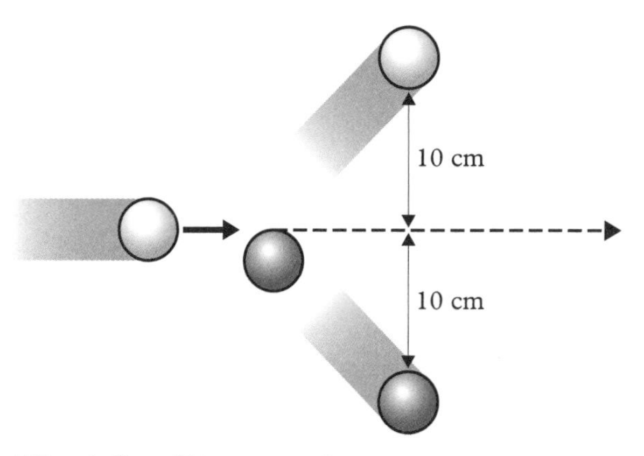

When balls collide at an angle

Tried it? Was I right? Of course I was. And you owe me ten bucks.

Anyway. Back to the physics. So although both balls go off at different angles, and they travel different distances left to right, at different speeds, if you tell me that

*Good pool players, however, do make the physics complicated. They also add in spin: partly to show how brilliant the human brain is at physics that is much too difficult for this book, and partly because that way they can get the cue ball into positions for their next shot that straight momentum would never allow.

red finishes 4 in. (10 cm) above the line, then I know that blue finishes 4 in. below, and all without looking or measuring.

Why? Well, as you've guessed, it's because momentum is conserved—and, more subtly, because momentum has direction, as we've just seen, and so it is conserved *in all directions*.

When just red was rolling, it had left-to-right momentum, and nothing up or down. This means that after the collision, our pool ball system, taken as a whole, still only had left-to-right momentum because momentum can't be created or destroyed. And therefore, after the kiss, the up momentum of blue must have been cancelled out by the down momentum of red, while the overall left-right momentum that was introduced by red was later shared between red and blue.

This momentum then gave the balls equal speeds *in the up-down direction* (because they have equal masses), and that speed was lost by both (to friction) at the same rate, and so in the up-down direction, they both travelled the same distance. Good, huh?

"But hold on a moment," I hear you say. "Those balls were rolling merrily along and they stopped. And something that's not moving has no momentum. So how on earth is momentum conserved when it has obviously been all used up?"

You can't lose momentum

The clue, in fact, is in the "how on Earth?"

In the last chapter, we learned—through those risky driving experiments—that as objects slow and stop, energy is being conserved, but through friction, kinetic energy is converted into heat energy (which is in some ways a kind of kinetic energy, as we'll see later, because it is created by the vibration of atoms). So playing pool actually raises the temperature of that pool table.

Momentum, too, is always conserved. No matter how things bang into each other, or rub up against each other, or are magnetically pulled together, the overall momentum of the system is unchanged. But momentum can't change into anything else, like energy can: It's always there, even if it transferred to something so big (like the planet Earth, for example) that we don't notice its momentum change.

The key to the difference between energy and momentum is once again that momentum is a vector: It has direction as well as magnitude. The vibration of atoms doesn't give an object momentum, because those atoms are vibrating randomly in different directions.

Remember how, at the end of chapter 2, we noted that the car's braking affected the spinning of the world, because of Newton's third law? Well, the same law applies as our balls stop. The balls are stopped from moving by the friction from the pool table's felt, and the equal and opposite force from the balls pushes the table, and hence the floor, and the country and eventually the whole world!

This is great news for hippies, who get some justification for their belief that everything is connected, man. But it's bad news for them, too, because the effect of a pool ball on the movement of the Earth is so tiny that it is impossible to measure.

In short, hippies can't teach us much about physics. But perhaps Clint Eastwood can.

The good, the bad, and the impossible

Just in case you're ever facing a six-gun-wielding outlaw in a graveyard where one of the coffins is packed with cash, it's worth looking at *The Good, the Bad and the Ugly* to find out exactly what won't happen.

First up, it is almost impossible to quickly draw a 150-year-old handgun and hit a person standing 55 yd. (50 m) away with a single shot. Heck, with those old guns you'd be pretty lucky to hit a barn door at that distance. But then, even if you got million-to-one-chance lucky, and did hit the bad guy, it is then completely impossible for the bullet you fired to knock that bad guy over backwards even though the recoil of your gun, which you're shooting from hip height, affects you not one bit as you stand there, cool as Clint.

After all, momentum has to come from somewhere. When your gun fires, and the bullet is blasted down the muzzle, its kinetic energy has come from a small explosion inside the gun. But momentum, as we've seen, can come only from other objects. So what gives your bullet momentum?

Initially, Clint and the bullet in his gun had no momentum. So, after he fired, they can't have had any overall momentum, either. So, whatever momentum the bullet had right after it was fired, Clint (the firer), should have had the same amount, but in the opposite direction. So, since the bullet hit Lee hard enough to knock him over backward, the recoil should have knocked Clint back, too, even though he was braced for the bang.

It's been around and it'll keep going around

So far, we've been looking only at one kind of momentum, which physicists call *linear momentum* because it's all about things moving in straight lines. But now it's time for a quick spin around the other kind of momentum: *angular momentum*. It had a large say in the creation of this planet and its rotation. And, because it keeps gyroscopes standing upright, it is also a vital ingredient in the artificial horizon instruments that tell airline pilots when they're flying straight and level—and when they are diving at full speed into the ground.

Like its linear cousin, angular momentum is never created and never destroyed. Once there is spin in a system, it's there forever. In this way, angular momentum is a bit like politics: The spin can be transferred from one object to another and it may be not be noticeable for a while, but it never goes away.

Angular momentum is also important in those slightly dodgy Olympic events, such as gymnastics, diving and prancing on ice, where you get medals for looking nice. Platform divers, for example, have a deep-seated understanding of the fact that, as they spread themselves out, they spin more slowly, whereas as they tuck themselves in, they spin more quickly.

Defying gravity

Let's try another experiment. First, take a wheel off your bike. Now, hold the wheel with two hands (one on each end of the axle), get it spinning quickly while upright, and then let go with one hand.

Come on, trust the physics: let go!

Amazing isn't it? Instead of falling over, your wheel is defying gravity, its angular momentum keeping it upright as you support it one-handed, on one side of the axle. Now you know why cyclists wobble like idiots as they start pedalling away from the lights but are far better balanced once their wheels are spinning quickly: it's all because the spin of their wheels keeps them upright.

Actually, your bike wheel's behavior is even weirder than it seems at first. After a moment, you'll realize that instead of falling over sideways, it wants to rotate around the point where you are supporting it. This behavior is even clearer if you support the wheel one on one side of the axle by hanging it on a piece of string. Then when you get it spinning, it will hang there, defying gravity, spinning, but also rotating gently around the string.

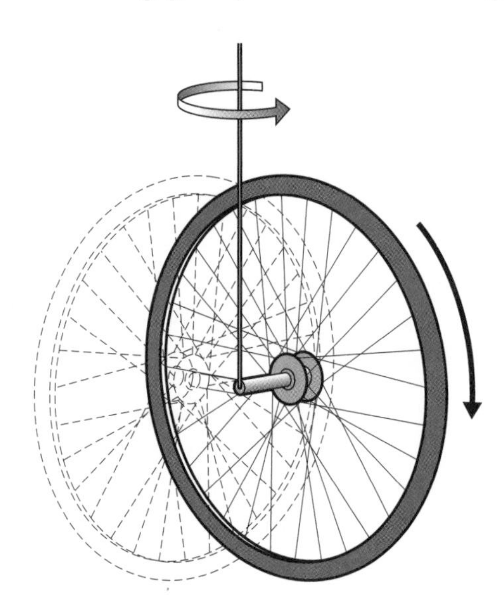

The reason? Well, instead of flat-out defying gravity, the wheel's spin subverts it.

Gyroscopes

The weird spinning-bicycle-wheel-on-a-string contraption you've just been playing with is a crude gyroscope. The great thing about gyroscopes is that the spinning wheel inside them means they're not affected if you try to rotate them. So a gyroscope will balance on the point of a needle, or, more usefully, remain level as you fly your aircraft up and down, and bank left and right.

Combine a few gyroscopes with some acceleration sensors (that measure precession), and you can build a navigation system that helps keep careful track of your accelerations and rotations. And, if you know where you started, that information will always be enough to tell you where you are and how fast you're going. Systems like this are used in aircraft automatic pilots and, more destructively, in long-range missile guidance systems.

A funny turn

Consider a point at the top of your bike wheel. If the wheel isn't spinning, the falling-over turning force applied by gravity and the string makes that top point fall down in an arc to one side. (Physicists and others like to call turning force "torque." More about that in a moment.)

If the wheel is spinning so that the top of it is moving away from you, there are no new forces involved, but the spin is already carrying our point at the top of the wheel downward, except that it is downward and away from you, rather than downward to the left.

Yet because the forces on our top point are the same as they were when the wheel wasn't spinning, the laws of physics say it has to get to the same place it would have if it wasn't spinning. And this is what happens: The spin of the wheel, added to the strange rotation around the string, gets our point on the wheel exactly where it should be, without the wheel falling—and so it doesn't fall.

Effectively, the wheel's spin turns the turning force caused by gravity through a right angle, so that it forces the wheel to rotate rather than fall. Physicists call this phenomenon *precession*: It's not a particularly useful term to remember unless you need an excuse for spelling procession wrong.

Torque isn't cheap

You may have noticed that automotive journalists love the sound of their own voices. But besides talk, they also love torque.

Torque, as we mentioned, is turning force. It's what causes changes in angular momentum, making an object spin more quickly or more slowly. It's also a measurement of a car engine's ability to turn the drive shaft. So if the supercar you're testing has an engine that produces a lot of torque, the car will be fast and powerful. But the relationship between power and torque isn't straightforward.

Car engines produce different amounts of power as they run at different speeds. They are generally at their most powerful when they are running quite quickly—maybe at around 6,000 revolutions per minute for a typical gasoline engine.

But what automotive journalists love is low-end grunt. Grunt comes from high torque at low revs: It's the turning force that the supercar's thirsty V8 engine produces as it spins quite slowly; it's what starts the wheels turning; it's what accelerates all that shining metalwork and those swooping lines rapidly and exhilaratingly away from a standing start.

Lots of power at high revs helps you scream down the highway at more than double the national speed limit; but torque at low revs gets you from standstill to speed limit in 4.5 seconds, your heart pounding as you're pushed back into your seat by the acceleration, a mighty grin on your face as you conquer time and space and creeping middle age.

Yu again

Before we're done with momentum, it is worth admitting that—despite what we found with our experiments in the pool hall—there *is* a way Jen Yu could have repulsed her attacker, much as she did in *Crouching Tiger, Hidden Dragon*, without breaking the laws of physics.

As Newton's first law showed us, the universe is lazy. Objects like to continue exactly as they are unless they get a proper kick in the backside from a resultant force.

To go back to our pool table for a moment, if we roll a Ping Pong ball into blue Jen Yu, she'll hardly move, but the Ping Pong ball will bounce straight off her. And don't think that this is because of friction. If we'd taken our blue ball up into orbit, set her floating in the middle of the room, and gently thrown our Ping Pong thug at her, the result would be exactly the same.

This little experiment shows us two things: first, don't use a Ping Pong ball as the cue ball if you want a decent game of pool; second, that it isn't only momentum that is important.

The lazy universe

We can say more about this tendency of the universe to stay as it is. We know that the bigger and heavier an object is, the more difficult it is to get it to change its movement (or get it moving if it isn't moving in the first place). An object that isn't moving doesn't have any speed/velocity, so it doesn't have any momentum. But it does like to remain at rest. And the heavier it is, the lazier it is.

Physicists call this resistance to change in motion "inertia," which can be a little confusing for the rest of us who tend to equate the inertia of a moving body with its momentum. But it is worth separating momentum and inertia.

Heavy things have great inertia: Whether they are moving quickly or slowly, or not moving at all, it is difficult to alter their motion (go push an oil tanker, if you don't believe me).

And light things can still acquire great momentum if they are moving very quickly. The Man With No Name's bullet (if he were a real nameless man, in the real world, firing real bullets, etc.) would weigh only 0.1 oz. (16 g). Throwing that at a bad guy wouldn't have much effect, but firing it at him at around 300 m/s would give him quite a jolt.

It turns out that we measure inertia in kilograms. An object's mass (which, on Earth, because of gravity, gives it weight) also gives it inertia. And for many things that are impossible to weigh (you can't, for example, put a planet on your bathroom scales), a calculation of their momentum—and therefore their inertia—gives us their mass—the measure of just how much stuff they have in them.

We'll see more about the stuff that makes mass in just a moment. After we've tied up one last loose end...

Secret weight problem

So was that *Crouching Tiger* scene realistic, after all?

Jen Yu may have looked like a svelte young kung fu fighter, but did she in fact she have a weight problem? We assumed in our earlier pool table experiments that Jen's attacker weighed about the same as her. But if instead she weighed much, much more than him, then our new experiment, with the thug played by a Ping Pong ball, would be a better indicator of the truth of that scene.

So, maybe Jen had massive weight problem. The kind of massive weight problem where she was something like a couple of tons overweight. Then even a heavyweight thug might bounce off her—if she was made out of something bouncy, and as long as her massive weight problem hadn't already caused her to crash through the floor of that rickety restaurant where she was sitting upstairs eating before she (and her attackers) kicked it all to pieces during their fight.

But how did she get to weigh that much eating low-fat rice and noodle dishes and drinking green tea? And how, if she weighed a couple of tons, did she manage to leap about like a flea?

Oh well. My advice is, don't watch an action movie if you want to learn physics.

5

Heat and Matter

In this chapter we'll learn all about matter and what it's made of. And then we'll see how what-it's-made-of explains how matter can turn from a hard, springy solid into an airy-fairy gas; why water is weird; why smoke gets in your eyes; and how life on planet Earth keeps us all under pressure.

Matter is the stuff all around us. It takes up space and it has mass: That's why it's filling up your cabinets and making your shelves creak under its weight (though of course those cabinets and shelves, and you and your house, and all the world are made up of matter, too).

Apart from having mass and volume, and creating storage headaches, what else does matter do? Maybe if we find some answers to that, we can find out a bit more about what matter is.

What's the matter?

Thousands of years ago, ancient Greek and Indian philosophers came up with the idea that if you kept dividing matter up into smaller and smaller pieces, you'd eventually end up with something fundamental: something that just couldn't be split again. That something was called the *atom*.

But it was a long time before the new science of chemistry began to give these ideas some experimental basis. In 1803, an English scientist named John Dalton noticed that certain elements could be combined with others in a ratio of small whole numbers. So if you had a big, well-equipped chemistry lab and piped 250 gal. (1,000 l) of hydrogen and half as much oxygen into a container, then threw in a lighted match, there would be a deafening explosion and all the gas, once it had cooled, would become enough fresh water to fill a large glass.

(If that explosion has made the water hard to find amid the general wreckage of your lab, get a mop—we're going to need that glass of water for the next part.)

If you use alternative volumes of oxygen and hydrogen (for example, the same volume of each, or twice as much oxygen as hydrogen), there will always be some hydrogen or oxygen left over. That's because water is H_2O: water molecules—the smallest components of water—are made up of two hydrogen atoms and one oxygen atom. So you need twice as much hydrogen as oxygen to make water.

Chemistry is elementary

Today, science has discovered 117 chemical elements, although only 94 occur naturally on Earth. You know many of them: hydrogen, helium, carbon, oxygen, iron, copper, silver, gold, chlorine, sodium, and neon are a few of the most familiar.

In chemistry, the atoms that make up these elements are basically as small as you can get. But they are rarely found sitting around by themselves—they're too sociable for that. For example, almost all the hydrogen on Earth is in water molecules because, as we just discovered, it takes very little persuasion to mix it up with oxygen and make up a cozy little threesome.

Atoms are so tiny that it is impossible to see them, even with a microscope. A pinhead is around 4,000,000 atoms wide. (Except that physicists have found that, like clouds, atoms don't really have fixed boundaries, so measuring them is difficult.)

Physicists have also found out how to trump the chemists' work by smashing the atom to make even smaller bits of matter. But let's not get ahead of ourselves. There's lots to find out about atoms before we start breaking them.

Ice breaker

Now we've made a glass of water, what else can we find out about it? Well, the obvious thing is that if we make it very cold, our water will become ice. If we then warm it, it will become water again.

In solid ice, our water molecules are pretty much frozen in place, packed tightly together and held by long-lasting bonds they form with their neighbors (although these bonds do allow them to vibrate around a central point).

As they warm up, the extra energy helps our water molecules vibrate more and more until they break free of these stable relationships to form a liquid. The molecules are still packed tightly, but their bonds with their fellows are fickle and fleeting as they jostle about like horny teenagers at dance club. Now they can flow over each other to fill whatever container they're in. (Note that this change of state—from solid to liquid—takes a lot of energy, which is why by melting, ice cubes can cool a drink much more than a similar amount of ice cold water could.)

Heat your water to boiling point (which takes lots more energy) and the molecules will gain enough oomph to escape the dance and become free spirits—in other words, they form a gas. In this state, our water molecules have broken all their bonds and are really speeding around, so they spread up and out in all directions until gravity hauls them back or they bump into something solid.

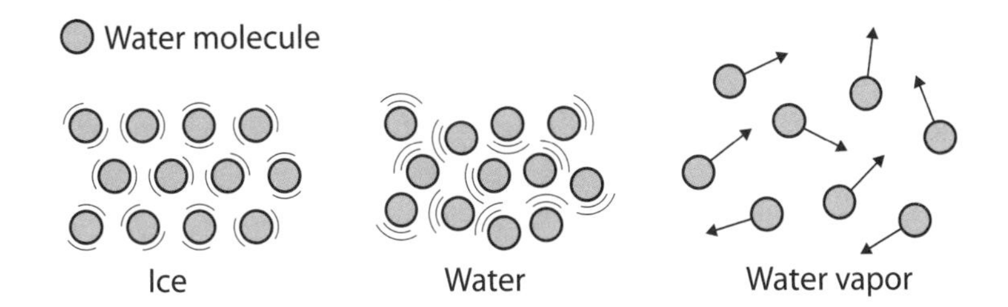

You can tell that gas molecules are much more spread out than those in solids and liquids because gases are relatively easy to compress (it only takes a bike pump). It is almost impossible to compress solids (unless, like sponges, they have a structure that's full of air) and liquids (which is why hydraulic systems work: try to compress oil at one end of a tube—with your car's brake pedal, for example—and it'll push back at the other—making your brake pads grip your brake discs).

Steamed up

The gas formed from water is called water vapor. Even though it took a combined volume of 375 gal. (1,500 l) of hydrogen and oxygen to make our glass of water, when heated that water makes around 125 gal. (500 l) of water vapor at room temperature. This is because it's not the size of the molecules that determine the volume of a gas, it's purely just the number of them.

Water vapor is as clear and as colorless as air. The steam we see coming from that saucepan (in which we're boiling away our precious cup of water) is slightly

States of matter

Solid, liquid, and gas are three states (although physicists like to call them "phases") of matter. But there are quite a few others, too, though they are much less common, and only created when there is enough energy around to break up the atoms themselves. They include plasma, Bose-Einstein condensates, and Fermionic condensates.

This knowledge is useful only if you feel like arguing with someone who tells you that there are three states of matter.

different: It, like the clouds we see in the sky, is actually made up of tiny drops of liquid water hanging in the air.

Soon all the water we made will be gone, boiled off and dispersed into the atmosphere. But we can bring some of it back. Water vapor will condense into water on a cold surface, the cold stealing away the energy of molecules that hit that surface, so that they can no longer fly free.

This is good news for us—water is amazing stuff and we're going to need it again in a minute.

Water: strange thing

Almost all solids expand slightly as they get hotter. That's why large concrete structures have those rubbery expansion joints in them. And almost all solids expand a little further as they turn into liquids. But water is a little odd.

Ice does expand slightly as it is warmed, but then it goes the other way and contracts as it turns into water. The shape of water molecules, and the fact that one side of them has a slightly positive electric charge and the other a slightly negative one, means that they can fit together more closely when jostling around in liquid form than as a solid (in which all those positive and negative charges line up in an orderly fashion, like a grid of mini magnets).

So water expands as it freezes: bursting pipes, but also causing ice to float, which allows fish to survive beneath it. Water also has many other properties (such as surface tension) that are found in few other liquids, and as far as we know, it is uniquely suited and vital for life as we know it.

But for our experiment, water is still a good way to find out about solids, liquids, and gases. And after all the trouble we had making our glass of water, it would have been a shame not to use it.

More about molecules

OK, it's not easy to believe that your still glass of water is full of jostling molecules. But if you mix a teaspoonful (5 ml) of tiny grains of pollen into your water and then look at them through a microscope, the evidence is right there before your eyes. You'll see those pollen grains jiggle as they're battered by the water molecules.

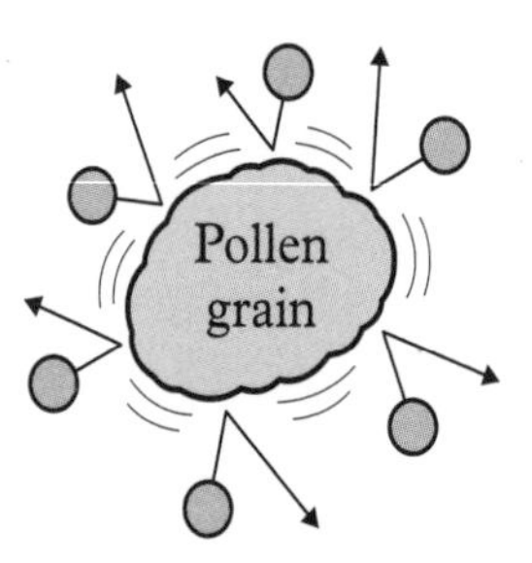

Brownian motion

This is called Brownian motion, after Robert Brown, the Scotsman who discovered it: You probably saw it at school. If our water is likened to a horny teenage dance, then the grain of pollen is like a giant balloon on the dance floor that is being continually bumped this way and that, but never very far, by the crowd of dancers around it.

In fact, molecules are 250,000 times smaller than pollen grains. We know this because Einstein did the math behind Brownian motion, which, if we measure our pollen grains, allows us to calculate the size of the water molecules. You can't see them, but they really are there.

Brownian motion can be seen in gases, too. Smoke particles in air (which is a mixture of 78 percent nitrogen and 21 percent oxygen, plus tiny amounts of argon, carbon dioxide, and water vapor) move like pollen grains in water. And that's just the start of the physical phenomena that can be explained once we realize that molecules and atoms are always moving.

A hot-air balloon fills up and then floats away because of a whole host of these effects. Come on, let's try it. You'll never have a better excuse to fly around in a wicker basket—with just the laws of physics for support and no control over where you go.

A lot of hot air

We've already seen how hot-air balloons rise because they displace a greater mass of air than they contain. Now we can discover why this happens.

Time for a quick thought experiment. And thought only, please, because this one is dangerous.

Imagine a sealed box full of air. Inside, free-spirited molecules are shooting around in straight lines at an average speed of 500 m.p.h. (210 m/s) until they bump into each other or, as is more likely because they're well spread out, into the walls of the box. This steady drumming of molecules on the inside of the box is what we know as *pressure*. It's a bit like what we feel from a strong spray of water, except those free-spirited molecules push out in all directions.

Now, if you put that box over a lighted fire, the air molecules will get fired up. They'll move more quickly, so they'll hit the walls of the container harder (free spirits don't like being kept in boxes). The pressure on the walls of the box rises. Keep your box on the fire long enough, and bang: It explodes. Told you it was dangerous—you can't lock up a free spirit forever.

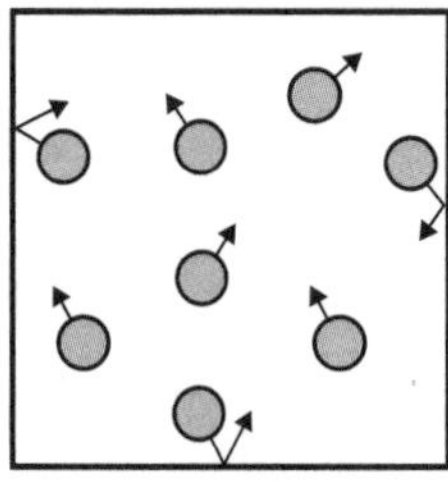
Low pressure

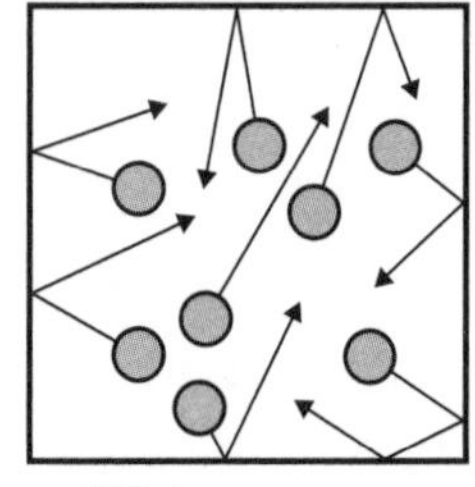
High pressure

Feel the pressure

Pressure is measured in Pascals, and sometimes p.s.i. (pounds per square inch). It's a measure of the force acting on a given area: So if you halve the area, you double the pressure. This is how snowshoes work: By spreading your weight (and remember, weight is force) over a wide area, they reduce the pressure on the snow and prevent you from sinking into it. If instead you went walking on the snow in high heels or on stilts, their tiny surface area would concentrate your weight into lots of pressure on the snow, and you'd fall straight through it.

But we're all under pressure anyway: 62 miles (100 km) of atmosphere presses down on us with 100,000 Pa of pressure. This is why suction cups work: When you attach the cup to a surface, some of the air is squeezed out, lowering the pressure inside; now the higher atmospheric pressure is pushing the suction cup to the surface harder than the cup is pushing away from the surface.

A bit about Blaise

The unit of pressure is called the Pascal, after French scientist and philosopher Blaise Pascal. Born in 1623, he did plenty of brilliant math and science from an early age, including building a mechanical calculator and essentially inventing probability theory. He was also instrumental in the invention of the hydraulic press, so it's appropriate that the unit of pressure carries his name.

After a vision in 1654 and an apparent miracle healing of his daughter in 1657, Pascal gave up all that science stuff and devoted his life to God, while writing arguments that reason was untrustworthy. He died in 1662, at age 39.

Blowing up a balloon

Now we know a bit more about pressure, let's try that box-on-the-fire experiment again, except with some sort of imaginary fireproof party balloon. Make it a red one with yellow lettering that says, "Happy Birthday."

Once you've blown it up and tied the end, the pressure inside equals the air pressure outside—that's why it stays at the same size. Now stick this fireproof balloon on the fire for a little while. What happens? As the air inside grows hotter, our free-spirited molecules start hitting the inside of the balloon harder—the pressure rises and so the balloon gets bigger.

Now, as the balloon blows up, the free spirits have more room, so they don't hit the walls quite so often. Eventually—if you take the balloon off the fire so that the air inside reaches a constant temperature—the reduced number of hits on the walls compensate for the extra energy of those hits. Once again, the balloon will reach a constant size. It'll be bigger, but inside and outside pressure will again be equal. All the fired-upness of those free spirits will have bought them a little extra room.

Careful with that fireproof balloon, though. That expanded air will be lighter than the rest of the air, and so it will try to float away. Something similar happens to the hot air heated by our hot-air balloon's burner: It expands and rises immediately. This process is called *convection*, and it's a common way for heat to travel. Columns of warm, rising air above hot objects are useful for filling hot-air balloons, or keeping birds of prey gliding while they look for small furry snacks. But they can be a problem, too.

Imagine you're back from a freezing trip in hot-air balloon. (Did you know that the reason it's cold up high is that the air pressure is lower? Can you see why?) Now you're back inside and there's a nice hot radiator on the other side of the room. So why is there a cold draft on the back of your neck?

Well, the hot air above the radiator rises, and as it does, it slowly cools. More rising air pushes it away from the radiator and eventually, when it's above you, it has cooled enough to fall—right down the back of your neck. Ugh!

But don't moan. You're not really cold. In a moment, well find out what it means to be so cold that you can't get any colder.

Absolutely freezing

Now we know that temperature is really just a measure of how much the molecules in matter are bumping around, we can think about what might happen if they stopped moving completely.

Well, we can think about it, but it can't happen: The third law of thermodynamics says it is impossible for matter to lose absolutely all of its thermal energy and so reach the complete lack of temperature that physicists call "absolute zero."

The strange thing about absolute zero is that it's only –460°F, or –273.15°C (and water freezes at 32°F/0°C). That is extremely cold; but when you consider that +523°F (+273°C) is a good temperature for cooking thin, crispy pizzas, and the middle of the sun is estimated to be at 27,000,000 °F (15,000,000°C), it doesn't seem that cold.

Then again, scientists do have ways of cooling things to temperatures very close to absolute zero, and it is in fact so cold that strange things happen—like, for example, the formation of those Bose-Einstein condensates we mentioned earlier.

Why springs are springy

Before we finish with the hot and heavy stuff and find out what makes light work, we should quickly mention a couple of the many other familiar things that are explained by the kinetic theory of matter (which just means that the molecules jiggle around as we've described). Let's look at why puddles evaporate without boiling and why springs are springy.

Puddles disappear even on cold days because it's the average energy of the molecules that give the puddle its low temperature. But that average disguises the fact that, at any time, the molecules are actually moving at many different speeds through their packed teenage dance club. And the ones that are lucky enough to get enough energy when they're near the surface of the water can—if they get a straight run—fly free, up into the sky, breaking their watery bonds and leaving behind their teenage angst (at least until they turn into rain or condensation). And so the puddle slowly evaporates.

Springs are springy because the atoms in a metal are all bonded, like the molecules in ice. Stretch them apart and the bonds pull back. (The molecules in ice are less tightly bonded and the pattern of their bonds is different from that of the atoms in a metal, so if you pull ice, it just breaks apart: it doesn't make a good spring.)

A small mistake

In this chapter we've been thinking of matter as made up of little bouncy balls. Well, it's not.

Don't dismiss this idea, though. It's what Newton believed. And, as we've just seen, it's a very useful way to think about all kinds of physical phenomena.

It's just that we have plenty of evidence that although atoms and molecules sometimes behave like bouncy balls, they are actually made up of lots more tinier bits, and that these bits are so tiny and so different from the matter cluttering up our world that almost everything about them seems strange and wrong.

And to start finding out about the world we can't get our hands on, we need to take a trip to the shore.

6

Waves

In this chapter, we'll see that all waves are similar: They travel through each other unharmed, reflect when they bump into some things, and bend as they enter others. And yet waves take many different forms. So we'll find out why wave power is tricky to harness, we'll calculate the speed of sound, and we'll hold proof in the palms of our hands that light is a wave.

But let's start at the seashore, because it is a great place to find out about the physics of waves. That's because—as you'll have guessed already—the sunshine, the waves on the sea, and the sounds of the seaside are all waves. So come on, grab your surfboard and we'll swim out to discover more.

Once you're through the surf, and sitting waiting for a nice big wave to ride back in on, you'll be noticing the most important feature of water waves: that they lift you up and down.

And there's another important feature of waves that's obvious, too: The waves carry energy to the beach (which is why they can push you along when you find one to ride), but the sea stays where it is. Sure, the surf plops up the sand a bit, but the movement of the waves and the energy they carry (toward the shore) is independent of the movement of any bit of the sea (which basically goes up and down with a bit of backward and forward so that each point in the sea actually goes round and round in a circle).

So there you go. You haven't even had to show off your surfing skills and you've discovered what a wave is: a transfer of energy without a transfer of matter.

But don't ride in yet. There's lots more we can discover out here about water waves, and—because all kinds of waves do the same wavy tricks—about other kinds of waves, too.

Interfering busybodies

For example, while you're out at sea moving gently up and down, you can make your own little waves by dipping your hand in the water. These ripples spread out on the sea on top of the bigger waves that you aren't riding. So it's clear that lots of waves can travel through the same stuff, in lots of directions, and all at the same time. They don't bump into each other like balls.

But they do interact in another way. Your ripple makes the big waves a little higher in some places, and a little lower in others. Ripples on a big swell are hardly noticeable, but if you drop a couple of similarly sized surfers into some reasonably calm water, it's clear that the ripples make a new pattern as they spread out, because in some places you get two troughs together (and the result is a doubly deep trough) and in others you get two peaks (and the result is a doubly high peak).

Sea power

Waves that are 3 ft. (1 m) high hit every 3-ft.-wide section of beach with enough power to run 10 strip heaters—which is why it is frustrating that we haven't been able to capture wave energy to generate electricity.

Part of the problem with wave power is the way waves carry it. The energy of a wave is proportional to the square of its height. So a 9-ft.-high wave has 3 x 3 = 9 times more energy than a 3-ft. wave. And when a hurricane brings 90-ft. waves, with 900 times the energy of the little waves you were generating power from, your clever wave power gadget is turned into something mangled and useless.

In yet other places a peak in one surfer's ripples meets a trough coming from the other surfer, and then at that point the waves cancel each other out. It seems as if there is no wave there—but of course the wave energy from both surfers is still travelling through that point.

Physicists call this interaction of two or more sets of waves *interference*. The poor surfers caught up in such wave interaction might have a slightly stronger word for it.

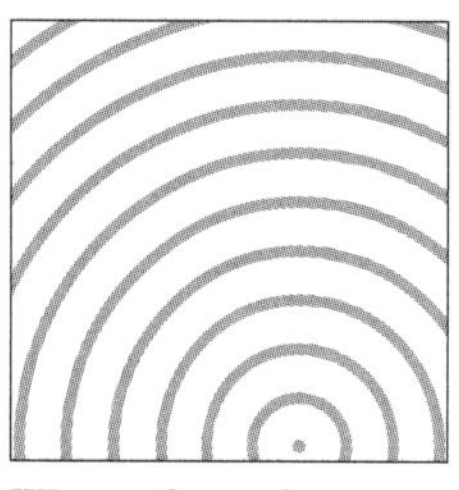

Waves from first surfer

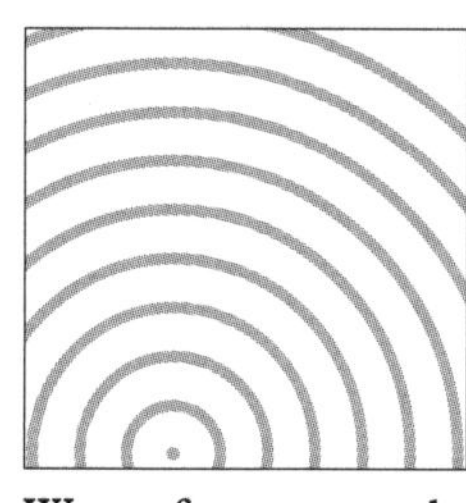

Waves from second surfer

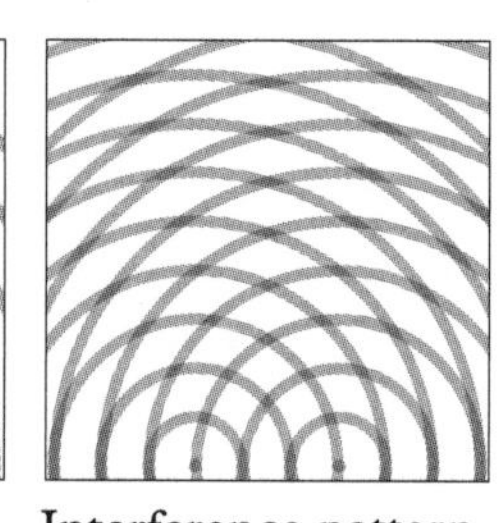

Interference pattern from the two sets of waves

Breaking waves

Waves travel at different speeds in different things. And shallow water is a different thing from deep water. Waves notice this difference, because as the water gets shallower they start scraping along on the sand.

This slows them down, but the slowing is more pronounced at the bottom where the sand is, and has less and less effect the farther up the wave you look. So the top of the wave carries on at its same old speed, and so the top starts to move ahead of the rest of the wave below, and eventually it moves so far ahead it falls over, and the wave breaks.

Turning a corner

One result of a wave moving from the deep sea, where it moves at one speed, to a shallow bay, where it moves more slowly, is that so long as it hits the boundary of deep and shallow at an angle, it will turn a corner.

This makes sense if you think of our breaking waves. Just as the top wasn't slowed as much as the bottom and so the waves broke, if part of a wave has reached shallower water, that part will slow down, whereas the part that is in deeper water will be moving faster, and so the wave will change direction. This is called *refraction* of the wave.

This situation is a bit like the way in which a bulldozer steers by making the caterpillar tracks on one side move more quickly than those on the other. If its right track turns more quickly than the left, that side of the bulldozer moves forward farther in any given amount of time than the left, and so the bulldozer turns to the left.

Mind the gap

We've already found one way to get waves off the straight and narrow, but there are others, too.

On a stormy day, with huge waves rolling in from the ocean, it's clear that the waves make it in through the small gap in the harbor wall and spread out, gently rocking all the boats as they sit at their moorings.

One reason for this is *reflection*. When wave energy hits a hard wall, it has to bounce off; so the wave is reflected and travels back through itself. Throw another surfer into a calm harbor and you'll see the ripples he makes bounce off the walls and spread out.

But if the waves are coming straight through a reasonably narrow gap in a harbor wall, you can see another wave effect: *diffraction*. Instead of just the portion of the wave that hits the gap continuing on inside the harbor while the rest of the water remains calm, the wave spreads out a little beyond the wall, and that spread grows the farther

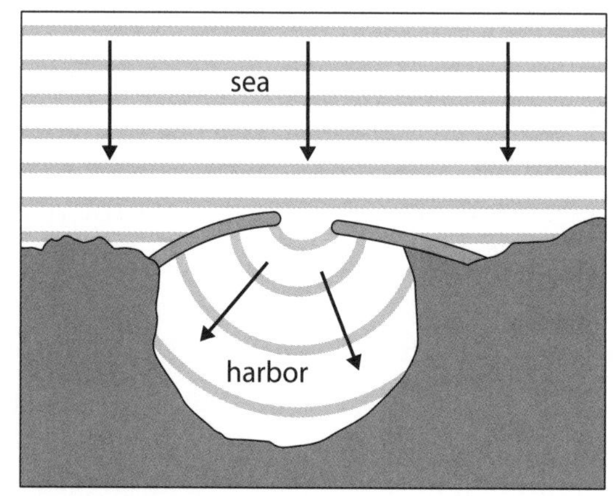

Waves diffracting in a harbor

the wave travels from the gap. The smaller the gap, the greater the effect.

Transverse and longitudinal waves

Water waves are *transverse* waves. They involve something moving up and down as the wave goes along. If you look at them from the side, they make that familiar wavy line, a bit like a long train of camels.

Longitudinal waves, on the other hand, involve something moving backward and forward in the same direction as the wave travels. But just as with transverse waves, the matter itself doesn't go far: just back and forth a little as the wave travels on.

Although these two kinds of waves might seem quite different, they do both display all the strange wavy properties we've been looking at. Both kinds of wave will reflect, refract, diffract, and interfere. And it's not just water waves that do this.

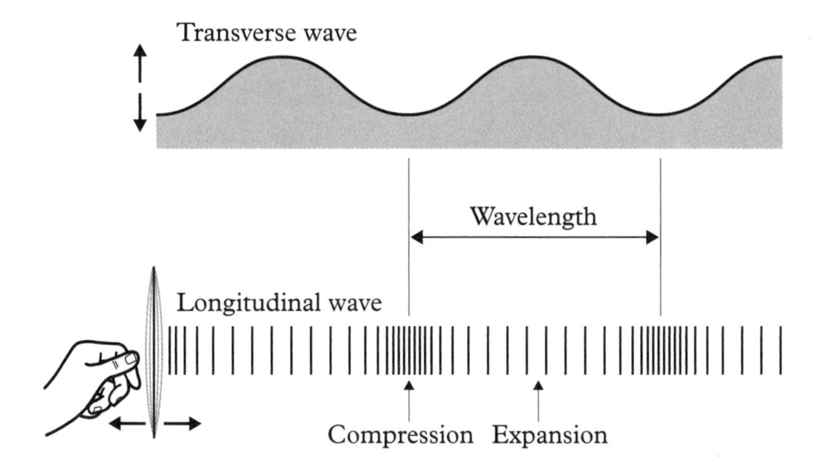

Sound thinking

Sound is a great example of a longitudinal wave. You can picture what's happening if you pluck a note on your guitar. OK? Ding! See, your G-string is vibrating: moving quickly toward you and away again. And as it comes toward you, it squeezes up the air molecules, creating a "compression." Then, as it moves away, it squeezes the air molecules on the other side, leaving the air on your side slightly spread out (and so at slightly lower pressure—a "rarefaction").

Then it comes back and you get another area of squeezed-up (or slightly higher-pressure) air traveling your way as the laws of conservation of energy and momentum ensure that the movement of one molecule is transferred to the next.

The Doppler effect

We've all heard the way ambulance and police sirens sound different coming and going. It's because of the *Doppler effect*: a phenomenon named after the Austrian physicist who identified it, long before sirens were even invented.

Think of a typical teenager's car, the sort that's as much a boombox on wheels as it is a mode of transport. And let's imagine that, every second, it throws one pulse of high-powered bass in your direction as you sit there on the beach muttering to yourself about kids these days.

Now, let's say our boombox-car is moving so quickly toward you that every successive pulse is released at a distance so much closer to your ear than the previous one

A tuneful note

Even though you may not be the best guitar player in the world, the regular vibration of that G-string, back and forth 196 times a second, means it makes a nice musical note.

Busy physicists don't have time to say "times a second" every time they talk about how fast a guitar string is vibrating or a wave is going through its full cycle from peak back to peak, or compression to compression; so instead they say talk about *frequency,* which they measure in *Hertz* (written as *Hz*).

So the open G-string on a guitar has a frequency of 196 Hz; those surfers still waiting out at sea have a frequency of 0.1 Hz (that is, every 10 seconds they are at the peak of another wave).

Now, if you press down on that G-string halfway down the neck, it will vibrate twice as fast when plucked—moving back and forth 196 x 2 = 392 times per second. Musicians will be able to tell that this new note is still G, but a different G, one an octave (that's eight full notes of the major scale) higher.

So that's math and music in perfect harmony. If you halve the length of the string, you double the frequency of the sound.

that it will spend half a second less traveling that ever-decreasing distance to you than the previous one.

Can you hear what's happening? Instead of your ear picking up a pulse every second, it receives one every half a second. That's twice as many pulses per second, which

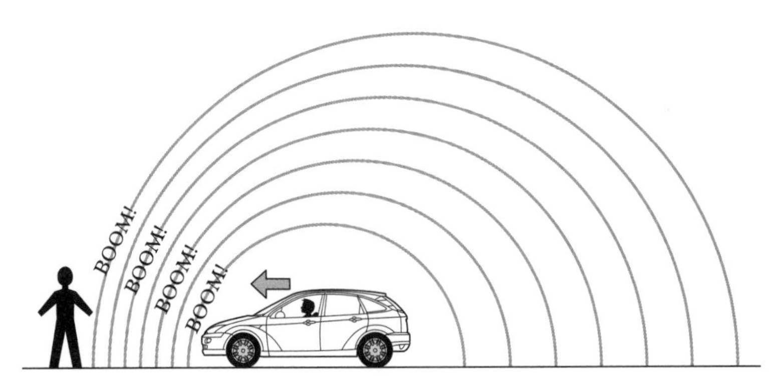

Doppler effect

means you hear that constant bass rhythm pumping twice as fast as the driver does (and the note will sound higher-pitched). Likewise, after it drives past, you'll hear the rhythm slow to half of what the driver is hearing (and the pitch of the sound will be even lower than what's rattling his fillings).

There is one important footnote to the Doppler effect: What we hear depends on the fact that the speed of sound in air is always the same.

Sound waves from something coming quickly toward you don't travel any faster than those from something that isn't moving. They're not like balls thrown forward from a moving car. This means the speed of sound in air is a *physical constant*.

Enjoying the rays

Light travels at 299,792,458 m/s in a vacuum. That's really quick. It's also a universal constant. It's always that fast, no matter where you are. That's why the length of a meter is

Electromagnetic waves

After it was discovered that electricity and magnetism were related (more about this in chapter 7), in the 1860s a Scottish mathematician named James Clerk Maxwell created and published a set of equations, known today as Maxwell's equations. These equations showed how electric charges create electric fields, and how electric currents create magnetism. Together they showed how electric and magnetic fields travel through space in the form of waves, and how they move at the speed of light (and how fast that speed is).

This was pretty good stuff, but best of all they showed that light is purely a combination of electricity and magnetism. That's why physicists call light an *electromagnetic wave*.

To us, it is special because we can see it. But it is different from many other types of electromagnetic wave only in its wavelength and frequency. The radio waves that bring us music and chattering DJs, the microwaves bounced around in microwave ovens to heat food, warming infrared,

based on it.* It's also, as we'll discover in a few chapters' time, one reason Einstein discovered special relativity.

For the moment though, we'll note that all this rushing around makes it much harder to get a handle on light

*In the 18th century the meter was defined as one ten-millionth of the distance from the equator to the north pole. Which is nice and neat, though unfortunately it was later discovered the calculation was one-fifth of a millimeter wrong. So it now has to settle for a less handy definition: one meter is the distance light travels in a vacuum in 1 divided by 299,792,458 seconds.

ultraviolet (which tans our skin), X-rays (which enable us to see the bones beneath our flesh), and dangerous gamma rays are all the same kind of thing. They're all electromagnetic waves like light.

Long-wave radio starts at a frequency of around 10,000 cycles per second (or Hertz) where the waves are a kilometer long (0.6 mile); whereas high-energy gamma rays go up beyond 10^{24} Hertz (with a tiny wavelength of 10^{-16} m). Somewhere in the middle are the frequencies that we see as different colors. Red light has a frequency of around 4.4×10^{14} Hz; blue a frequency of around 6.4×10^{14} Hz.

The more you think about this, the more amazing it is. It's worth repeating: All these invisible forms of electromagnetic radiation—which is created by the stars and heaters and radio transmitters—are basically the same kind of thing as visible light (better known to most of us as "light" because obviously, invisible light isn't light. It might cook your dinner, but it's not going to help you see in the dark).

than on sound, which is one reason physicists had a long argument about whether light was in fact made up of waves or particles.

In the dark

The Greeks started the confusion. They thought something came out of our eyes and lit up what we looked at. Explaining why we couldn't see in the dark was always tough for the Greeks.

In 1670, Newton said light was made from particles (or, as he called them, *corpuscles*). That made it easy to explain reflection and the fact that light travels in straight lines and through vacuums (especially for Newton, who, as we've seen, was very good at the physics of motion). Light could now travel from the sun, bounce off things around us and then enter our eyes. In the dark, there was no light, and so nothing reaching our eyes. But Newton did find it tricky to account for refraction and those other weird wavy properties.

Other scientists, including the Frenchman René Descartes (of "I think, therefore I am" fame) and the Dutchman Christian Huygens believed that, because it could be diffracted and refracted, light was more likely to be made up of waves.

The debate raged for over a century, until a bright Englishman named Thomas Young, who could speak fourteen languages by the time he was 14, came up with the not very elegantly titled *double slit* experiment.

Fringe benefits

What Young did was to use light waves of a single color, and *two* very narrow slits, 0.004 in. (0.1 mm) apart, for the waves to diffract through, instead of a single gap. (The thinness and closeness of the slits is important because visible light has a wavelength of around 0.0005 mm.)

The result was that, because there were two slits for the light to come through, it was as if Young had created two separate but identical sources of light. And when the light waves spread out from these slits by diffraction, they interfered just like water waves, creating some areas where the waves reinforced each other, and others where they cancelled each other out.

Best of all, this interference could easily be seen with the naked eye. In a dark room, Young's slits make a pattern on a screen: a central bright spot, with successive fainter blobs of brightness (called *fringes*) slowly fading out on each side. Physicists can even use the spread of this pattern to calculate the wavelength of light.

So there you have it: one light experiment, two wave-related effects. Particles can't diffract or interfere, so poor old Newton's theory was blown out of the water.

If he hadn't been dead, he'd have been furious!

Spectacular light show

Here on the beach, the fact that light is a wave is obvious.

Let's start with those binoculars that you're using to study the fine array of surfing talent sitting out there on the waves. These use lenses. And lenses make things seem bigger by refracting the light so it bends, because light travels more slowly in glass than in air.

Also, can you see that spray bow above the waves? (It's that rainbow formed in the sea spray when the sun is behind you.) It's there because the white light coming from the sun is really made up of many colors. And light of different colors is refracted different amounts (because it has different wavelengths). So when white light goes into a drop of water (and refracts), reflects off the back of the drop, and then comes out the front (and refracts again), this double refraction causes it to be split so much that a rainbow appears.

Can I be invisible?

In theory, if you bend light around something and then straighten it out again afterwards, that something would become invisible. That something would be a bit like a rock in a stream: a little way downstream of the rock, the water has settled down, and there is no way to tell (by looking at the stream) that it ever passed a rock.

Theory, of course, is one thing; practice, quite another. But in 2006 and 2009, teams of scientist in the United States and the United Kingdom made newspaper headlines when they claimed that they really had made objects invisible using light-bending cloaks made of "metamaterials"—substances engineered to have a precise structure, such as tiny hairs or holes, on a scale similar to the wavelength of light.

However, the first "cloak" was actually a heavy and completely-not-invisible metal cylinder that only bent microwaves. The second was almost invisible—but only because it was a hundredth of a millimeter wide. And again, it had no effect on visible light. It only worked on infrared. Many other scientists pointed out that it is difficult to see how these "cloaks" could ever work for more than a few very specific wavelengths (and therefore colors) of light. The metamaterial would have to be very ingenious; otherwise, like raindrops, it would split white light into a spectrum as it bent it, and you would end up hiding under a rainbow.

So, for the foreseeable future, invisibility is out of reach for us mere mortals (though as 90 percent of the universe is invisible anyway—see chapter 10—perhaps that doesn't matter).

The color of the sky is also a clue to light's waviness. The sky is blue because blue light, which has a shorter wavelength than red and yellow light, is, because of that wavelength, scattered by the air molecules bouncing around in the sky. So whichever direction you look (as long as it's up), some of this scattered blue light reaches your eyes, and the sky looks blue. Most of the red and yellow light travels directly to the surface of the Earth and is reflected and absorbed by the sand, the sea and, of course, that surfing talent.

The clincher for light being made of waves is this: You can do your own single-slit version of the double-slit experiment. But we'll get to that in a moment, after a quick look at how the waviness of light could help us all disappear.

Two fingers to light particles

Young used two slits because it clarifies the interference caused by diffraction. But you still get an interference pattern with a single slit because the light from different sides of the slit travels different distances and still arrives in or out of sync. So here's the handy version of the experiment.

Ready? Hold two fingers very close together so there's a tiny gap between them that you can barely see through. Now look toward something bright, like that white sea wall (not the sun). And there (by the laws of physics and the fact that light is a wave), in the gap between your fingers and running parallel to them, will appear faint dark lines of destructive interference ("dark fringes"). You can see they aren't due to blurred vision if you move your fingers apart a bit farther and watch them disappear.

Isn't that amazing? And isn't it even more amazing that Newton's theory of light being made up of particles was believed for a hundred years?

Well, yes, it is. But there is one thing even more amazing than that: In chapter 9 we will discover that Newton was, in fact, right. Light might behave as a wave, but it *is* made up of particles; only now we give them a fancy name. We don't call them corpuscles (which sound like the sort of nasty blisters that might have afflicted medieval alchemists). We call them *photons*.

7

Electricity

In this chapter we'll learn about static electricity, batteries, voltage and current, Ohm's law, the relationship between electricity and magnetism, and DC and AC current. Put them together and you get (a) the building blocks of our powered-up, gadget-crazy world and (b) some really dangerous physics.

Today, one form of electricity is regularly rediscovered by shoppers in shopping malls, who get a shock from touching a metal elevator button after a couple of hours shuffling around on hard-wearing carpets (though it's a mild shock compared to the one they receive when they open their credit card bills a few weeks later).

Electricity of all kinds is essentially the movement of *electric charge*. And electric charge is created by something having more or fewer tiny negatively charged particles, called electrons, than it should. (We'll talk more about electrons later.)

Charge builds up because different materials behave in different ways toward electrons. Some, like certain

Franklin's Kite Experiments

When Benjamin Franklin wasn't plotting with the French to end British rule and found the United States, or working to abolish slavery, it is said that he liked nothing better than a bit of extremely dangerous practical physics, such as flying a kite into thunderclouds to collect electric charge.

This charge was conducted to the ground along the kite's dampened string, and the tiny sparks that jumped from a key tied at the end showed that this electricity was the same stuff as the static electricity that had been discovered long ago by the ancient Greeks, who found that their amber jewelry attracted dust because it picked up a charge after rubbing on their clothes.*

Franklin's kite demonstration is so risky that we won't even try it as a thought experiment. But Franklin was aware of the danger, and he certainly didn't try it when lightning was flashing. In fact, it's possible that he never did the experiment at all, and simply wrote it down as a good idea. Others, including a physicist named Georg Richmann, proved that in fact it wasn't a good idea. Richmann was killed by lightning during a similar experiment.

carpets, are inclined to collect extra electrons if they get the chance, and so become negatively charged. Others, like leather shoes and human skin, are happy to give away electrons and become positively charged.

*In fact, the word electricity comes from the Greek work elektron, meaning amber.

The electrical charges that result from this trading of electrons are static electricity—electricity that isn't flowing. But the charge does flow when the unfortunate shopper touches an electrical conductor, such as that metal elevator button. This brief flow of charge is called *electrostatic discharge*—the discharge of static electricity. This is what gives our shopper the (small!) electric shock.

Electric shocks through metal fixtures might be an annoyance to bargain hunters, but sometimes it can be very useful. Benjamin Franklin's knowledge of electricity led him to invent the lightning rod: a metal strip that could take the electrical charge from lightning straight into the ground, diverting it before it entered and wrecked tall buildings with fires and explosions.

At the time, churches, as the tallest buildings in town, were often struck by lightning. In fact, at one time people were advised to escape from thunderstorms by going anywhere *except* a church. Today lightning rods are a common sight on tall buildings, and ships and aircraft have lightning protection that works using the same principle.

Staying positive

It wasn't until 1896 that electrons were discovered, by the British physicist J. J. Thomson. But for a long time it had been known that if you used a powerful battery to give a strong negative charge to a piece of metal at one end of a tube containing nothing but a vacuum (that is, containing nothing at all), and a strong positive charge to a similar piece of metal at the other end of the tube, rays of something mysterious would shoot from the negative cathode to the positive anode.

When life gives you lemons, make batteries

It's quite easy to make a simple battery cell with some ordinary household objects. Take a lemon and stick a piece of zinc in near one end (we'll use a galvanized nail). Stick a piece of copper (like a copper coin) in near the other end. Make sure both pieces go into the flesh of the lemon but don't touch each other.

The two metal parts are called *electrodes*—they're the parts which electric current will flow from or to. The zinc (nail) electrode is the *anode,* or negative terminal, while the copper electrode is the *cathode,* or positive terminal. In a circuit, electrons will flow from the negative anode to the positive cathode.

The lemon battery works by a chemical reaction—the acid in the lemon dissolves the zinc, releasing electrons at the anode and thereby making it negatively charged,

Thomson showed that these rays were made up of tiny particles 1,000 times lighter than a hydrogen atom, and that they were the same no matter what substance you made the cathode from. He also discovered that these same particles could be produced by shining the right kind of light on certain metals and by radioactivity. They came to be called electrons.

But plenty of inventors hadn't waited for the physicists to "discover" what they had been playing with for years. The first electric light was demonstrated in 1803 by British inventor Sir Humphrey Davy, and by 1880 Thomas Edison started selling practical lightbulbs in the

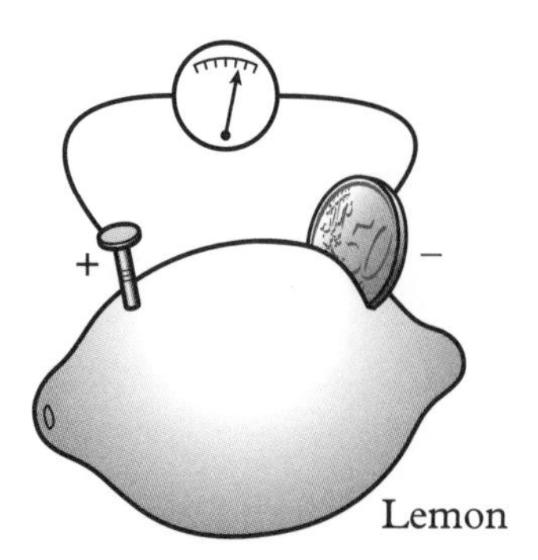

while a copper-acid reaction at the cathode absorbs electrons, giving it a positive charge. Unfortunately this battery is very weak (the lemon's citric acid isn't very strong, after all)—so weak, in fact, that to see it working you'll need to either use an electronic multimeter, or make several lemon batteries and use them all at once to power something. But be warned—you'll need nearly 10,000 to power a flashlight bulb.

United States. Soon electric gadgets were helping us get around, get fed, clothed, and watered—and get out the message about just how many new kinds of electric gadgets could be built in the bright new electrical world.

The only problem was that all these new gadgets needed power. Static electricity is good for electrocuting kite fliers and allowing kids to shuffle their feet on carpeting and then shock their siblings, but it is only when electric charge flows along conductors, such as copper wire, that it is useful.

What was needed was a way of getting all those electrons moving—to create electric current.

Ohm time

The laws governing current, voltage, and electrical resistance were discovered in 1820 by a German school teacher and physicist named Georg Ohm, after the Italian Count Alessandro Volta had helped by inventing basic batteries.

Ohm found that a battery forces charge to flow through a circuit because it applies a *voltage*. The voltage of a battery is the difference in *electric potential* between its electrodes. Electric potential is just a fancy way of saying "amount of electric charge." So if you took your lemon battery and replaced your electrodes with metals that produced and absorbed electrons even better than zinc and copper (when you stuck them in a lemon), then your anode would be even more negatively charged and your cathode even more positively charged, so there would be a bigger difference in electric potential, and so the battery would have a higher voltage. Whew! Got that?*

The electron flow around a circuit is called electric *current*—more voltage, all else being equal, means more current. But the electrons don't really want to flow around the circuit—they were quite happy where they were—so a circuit is said to have *resistance*. The more resistance, the less current is allowed to flow.

You can think of the whole thing as being a bit like a bike wheel, with the rim and tire standing in for the electrons. The voltage applied by the battery is like the force applied by the pedals: It causes the whole wheel to turn (so all the electrons in the copper wires begin to move at once, at a speed of a few inches per hour). The resistance

*Another way to raise the voltage might be to use a stronger acid than lemon juice.

Ohm's law

Ohm's law is expressed in this equation:

Current (measured in amps) = Voltage (volts)/Resistance (ohms).

This equation simply states that you can find the current flowing through a circuit by taking the applied voltage and dividing by the circuit's resistance. More voltage means more current; more resistance means less current.

of the circuit is like your hand slowing the wheel as it spins, with the rotational energy of the wheel being converted into heat by friction so that it warms your hand.

Ohm's discoveries are pretty straightforward. Ohm's law says that if you double the voltage across something that resists current flow (such as the filament of a lightbulb) you double the current (which is basically the flow of electrons through the circuit). It holds true as long as your circuit doesn't heat up. Then again, if you put current through a lightbulb, it does heat up, so double the voltage doesn't quite produce double the current.

Also important is the amount of power that the battery delivers to the bulb. This is given by multiplying the current by the voltage. So, if you can double the voltage and the current, you can quadruple the power delivered to the lightbulb. (Until your bulb burns out, anyway.)

A flow of charge in one direction, as in these examples, is called direct current (or DC). But, as physicists studied electricity and magnetism in the 19th century, one odd

Electric Power

The equation for electric power is very simple:

Power (measured in watts) = Voltage (volts) x Current (amps).

As with other simple equations, this can be easily rearranged. So Current = Power/Voltage and Voltage = Power/Current.

genius, Nikola Tesla, who came from Serbia but settled in New York, would discover that it was much easier to generate and distribute another form of electricity, where the electrons don't flow around a circuit but instead rock back and forth in once place, creating alternating current (AC). But first, someone had to discover the link between electricity and magnetism.

The attractions of electricity

In 1820 a Danish physicist, Hans Christian Ørsted, noticed that the needle of his compass moved when the electric current in a wire near it was turned on and off.

This was a very important discovery. It showed that, just like magnets, electric currents create magnetic fields. So, for example, the conductors that carry them can be attracted to some metals, such as iron; they can be repelled by other magnets or conductors that have the same polarity (just as the north poles of two permanent magnets repel each other); and they can make pretty patterns with iron filings on a sheet of paper as they move to follow the lines of force in a magnetic field.

The effect is even better if you wrap a coil of current-carrying copper wire around a short iron bar: When the current is on, you have a strong magnet, but when it's off, none at all. Electromagnets, as these devices are called, are very useful. For example, they make the fabric cones in loudspeakers vibrate (so you can listen to your favorite band and damage your hearing all at the same time), and they pull items containing iron out of household waste so it can be recycled.

The strange thing is that the movement of electric charge actually explains all magnetism. Permanent magnets, like the one in your compass, are magnetic because of the way the electrons in the needle are permanently moving in sync, a bit like they would be in an electric current.

Signs of movement

The fact that electromagnets can vibrate speaker cones and pick up steel cans from garbage gives us a clue that electricity can be used to create movement.

In 1821 a great British experimenter, Michael Faraday, was the first to make use of the fact that the magnetic field around a conductor will cause another magnet to turn. But his demonstration of the effect required that the wire carrying the current be dipped in a bath of toxic mercury, which made it an unlikely candidate for the development of electric motors.

Faraday also discovered that the process worked in reverse. If you moved a conductor through a magnetic field, a current would start to flow in the conductor. What's interesting is that the strongest magnet in the world can't make a current flow unless you move it. But the faster you move that conductor, the greater is the current *induced* in the conductor. So spinning a conductor—a coil of wire is best—in a magnetic field is a great way to generate electricity.

All this theory helped lots of inventors improve on Faraday's ideas, until in 1869 Zénobe Gramme, a Belgian electrical engineer who struggled with reading and writing and couldn't do advanced math, invented the first generator that could make enough power to sell. And when Gramme accidentally connected one of his efficient generators (that was generating electricity) to another (that wasn't) and spotted that the shaft on the second turned, he realized that he'd also invented the first usefully powerful electrical motor.

Soon, the first commercial power stations were being built. But still, the electric age was not quite born. One man, Thomas Edison, was holding everything up. Part of the reason was that he, too, wasn't great at math. And part of the reason was that he owned a lot of patents and made a lot of money off of direct current. He didn't want AC rocking his comfortable boat.

Edison tried a lot of stunts, including electrocuting an elephant, to convince people that alternating current was dangerous. He also exploited and ignored Nikola Tesla, who for a while ended up digging ditches for Edison's company. But Tesla was a genius. He had done the math (AC is much more complicated than DC), and his AC designs—particularly of motors, generators, and power transmission systems—won out all over the world, even if no one wanted to build the death rays and another strange machines he proposed in his later years. Edison, who had plenty of other patents and had started movie piracy as a sideline, merely ended up rich (and famous as the inventor of the lightbulb—which he didn't invent).

So what was the big advantage of alternating current anyway?

AC/DC: but only AC really rocks

Alternating current (AC) is much more complicated than direct current (DC). The voltage is constantly moving between positive and negative; the current therefore flows one way, and then the other. The AC that's piped into some houses causes the electrons in its wires to rock back and forth 50 times a second. This makes the math complicated and causes strange effects. For example in a thick conductor, AC flows only through the surface of the wire—so the kind of high-current conductors used by power stations are usually hollow.

But AC has one huge advantage over DC. Because it is constantly changing, it is easy to change the voltage with a transformer, and as we'll see, that makes it easier to transmit over long distances, as in, say, a power grid.

Once your power grid includes transformers, you can make use of the fact that high-voltage AC can efficiently be sent many miles through a national power grid at 400,000 volts before being stepped down by a transformer to the 220 volts that come into most U.S. homes. Why use such a high voltage in the power grid? So that the electric current in the grid is low.

Remember that electric power is the voltage multiplied by the current. So for a given amount of power, you can use a low voltage and a lot of current, or a high voltage

Transformers

A transformer is a very simple device, consisting essentially of two coils of wire next to each other. AC current in the first coil (called the primary coil) creates a magnetic field, which induces an AC current in the second (or secondary) coil.

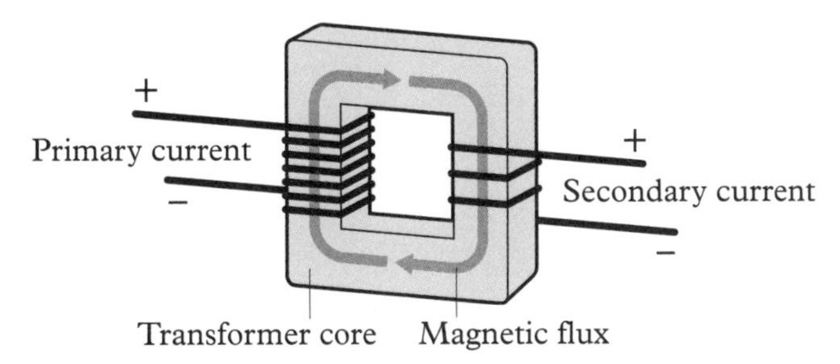

You can't use a transformer to transform DC current, as it's the constant changing of the AC current that produces the magnetic field. All you will do is melt the fine wires in the coils, so don't try it!

and not much current, or something in between. But why is it good for the current to be low?

Let's go back to our bike-wheel thought experiment. Put the bike in low gear and turn the pedals—this is like using a high voltage to produce a low current. Now place your hand on the tire to act as a resistance. No problem, right? Now put the bike in high gear—to produce lots of "current" with a small "voltage"—and try again. Ow! Friction burn!

How power stations work

In their most basic form, all power stations use a turbine to convert *kinetic energy* (energy that is due to movement—for example of steam or wind or water) into electricity. The source of the power—whether it's fossil fuels burned to make the steam, the wind, or water flowing through a hydroelectric dam—causes the turbine to move a large magnet around a coil of wire, which, according to the laws of induction, causes an electric current to flow in the wire.

It's the same with electric cables. All cables have some resistance, so put a lot of current through them and they'll heat up, throwing a lot of power away. Crank up the voltage, though, and you don't need so much current, so you reduce power losses from heating cables. And the power grid transmits a lot of power, so obviously it will use very high voltages to keep those currents down.

DC power stations, on the other hand, could be located no more than a couple of miles or so from the homes that used their power. Any farther away and they would lose too much power through cable heat loss. Either that or use high voltages that would be very dangerous in the home—at power grid voltages, electricity will happily jump short distances through the air.

So Tesla's AC systems won out, revolutionizing life. Starting in the early 20th century, you no longer needed one steam engine for every pump and train and machine. The electric age had begun.

8

Relativity

This chapter is all about special and general relativity, the concepts that Albert Einstein used to revolutionize our understanding of everything. Since Newton's time, people had thought the universe was neat and orderly, that it ran like clockwork. But Einstein showed that that's just how it seems. If you look carefully, everything is weird—which is why nuclear bombs go bang, and you can never beat the speed of light.

Albert Einstein was born in 1879. As a youngster he clashed with the authorities at school. At age 17, he changed nationalities to avoid military service. In 1900, he finally got a degree in math and physics. But he couldn't get a university job, so he became a patent clerk.

That hardly sounds like the résumé of a genius, but Einstein was stubborn. He knew he had some good ideas, and he didn't give up on them. His patent work helped because he looked at new kinds of electromagnetic devices, but most important, Einstein was very creative.

He knew that he had to think in a different way to solve the problems facing physics. And though the work of other physicists had given him many clues to follow, he couldn't rely on falling apples like Newton had. Physics had to go somewhere new. And so Einstein (like us) did physics by thought experiment, looking for general, logical truths about the universe, and trying to understand what they implied.

Then came 1905, Einstein's miracle year. After a day at the office, Einstein would go home to his wife, Mileva, a trained engineer, and to his 1-year-old baby son (though he admitted he wasn't a great family man). And there, within 12 months, he found the energy to write and publish four startling, revolutionary papers on physics.

And the first and most important principle that those papers presented was *special relativity*.

You don't know where you're going

Relativity wasn't entirely Einstein's idea. For example, all of physics is based on the idea that the laws of physics are the same at all times and everywhere. And Galileo broadened this idea so that it covered steady motion.

In the 1600s, the church told Galileo that the Earth couldn't be rotating to the East at hundreds of miles an hour because (a) God put man at the center of the universe, and (b) if it was rotating at such a ridiculous speed, any falling apple would move down and to the West. In reply, Galileo told the churchmen to go away and shut themselves in a windowless ship's cabin—and there do a long list of experiments.

As long as the ship moved at constant speed, in any direction, Galileo argued, apples would still fall straight down. In fact, he said, once in the cabin, it is impossible to tell which way the ship is sailing, just as we can't know which way the Earth is rotating, other than by looking at the stars.

Others developed this idea that events are relative to the observers that see them. For example, just because you're in the Back of Beyond doesn't mean you're a long way away from me. I might myself be taking a short break just around the corner, in Beyond.

It's a frame-up

Similarly, if you're driving down the highway and pass a police car at a speed of 22 m.p.h. (10 m/s), you might wonder why it comes after you, sirens blaring, and you get a hefty fine and maybe three points on your driver's license. But of course if the police car was already doing 68 m.p.h. (30 m/s) when you passed it, that means, as their clever on-board camera shows, that you were actually doing 90 m.p.h. (40 m/s).

In physics at least this is a relatively uncontroversial bit of relativity. But that doesn't mean that all of relativity has always been uncontroversial. Back in 1905, Einstein was about to tear apart Newtonian physics and make relativity much more interesting.

Lighting the way

As the 1800s ended, it was becoming clear that light was special. It wasn't just that no one could see the ether through which light was meant to travel, and that light's speed (in a vacuum) was always the same: it was also becoming clear that the speed of light itself was important, for example because various equations suggested that it is impossible to travel faster than light. So scientists started looking more closely for evidence that proved ether existed, and to see how it might affect the speed of light.

And so Einstein took a bold step. He ditched the idea of ether and, building on the work of others, made the constant speed of light the centerpiece of special relativity.

First of all, it's worth realizing just how weird this idea is and how it messes up the nice solid Newtonian universe we know and, on pleasant days in the apple orchard, generally love.

Let's get you off Galileo's boat and onto a train, because Einstein used trains in his thought experiments. Let's say your train is moving east at 75 m.p.h. But that doesn't matter to you. Whether you throw your apple forward or back, it moves away from you at 25 m.p.h.

Now, as good old Albert watches from the platform, he sees your apple move at different speeds backward and forward. Relative to him, when you throw your apple forward, it moves forward at 75 m.p.h. plus 25 m.p.h., which is a whopping 100 m.p.h. But when you throw it backwards, it merely moves forward at 25 m.p.h. less than the train's speed; that is, at 50 m.p.h.

All this is fairly obvious. But Einstein said that light is different. If our apple, instead of acting like an apple, acts like a photon of light, it doesn't matter which way you

What's the ether like?

Everyone knows that sound waves travel through air (and other substances) and water waves travel through water—but what do light waves travel through? What is this invisible stuff—which physicists used to call *ether*—that brings the sun's light and energy to us? Toward the end of the 19th century, Albert Michelson and Edward Morley spent six years carefully building an intricate device to investigate the ether and answer this question.

They knew that the Earth is speeding through space, spinning and circling the sun. And so it should be travelling through the ether, too. In one direction, therefore, the speed of light should seem faster relative to a scientist on Earth, just as the wind seems to blow harder if you run against it. And in the opposite direction the speed of light should be slower.

But when Michelson and Morley ran their intricate experiment, it failed completely. They tried again and again, over a period of years, but with no luck. Whichever direction they chose to look in, the speed of light was exactly the same. There was no evidence at all for the existence of ether.

throw it: it always passes Albert, who's still there on the platform waiting for his train, at 75 m.p.h. What's more, relative to you, every photon of light you throw out goes away from you at 75 m.p.h.

If you don't understand this, don't worry. It makes no sense with apples. Let's try it with those little packages of light known as photons.

Time to wait

Poor old Albert's been waiting around on that platform for a long time. And as we'll soon see, he has discovered that time isn't quite as dependable as most of us think. If, for example, that train platform is somewhere in outer space near a black hole, he could be there approximately forever without seeing a train.

So let's give him something useful to do: another thought experiment. We need two tall glass boxes—one for you and one for Albert—each with two mirrors inside, one on the top face and one on the bottom. And in those boxes, bouncing in sync between these mirrors, you each have your own tiny photon of light.

Now, if your train is stopped at the platform, and because you and Albert have fantastic eyesight, you can see your photons bouncing up and down together. So far, so simple. But what happens if we try the same thing while your train is moving at 90 percent of the speed of light?

On the fast train

Here you come. (Don't get your hopes up, Albert. It's not your train.)

As you look at your box, your photon is bouncing up and down as before. No problem. But what does Albert see? He sees your photon move diagonally, in a series of zigzags. It has to, because after it leaves the middle of the bottom mirror, it travels up and hits the middle of the top mirror—and that mirror (along with the train and you and the box) has moved forward a bit as it traveled with the train.

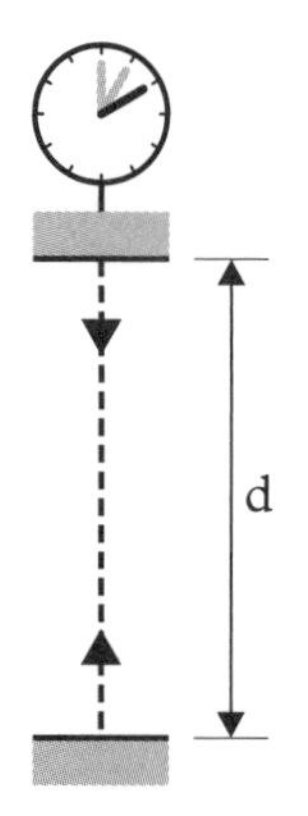

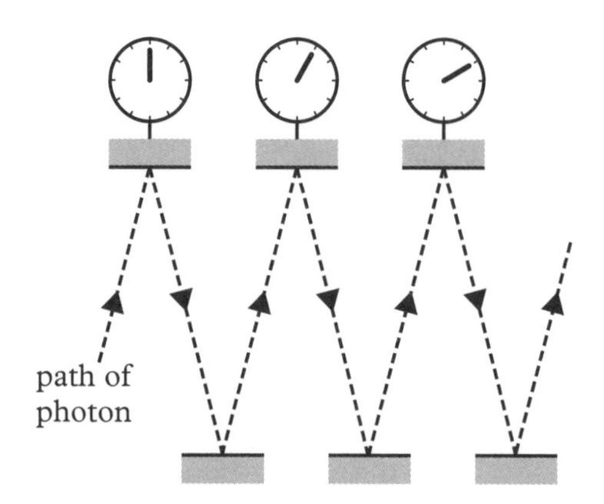

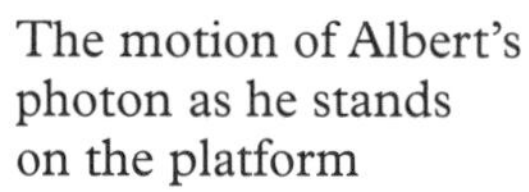

The motion of Albert's photon as he stands on the platform

What Albert sees your photon do as you move

But this is where it gets interesting. That diagonal path that Albert sees your photon take is like the long side (hypotenuse) of a right triangle, because it has gone up and across a little bit. And, of course, this long side is longer than the path you see the photon take because for you, it only goes up. In fact, if your train is moving at 90 percent the speed of light, that path is roughly twice as long.

This is much the same as what happened when you were throwing your apples forward at 25 m.p.h. just now. If something moves a greater distance in the same amount of time, it must be going more quickly. So if your photon was an apple, Albert would simply see it move faster than you see it move.

Except, of course, that light can't go faster. And so something has to give. As Einstein discovered, that something that gives is time (and actually distance, too, but we'll just worry about time for now and ignore the fact that superfast travel makes you shrink a bit). Time gives up being constant. Because you're moving relative to Albert and because, as Albert sees it, your light has farther to travel between bounces (and because it has to travel at the same speed), *time for you must run more slowly than for him.*

Of course, you can't tell that time is running more slowly for you. Your watch still seems to tick as constantly as ever. But if your train is going past Albert at 90 percent of the speed of light, as he sees it, for every *five* bounces of the photon in your box, the one in his bounces *ten* times.

And it's not just an effect on photons. Deep in the laws of physics (and Einstein did do the math), time really does slow down as you speed up. So, according to Albert's measurements, your watch would tick more slowly, and if he could see you doing a little dance of physics happiness in time with your bouncing photon, he'd see you doing it all in slow motion.

Even at low speeds this happens. It's just that the effect is so small that we can't see it. But if your train is moving at 75 m.p.h. and you throw your apple forward at 25 m.p.h., and Albert on the platform measures its speed with his new Super Accurate Apple Speed Measuring Device (which he's just invented), he'll see it moving forward at a tiny bit less than 100 m.p.h.

So once you accept special relativity, you have to accept that many other things in physics change.

Faster than the speed of light?

Your fast travel slows down your time, relative to stationary Albert on the platform—but relative to you, on the train, it's Albert's time that has slowed. One result of this confusion is that some things, which look like they're

That famous equation

The equation that tells us how energy and mass are related—and how much energy is hidden in all the solid stuff around us—is the most famous equation in physics, which Einstein discovered in 1905:

energy = mass x speed of light squared, or as it is more commonly written:

$E=mc^2$.

happening at the same time to you, will look like they're happening at different times to Albert.

Hold on a minute, you say. This makes no sense and it's all based on not being able to go faster than the speed of light. But who says we can't travel faster than the speed of light? In your thought experiment you've built a super-powerful rocket. And here you are, blasting off into space. What stops you from going faster and faster and faster—to the speed of light and beyond?

Well, one way to look at what happens is to look at kinetic energy: the energy a thing has due to its movement. Kinetic energy is related to the mass of an object and its speed squared (see pages 379–381).

According to relativity, the faster you go, the more difficult it becomes to go even faster. But you're still adding kinetic energy with all that rocket power you're using. So if your kinetic energy is increasing and your speed isn't—then your mass must be.

At low speeds, which in relativity means speeds less than a third of the speed of light (which, you'll remember, is nearly 670,000,000 m.p.h., or 300,000,000 m/s), it's almost impossible to notice this effect. But as your rocket's speed increases beyond 224,000,000 m.p.h., or 100,000,000 m/s (much, much faster than any human being has ever gone), all your extra pushing just makes your rocket heavier and heavier and even more difficult to push. And that's why you and Albert and I can never travel faster than the speed of light—even in a thought experiment.

New killer power

Once you've discovered that $E=mc^2$, it is obvious that all you need is a way to convert mass directly into energy, and you will get a very large amount of energy from a very small amount of mass (because the speed of light is very large). Then we can stop drilling for oil and digging for coal and warming the planet, and make as much energy as we need, because we can always spare a bit of mass—especially around the waistline.

Unfortunately, controlling that mass-into-energy conversion is tricky, especially since once you find some way of getting the process going, lots of that energy tends to come out as highly dangerous forms of radiation.

So it's easier to make nuclear bombs (which convert some mass from the nucleus of an atom into a huge, energetic bang and a lot of dangerous radiation) than it is to make a nuclear power station, which also makes energy from mass, but also, unfortunately, makes radioactivity.

The bomb dropped on Nagasaki at the end of World War II converted just 1 gram of mass into energy. But it killed 40,000 people immediately, and another 40,000 died from injuries and radiation in the following few months. And many more died of cancer and other diseases caused by radiation in the years since 1945.

Floating and falling are the same

Making relativity special (and Einstein's other 1905 stuff that we'll find out about in the next chapter) might have been enough for some scientists. But Einstein wasn't satisfied. By 1907 he was making progress on a new, more general kind of relativity theory that included gravity. He called it *general relativity*.

Newton had done a good job with gravity. He used the movement of the planets to come up with mathematical descriptions of gravity that are still useful today. And he realized that the force of gravity was a universal. Just as it made the apple fall toward the Earth, it made the moon fall toward the Earth (except that the moon keeps on missing because it's going pretty quickly, and so it ends up flying around and around). In the same way, the Earth and the other planets in the solar system fall toward the sun, but keep missing.

But what Einstein realized in his thought experiments (and published in his 1916 paper when he had it all figured out) was that there is no difference between what the moon or a skydiver feels in free-fall—and what you'd feel if we stuck you in a spacesuit and sent you out of our galaxy into empty space, where gravity is very weak. (Except that when you're out alone in the space beyond our galaxy, you may feel a bit worried about how you're going to get back to Earth, given that you can't travel faster than light and, even at the speed of light, it would take you 30,000 years to get home.)

The similarity of free-fall and floating where there is no gravity becomes clear if we ignore the effect of wind resistance and consider what happens to apples dropped by the skydiver and by you in deep space. What happens is that those apples just seem to sit where you let go of them. Alternatively, if you or the skydiver gives them a push, they continue on in whichever direction they were pushed.

So, what Einstein realized is that when you're in free-fall and accelerating along with gravity, it is impossible to see any effects from gravity. It no longer affects you at all.

And then he came up with another thought experiment.

Sitting down is like blasting off

What, Einstein wondered, is the difference between sitting in a comfy chair in the windowless cabin of Galileo's ship (which is moored in the harbor) and sitting in a similar comfy chair in your similarly windowless spaceship that is accelerating at 9.8 m/s^2 as you begin that 30,000 light-year journey back home from the Back of Beyond? (You've chosen to accelerate your spaceship at 9.8 m/s^2 because it's the same rate that the Earth's gravity accelerates falling apples and everything else.)

And the difference that Einstein came up with is that *there is no difference* that you can detect. For example, in both places, if you get out of that comfy chair and onto a set of bathroom scales, they will say that you weigh the same. And an apple you drop in either place will pick up speed at exactly the same rate: 9.8 m/s^2.

Einstein explained this with lots of complex math, but you can get a good idea of his results when you understand that mass, instead of making an invisible force called gravity, instead makes space and time curve. Every object in the world curves space and time, and big things curve it more, and these curves are like pits around the objects that create them. The curvature of time and space—the pits, as we've labeled them—then cause other objects to move (as if they were rocket-powered) because they slide into them.

Falling into bed

One way to picture the curvature of time and space and the movement that it causes is to think of space as a cheap old mattress on a cheap old bed, the kind that sags a lot when you lie on it.

Whoever gets into bed with you will enter your gravitational field (which is the bit of space and time—that is, mattress—that you've curved). Once that person is on that curved part, they'll slide into your pit and there'll be two of you down there, and with their mass added that gravitational pit will be even deeper and more difficult to struggle out of than it was.

If a couple of children, the dog, and Grandma then also climb on the bed and roll into the pit you've made, then together you've pretty much created your own black hole: an area of space and time so curved by a huge and compact mass that it is impossible for anything—even light—to escape its gravity.

I don't believe it!

And neither did many scientists in the early 1900s. After Einstein, nothing was quite what it seemed anymore.

In Einstein's math, instead of space and time being, well… space and time, they are just aspects of a single curved, four-dimensional system, which includes our three usual dimensions (up/down, left/right and in/out) along with time. The system sucks up the force of gravity, too. So, instead of the moon orbiting the Earth because of the pull of gravity, the moon (as far as the moon is concerned) has no forces acting on it and is continuing along a nice straight line. It's just that with space and time curved by gravity, that nice straight line is basically a squished circle.

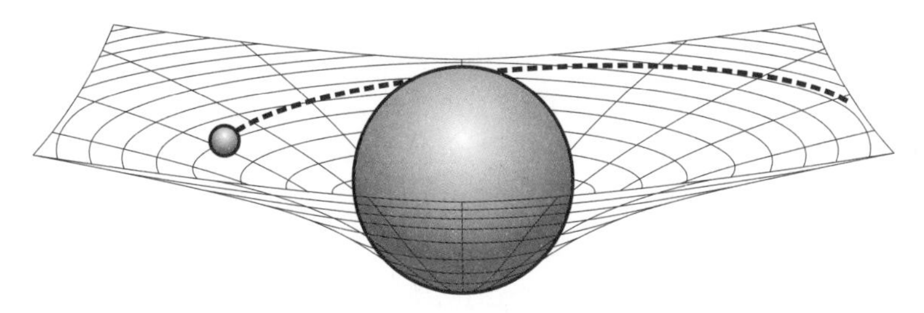

How space is curved by a massive object

And mass, for such weighty stuff, is no longer solid, dependable, or necessarily that weighty. Mass, energy, and—it turns out—momentum, are simply three different ways of looking at the same thing. So all three are sources of gravity. (And, to make it even more complicated, the related quantities of internal pressure and tension are also gravity sources.)

We've already seen how going fast makes you massive. So does being energetic or under pressure. It's almost as if you go on a diet and turn all your excess weight into energy and higher blood pressure and find that, because energy and pressure have mass, you weigh exactly the same as before you took out that expensive gym membership.

Yes it's complicated and unintuitive, and some people didn't like it, but the predictions that Einstein's theory made, and the way it agrees with all kinds of measurements and experiments, are remarkable. It simply has to be right.

Bending starlight

Newton's law of gravity predicts that the planets orbit the sun in perfect, fixed ellipses. But general relativity predicts that those ellipses themselves will slowly rotate around the sun. This effect had been noticed in the orbit of Mercury before Einstein explained it, and soon after Einstein published his new theory, astronomers were able to start confirming that all planets in the solar system had relativistic orbits.

That was only the start of the evidence. Einstein predicted that intense gravitational fields bend light—and in 1919, when this deflection was measured, Einstein became an international star and part of popular culture. Meanwhile, a number of competing theories from other eminent physicists were discarded for good.

General relativity also predicted that gravity—like movement in special relativity—affects the passage of time. The more intense the gravitational field around you, the more slowly time will run for you. Again, this isn't saying just that your clock will run more slowly—though it will—it is saying that time for you really is slower than for someone feeling less gravity. Time spent in a high gravity

General Relativity and GPS

The strange result of gravity on time is well proven. For example, compared to the interminable time you experience while stuck in a traffic jam, time literally runs faster (because gravity is weaker) in the orbiting GPS satellites that help your GPS system get its fix. GPS relies on very accurate timing, so the clocks in GPS satellites are built to take the physics into account. On Earth, they tick 39 microseconds a day more slowly than accurate Earth clocks. Then, when they're in orbit, they tick at exactly the same rate as Earth clocks.

field is a bit like time spent in a bar doing physics on a pool table. You think you've been in there barely half an hour, with hardly enough time to finish your experiment, let alone your drink, but outside it's 6 hours later, it's cold, it's dark, and your dinner has been fed to the dog.

Black holes and a big bang

Besides making the specific predictions that we've looked at, general relativity turned out to apply really well to the universe as a whole. Once it was confirmed, it revolutionized cosmology and astrophysics, the sciences that try to explain the entire universe and how it came to be here.

For example, general relativity is an integral part of the theory that says the universe was born in the Big Bang. It also predicted black holes long before we'd built the technology to go looking for them.

A black hole is a place—a collapsed star or a bunch of them, squeezed together—where intense gravity slows time so much that if you were to fall into one, we'd see you move more and more slowly as you approached what's called its *event horizon*. But even if we watched forever, we'd never see you actually cross it and fall into the hole. Instead, the light from you would slowly fade and change (it would, in fact, be *red-shifted* as if you were moving away very quickly; see page 494).

However, that doesn't mean that a quick dive into a black hole offers you a way to take time out and come back in a few thousand years. Remember, relativity says that you can't see time speed up or slow down for yourself. So you'd cross the event horizon without noticing anything odd, except that you wouldn't be able to turn around and escape. And then…well, we're not sure exactly what happens then. But with all that gravity, it's likely to be a crushing experience.

Newton versus Einstein

All in all, Einstein's theories of relativity showed how the laws that Newton and many other classical physicists had discovered were merely *just about* right. And in physics, just about right is, in fact, wrong.

Nevertheless, you can't argue with the fact that Newton created modern physics. Newton's system described the behavior of the entire cosmos, and while others before him had invented grand schemes, Newton's was different. His theories had math. They made specific predictions that could be confirmed by real experiments. In a way, Newton was lucky: he made such a big impression because he was first. And in a way, it doesn't matter that we now have better versions of his just-about-right laws. Engineers and some other scientists are quite happy with just-about-right. Newton's laws, and lots of the math that he figured out, are still used regularly.

Unless you start traveling faster than about a third of the speed of light, or shrink down to the size of an atom, Newton's laws cover just about all the running, jumping, throwing, and hitting you can get away with. Where they fall down is if you want to understand what makes the universe tick and where it comes from.

In this regard, after 1905, everything in physics was different (though it took some physicists many years to accept the new ideas, and some never did). Newton's reign as chief physicist genius of all time was over. He couldn't compete with Einstein, a man who almost single-handedly changed how we think of space and time. Especially when, as we'll find out next, Einstein went on to almost single-handedly change how we think about matter and atoms, too.

9

Quantum Physics

In the first few decades of the 20th century, physicists made huge leaps forward in their understanding of light and atoms. Einstein started everything off, but this time there was also a host of other brilliant men who helped us realize how, if you look closely, the world is unbelievably odd: Elements have fingerprints, energy comes in indivisible chunks, light is both a wave and a particle, and some things can be in two places at once.

At the start of the 20th century, as we've seen, physics was in a mess. The speed of light was one big problem. But there was also a little problem that was just as big: the atom.

Chemists had produced good evidence for the existence of atoms. And at everyday temperatures, as we've seen in chapter 5, Newton's laws could be applied to large numbers of atoms and molecules to predict the behavior of gases and solids.

But throughout the 19th century, physicists had been discovering areas where the combination of Newton's laws and the theory of matter (that said it was made up of little bits called atoms and molecules) did not work. For example it would predict that if your toilet seat was really cold (around absolute zero), its specific heat capacity would be so low that it would warm up instantly as you sat on it. And we all know that can't be true.

These problems led many people to believe that atoms were not real. Chief skeptic was an Austrian physicist and philosopher, Ernst Mach. He argued that, because atoms couldn't be seen, they didn't exist. For him they were no more than an occasionally useful idea.

But Mach was wrong. Clever arguments and fancy philosophy are no match for physics and experiments. And they certainly weren't a match for Albert Einstein.

Yet in what came to be called quantum physics, Einstein outdid even himself. Some of the ideas about atoms and light and matter that he and a few other very clever physicists discovered are so strange that even Einstein could never really get his head around them. He thought his theory went so far against common sense that it was just a stepping stone to something more sensible, and he spent many unsuccessful years trying to find it.

So don't worry too much if what we discover in the next few pages seems a little odd.

You can't be serious

Einstein was a realist. He believed that there must be a single theory that could prove the existence of atoms and accurately predict how groups of them would behave.

And, as the greatest genius in physics, he had the brainpower to start creating it.

All of Einstein's 1905 papers in the German scientific journal *Annalen der Physik* caused debate and argument. In the second paper, Einstein did the math that made sense of Brownian motion. In the third, as we saw in the last chapter, he announced his theory of relativity. In the fourth, he discovered that mass and energy were related by the famous equation $E=mc^2$ and paved the way for nuclear bombs.

But it was Einstein's first paper of 1905 that most shook up physics and physicists all over the world. It was not-very-snappily called "On a Heuristic Viewpoint Concerning the Production and Transformation of Light" (*heuristic* means explorative), a title that highlighted the fact that even Einstein wasn't entirely convinced by his reasoning. And in it, he set forth the revolutionary proposal that light can be two different, contradictory things at once.

Don't open that oven—it's a can of worms

In 1900, a couple of British physicists realized that the accepted laws of physics predicted that if you looked into a hot oven, you'd immediately be burned to pieces. This was obviously wrong, and Einstein's first paper of 1905 started to explain why.

The only problem was that this explanation seemed more impossible than the paradox it was meant to solve. It took nearly 20 years before the majority of physicists began to accept it.

Black bodies

A black body is a physics term for an object that completely absorbs all frequencies of electromagnetic radiation. Black bodies exist only in thought experiments (although we can build close approximations), but thinking about them produces the math that helps us figure out things like the temperatures of stars or how the greenhouse effect is affecting the climate.

As a black body gets hotter, it emits higher frequencies of electromagnetic radiation. At first that radiation is invisible, but from a few hundred degrees C up, it appears red, then yellow, and so on through the visible spectrum.

You can see the same effect with a regular lightbulb on a dimmer, because the bulb's filament acts like a black body. At minimum power, the light from the bulb will appear somewhat red. Slowly turn the power up, and as the bulb gets hotter, the light will turn orange, then yellow, then eventually white at full power.

The biggest problem was that Einstein's new theory suggested that light (and all other electromagnetic radiation) is both a wave and a particle. For a realist in particular this was a terrible result, because waves do wavy things (like pass through each other unharmed), and particles do martial arts on pool tables.

It was about as bad as telling physicists, "I've found a theory that says something can be in two places at once." In fact it turned out that in a way, this was exactly what Einstein was telling them. No wonder so many of them hated the idea.

Chunks of energy

It makes sense that a hotter object makes a brighter light because, as we know, hotter things have more energy. So a 100-watt lightbulb is brighter than a 40-watt. But why doesn't the radiation come out of a black body in equal amounts at all frequencies, so that to our eyes, it always looks white, whether it's dim or not? Why is it that at lower temperatures, lower-frequency radiation is more common, so the black body looks red?

The man who came up with the answer—even though it made no sense to him—was German physicist Max Planck. He spotted that the only way to make the math work was to assume that the vibrational thermal energy of atoms can be released only as light energy in chunks of certain sizes, and that at higher frequencies these chunks would have more energy, because higher-frequency electromagnetic radiation carries more energy around.

The upshot of Planck's discovery is that if you have a quantity of light energy and keep dividing it in half,

Planck's constant

Planck also discovered that the size of these tiny chunks is given by multiplying the frequency of the light by a very small number, which came to be called Planck's constant. (Physicists write this as $E = hf$.) Planck's constant is usually represented by the symbol h, and its value is 0.00000000000000000000000000000000006626 Joule seconds (usually written as 6.626×10^{-34} Joule seconds).

eventually you reach a small amount of energy that cannot be divided any further. Planck called this tiny chunk of energy a *quantum*.

Now, at high frequencies these chunks become quite large, because the frequency of the radiation becomes large. This is even clear in visible light: the deepest violet light we can see has double the frequency of the darkest red; so chunks of violet light must have double the energy of chunks of red light. Once you know this, it is clear that unless our black body (or bulb filament) is very hot, very few of the hot little atoms in it will have enough thermal energy to make chunks of blue light, and so red light is more common. (Remember that all the atoms in a hot black body have different amounts of energy, but it's the average energy of all the atoms that gives the body its temperature.)

So by inventing the idea of the quantum, Planck came up with a partial explanation for why hot bodies glow red and really hot ones glow white. But it was only after Einstein got ahold of the idea that it became part of our picture of how the world works.

Photon torpedoes

If you shine light and ultraviolet on to a piece of metal, the light can knock electrons out of the metal. In a physics lab, these can easily be collected and the number being knocked out can be measured.

Back in the 1900s, this photoelectric effect was making physicists rather uncomfortable. The wave theory of light suggested that as you turned up the brightness of the light, you should eject more electrons, because brighter light has more energy.

But in their experiments this didn't happen. If you shine red light onto a piece of potassium, no electrons are ejected, no matter how bright you make the light. But if you change the light to violet, you can turn it down low and still electrons will be ejected.

Einstein had the genius to see that, if light was made up of tiny quantum particles (which we now call photons), the photoelectric effect is easy to explain. As Planck had shown, it's the frequency, not the intensity, of the light that determines its energy. So Einstein's 1905 paper suggested that low-energy red photons don't have enough energy to knock any electrons out of the potassium, no matter how many of them you throw at it. But even a single ultraviolet photon has enough energy to knock an electron out.

Testing times

This explanation of the photoelectric effect may seem obvious now, but at first, hardly anyone believed Einstein. One American physicist, Robert Millikan, was so annoyed and so wedded to all the evidence that light must be a wave that he spent *10 years* carefully testing the photoelectric effect in order to find something wrong with Einstein's theory. But his careful experiments only ended up confirming Einstein's ideas in every single detail.

For this useful work, Millikan won the Nobel Prize for physics. Which just shows that in physics, you can get it right even when you're wrong.

Slowly but surely, physicists began to accept Einstein's radical ideas. It helped that other brilliant thinkers used and developed the idea that light comes in packets called photons to explain many familiar effects, including how light can be produced by various substances even when they're cool, or at least not very hot. (A few examples are neon lights, glow sticks, and the Northern Lights—where the dark skies above the magnetic north pole glow with spectacular green and red curtains of light.)

Fingerprint physics

All elements, when turned into a gas and heated, give out their own distinct color. And if, using a prism, this color is separated out into a spectrum, there will be bright colors in some places and no color at all in others: a fingerprint that is unique to every element in the universe. This is particularly good news for astronomers, because it means that simply by looking at the light that the sun and other stars send us, they can learn a great deal about the substances that make them up.

The simplest case is hydrogen (because, it turns out, hydrogen is the simplest element—it has just one electron scooting around just one proton). If you heat hydrogen until it glows and then, using a prism, spread out the light it produces into what would be a rainbow (if it were from a white-hot black body), all you see are four bright lines of color: red, blue-green, blue, and violet. The rest of the rainbow is dark.

But if you then let your hydrogen cool, and shine a white light through it, and then through the prism, you get almost the whole rainbow of colors—except with thin dark lines at exactly the places where the bright bits were at the time the hydrogen was heated.

So hot hydrogen emits red, green, blue, and violet light, and cool hydrogen absorbs that light.

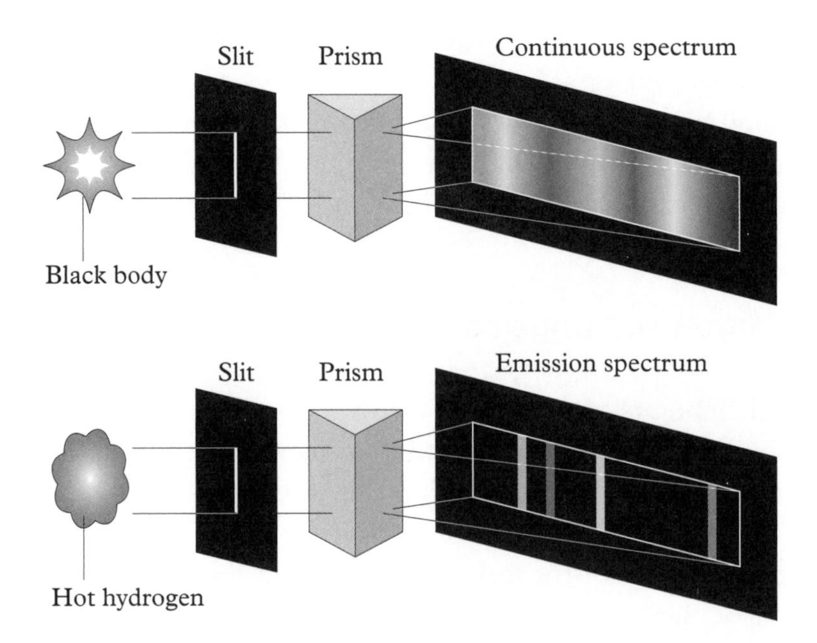

In 1885, when Swiss schoolteacher Johann Balmer looked at the frequencies of these four bands of light, he realized that they fit a pretty simple mathematical formula. (He was also able to predict that other frequencies of electromagnetic radiation would be emitted—as ultraviolet and infrared, and so on—and years later, physicists with new technology discovered these.)

Because Balmer's equation was so simple, it seemed likely that it had something really important to say about what happened inside atoms. The only problem was that nobody knew what that thing might be for another 27 years, until Danish physicist Nils Bohr arrived in Manchester, England, to work with Ernest Rutherford, the man whose experiments had given us a picture of the atom as a tiny positive center surrounded, at a large distance, by negative electrons.

Inside the atom

After J. J. Thomson discovered the electron in 1897, it was thought that atoms were like a "plum pudding," in which electrons (the plums) were surrounded by a "pudding" of positive charge, which held them together.

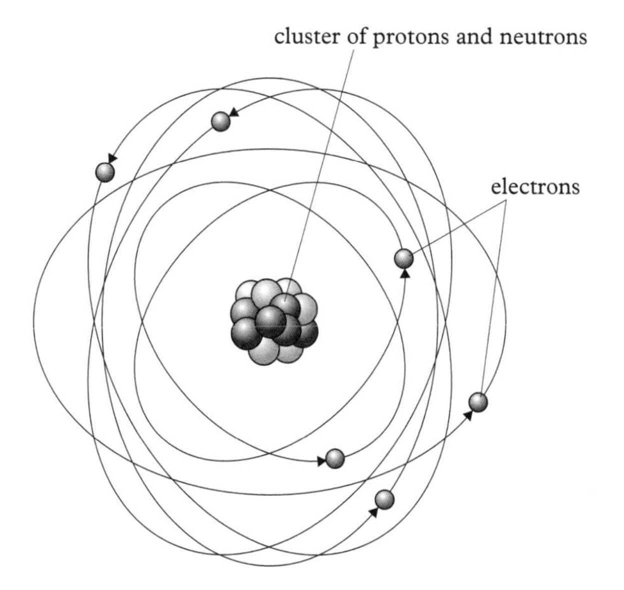

Carbon-12, with six protons and six neutrons in the nucleus

This changed in 1909 when Rutherford, a New Zealander who came to be known as the father of nuclear physics, directed alpha particles at a thin sheet

Great explanations

But back to Bohr. The Dane had arrived in England in 1911 with little English, but a big dictionary, the complete works of Charles Dickens, and the ability to work very hard.

of gold foil and measured how they were deflected. Under the plum pudding model, most of the alpha particles should have been deflected just a little as they made their way through the pudding of gold atoms. What actually happened was that most went straight through with no deflection, but a very small number bounced almost straight back.

This shocking result led to our understanding of the atom as a small, dense, positively charged nucleus orbited by electrons. Rutherford did the math and found just how little space the nucleus takes in the atom—it's so small that, if you could crush up all the human race, and do away with all the electrons, and overcome the huge repelling force of all those positive nuclei, you could fit us all into a block the size of single sugar cube (though he didn't put it quite like that).

The nucleus itself is made up of smaller particles—protons (which are positively charged) and neutrons (which have no charge). The number of protons determine what element the atom is, while the number of neutrons affects how stable it is—too many or too few neutrons and the atom may break apart or *decay*, resulting in radioactivity and radiation.

It didn't take him long to revolutionize our understanding of the atom. He knew that electrons couldn't just keep floating around the atomic nucleus by themselves—there needed to be something to stop them from radiating away all their energy (as light, ultraviolet, etc.) and falling into the middle with a universe-ending bang.

His first brainstorm was to combine Einstein and Planck's idea of energy chunks with Balmer's equation that described the emission spectrum of hydrogen. His idea was that electrons can sit only at certain fixed quantum distances from the nucleus. When they get more energy (from heat, for example) they become "excited" and move further away from the nucleus, say from level one up to level four. (It's a bit like your having more potential energy when you're sitting upstairs.)

But like you, electrons can remain excited (or upstairs) only for so long. After a while they fall back to a lower energy level closer to the nucleus (falling, say, from level four to level two), and releasing their extra energy as a chunk of electromagnetic radiation (in this case as a photon of blue-green light).

Because the various energy levels that an electron can sit in are fixed (like the stories in an apartment building are fixed), the packets of energy emitted as they move between them are fixed, too—and therefore so are the frequencies and colors. In hydrogen, for example, the fall from level four to level two always gives off that blue-green photon. And this creates the colorful elemental fingerprints that physicists and astronomers see in their experiments.

Exciting times

Bohr's idea also explains why gases absorb certain frequencies of light. It's like emission, but in reverse. As the light photons hit the atoms, only those that have the right amount of energy (and therefore the right frequency of light) can be absorbed. So if a hydrogen electron is on level two and a blue-green photon hits it, it has just the right amount of energy to be absorbed, and the electron will jump up to level four. Yellow photons have the wrong energy for hydrogen electrons, and pass straight on through. (It's a bit like a crowd at a basketball game. Only the blue-green team's baskets get the blue-green half of the crowd excited. They don't even bother with polite applause when the yellows do something good.)

Einstein and Bohr, on the other hand, did receive polite applause for their work on quantum theory. And so did the increasing band of geniuses around them. But this was faint praise for the enormous and complicated advances made in physics as quantum theory was rapidly discovered and refined between 1900 and 1928 (especially when you consider that many of the contributors—including Werner Heisenberg, Erwin Schrodinger, and Paul Dirac—are definitely in the top 10 physicists of all time).

For example, Lederhosen-wearing, mountain-climbing German genius Heisenberg discovered that once you start poking around at the quantum level, there are real boundaries to what you can find out about photons and electrons. His *uncertainty principle* says that if you find out where exactly a photon is, then you can't tell how fast it is going (and vice versa). And this is not because our measuring systems aren't good enough. Instead, measuring one quantity (speed, for example) must affect the other (position, for example), so it can't be known exactly.

Part of the reason that these men didn't receive the worldwide fame they deserve is that the more you learn about quantum physics, the weirder and more difficult to grasp it becomes. And partly the problem is that the experiments that support it aren't easily explained either. But in 1986, all that changed. Laboratory technology was finally good enough to carry out the most important experiment in quantum physics—the one that, almost on its own, makes sense of the whole nonsensical subject.

Quantum physics laid bare

I'm sure you remember our day on the beach: the sun, the surfers, the double slit experiment, which seemed to prove that light is made up of waves, not particles, because the light waves interfere and cause a diffraction pattern. You even made diffraction fringes in the gap between your fingers.

But what happens if you try the same experiment with single photons of light? If you take a very dim laser beam that sends out those single light chunks, one at a time, and you let them pass through two slits, what happens then? At this, its barest, loneliest point, does light behave like a wave or like a particle?

Well, the clever, amazing answer, the one that brings the abstractions of advanced quantum physics into the real world, is that light really is a wave and a particle: both, and at the same time, too. And if you poke at it to try and find out more, well then it just collapses and is one or the other—depending on what you do to it.

OK. Here's the experiment. We set up our dim laser, our narrow slits, and behind them a piece of sensitive photographic film, so that the arrival of each individual photon of light will be recorded. We turn our apparatus on. The first photon is produced. It speeds through. Bang.

It hits the film and leaves a mark. A single mark. It is after all a single photon. Aah! It's a particle!

But where is that mark? Well, you can't predict where it will be. But it is unlikely to be in a straight line from the laser, through a slit, and onto the film. Somehow that confounded particle has interfered with itself and not travelled in a straight line. What's more, if you leave the apparatus running for a few hours, the pattern that appears on the film is the familiar fringes, those exact same regions of dark and light that prove that interference is taking place.

And whether you run the apparatus for hours and let a million photons through one at a time, or turn up the light and blast them all through in a microsecond, the pattern is the same. More photons arrive where the light interferes constructively, fewer where it is out of sync, and cancels itself out.

The answer is inescapable. Each lonely photon travels through both slits at the same time and then interferes with itself, just like any good wave! Photons can be in two places at once, BUT (and this is a very big and important but, as you can see) if you start checking for them at the slits, you find that they really do go through one slit or the other.

In a way, it makes no sense. But it is what happens. Maybe there is no more to say than that.

But what does it mean?

In quantum physics, meaning is hard to come by because things seem so odd to us. What, we wonder, does it mean for everything to be both a wave that goes through both slits and a particle that goes through one? What does it mean when you say that we can never be sure about where a particle is and how fast it is moving?

It doesn't help that quantum physicists themselves aren't in complete agreement about how to explain their discoveries. The Austrian, Erwin Schrodinger, got so excited by some of his many love affairs that he came up with lots of important quantum math. But in an effort to challenge the way we see quantum physics, he also came up with his famous thought experiment, in which a poor cat, shut in a box and at the mercy of a chancy quantum event, is both alive and dead until a physicist opens the lid and forces it to be one or the other. For years, we were expected to believe that a cat could really be both alive and dead. Today, though, Schrodinger's cat is being retired. Many physicists are coming around to the commonsense idea that, although quantum events can defy logic (so our single photon can go both ways through the apparatus at the same time), cats can't. They are dead and leaving their hair in one place or else they are alive and leaving it everywhere.

Of course, our problem with quantum physics may be due to the fact that it is only 100 years old and most of us aren't familiar with it yet. Maybe it's like a new pair of shoes that haven't been broken in. After all, it took centuries for most people to accept that the world is round and that it revolves around the sun, despite there being easily available evidence for those theories even before we invented frequent flyer programs and space travel. (For example, when a ship comes over the horizon, it doesn't just appear as a dot and grow as it would on a flat planet. Instead, you see its masts first, and slowly the rest is revealed.)

Really weird

Scientists certainly have few problems with the effects of quantum physics. They are still adding to the long list of things that it explains, in physics, chemistry, and even biology, where it is shining new light on how our brains work. Paul Dirac used it to predict the existence of anti-matter before it was discovered in the laboratory. And engineers use the advanced equations when they're building microchips and working on new kinds of computers. We even know that basic light and power switches wouldn't work without quantum physics (and an effect called quantum tunneling).

So quantum physics is useful and well proven. The only problem is, it still raises questions that even the best and most brilliant physicists can't always answer.

10

The Universe

One of the great things about physics is that in spite of all the wonders we've discovered (and in this little book we have barely scratched the surface), there is still lots we don't know. There's also lots that we sort of may know but aren't quite sure about: stuff that causes debate and argument at physics meetings and on the Internet—and that leads physicists to spend piles of money building bigger and better particle accelerators so that they can make even bigger bangs and smaller particles when they smash things up.

What's more, most of these hotly debated questions are so hotly debated because they touch on important and fascinating theories about the history and origins of the universe and our place in it. And that's two excellent reasons these questions are worth a look.

So, let's finish up by thinking about, among other things, the causes of the Big Bang, the possibility of time travel, and the makeup of dark matter: the questions that can flummox even a top physicist.

How big is the universe?

Our sun is one among hundreds of billions that make up our Milky Way galaxy, a vast cloud held together by gravity, with maybe 100 billion stars, plus more clouds of gas and dust, and, we assume, many hundreds of millions of planets (though, because planets are small and dark compared to stars, we've only been able to spot around 500 so far).

On a clear night, far away from the bright lights of the city, you can often see the Milky Way. It's an arch of white light across the night sky, with its center around the constellation Sagittarius (the one that's supposed to look like a mythical half-man-half-horse centaur, preparing to fire a bow and arrow). The milkiness of the Milky Way is made up of those hundreds of millions of far-away stars, and we see them form that milky band because the Earth is on the edge of things, near the edge of the flattened disc of our galaxy, in a side road off one of its four major spiral arms.

Our galaxy is huge: It is around 100,000 light years across. In comparison, the sun is just 8 light minutes away—and you could fit a million Earths in it. The next nearest star, Proxima Centauri, is 4 light years away. But, the next nearest galaxy, Andromeda, discovered in 1925 by the U.S. lawyer-turned-astronomer Edwin Hubble, is 2.5 million light years off.

However, the actual size of the universe is a mystery. We can see 46 billion light years out into space, but, as we shall see, the universe probably extends far beyond that.

Is the edge of the universe a red-light district?

You'll remember from when we looked at waves that, just after a teenager in a boombox on wheels passes you, you hear the pitch of that bass he's pumping out become even lower because of the Doppler effect (see page 432). As relativity predicts, the same happens with the light from stars that are moving quickly away from us: the light waves from them seem to us to have a lower frequency—and therefore appear redder—than they would have been for someone not moving relative to the star. (Physicists say the light from retreating objects is *red-shifted.*)

It turns out that the farther out into space we look, the faster the galaxies are moving away from us, on out to the farthest galaxies we can see, which are now that as-far-as-we-can-see 46 billion light years away. The red shift of the light from these most distant galaxies tells us that they're moving away so quickly that the light we now see left them when they were just 36 *million* light years away from us. (Beyond these galaxies, we calculate that there are galaxies moving away from us so fast that the light from them can't ever reach us.)

This all means that everything in the universe is not just getting farther away from us: It's getting farther away from everything else, too. So the whole universe is expanding, which means it must once have been smaller. If we run time backward, we come up with a date, 13.7 billion years ago, when the entire universe was very small and very dense. (The Earth, by contrast, is just 4.5 billion years old.) So we need some event to create that small dense universe and turn it into a rapidly expanding one.

That event was christened the *Big Bang* in 1949 by the British astronomer Fred Hoyle. (Hoyle actually used "Big Bang" as a snappy way to refer to a theory he thought was totally wrong. Unfortunately for Hoyle, it was his alternative theory that was wrong.) But it wasn't until 1967 that proof of the Big Bang was discovered: It's called *the cosmic microwave background* (or CMB for short).

Why do I feel this warm glow?

If it isn't caused by your enjoyment of physics, it may be due to the Big Bang.

As we saw when we looked at matter, something squashed and dense (like the universe as it was being born) must also be very hot. And hot things give off energy as electromagnetic radiation. And hot things as hot and big as the Big Bang give off a great deal of that radiation. In fact, the Big Bang gave off so much energy that, although it's now quite weak, it is still all around us—as the cosmic microwave background, a slight warm glow that fills all of space (if you look using a radio telescope).

We know the CMB is the afterglow of creation because it's special: It's the same in all directions, and its spectrum, with microwaves as its most common component and little visible light, is that of radiation from a black body (see page 477). Nothing but a hot, dense, uniform, exploding plasma-thing-that-will-be-a-galaxy could have made the CMB.

So, the universe began with a bang. Then it became a rapidly expanding bundle of dense, hot, opaque gas-like plasma, until, after about 380,000 years it had cooled enough for atoms to form. At that point, it became transparent, so that all the heat radiation flying around could keep flying around. And that's what our CMB is: a post–Big Bang glow.

The CMB is almost the same in all directions, but there are tiny differences in temperature here and there, which correspond to tiny differences in density. Those differences were vital, because as the universe expanded and cooled, the slightly denser areas had greater gravity, so they pulled in more gas and became denser still, and slowly the galaxies and the stars within were formed.

In the stars, 10 billion years of nuclear fusion then turned the hydrogen and helium of the early universe into other elements, until they used up the hydrogen. At this point, most of these poor dying stars would have swelled up into what we call red giants (even though they're usually orange). Then, after just a few million years, the red giants would have thrown their outer shells off into the galaxy, spreading around all kinds of useful stuff that gathered to build new, more complicated stars, as well as planets packed with useful stuff like oxygen, carbon, iron, and uranium.

Can we escape?

As we look out into the universe—and we can now see evidence for about 125 billion galaxies—it looks the same in all directions. There is no edge and no center, and the uniformity of the CMB also suggests that there is no center. So although the term "Big Bang" is snappy, it does give us the wrong idea. In a way, the Big Bang wasn't an explosion *in* space, it was the explosion—and the creation—*of* space.

Today it seems likely that wherever you sit in the galaxy, you will see all the universe expanding away from you. Yet this is not just because all the other galaxies are traveling through space. Instead it is because, as Einstein discovered, space-time itself can change shape, and the expansion of the universe is due to the expansion of space itself.

This is why, when you add up lots of expanding space between us and them, some galaxies can be moving away from us at speeds faster than light without breaking relativity. This is also why, although the universe is probably not infinite, it is unlikely (even if you could go faster than light) that you could ever find the edge. Instead, you'd curve around and (eventually) find yourself back where you started.

What caused the Big Bang?

So far, we have direct evidence for what the universe was like after 380,000 years. Is that as good as physics can do?

Actually, with theory and with experiments in particle accelerators that mimic tiny bits of the early universe, we think we can look back much further. A second after the Big Bang, protons and electrons, and the other building blocks of atoms, had begun to appear in an 18,000,000,000°F (10,000,000,000°C) super-hot soup of subatomic particles. Further back still, after a tiny fraction of a second, the forces and laws that hold the universe together (including gravity and electromagnetism) had appeared. Back then, our soupy universe was hotter still, though it was starting to cool as some of the huge energy from the Big Bang began to be frozen, by the power of $E=mc^2$, into the first raw building blocks of matter.

And before the soup course there was just the oven: the Big Bang itself, a huge flash of energy that may have been caused by a strange kind of field (that's a field like a magnetic field, not one with grass and a cow it) called the *inflaton* field.*

This inflaton field, which basically came out of nothing, very quickly swelled the new universe from a tiny size (where the random effects of quantum mechanics were important) to one where the randomness was so spread out as to be almost invisible—except as those tiny but important variations in the CMB that tell us how the stars were formed.

Sounds crazy, doesn't it? But behind this story is a powerful theory, which was invented by the American theoretical physicist Alan Guth in 1979. And the math of the story—and the way it predicts exactly the minute variations in the CMB that we can measure—means that it holds up very well. Today, among physicists, inflation theory is pretty well tested and accepted.

Is this the only universe?

Inflation theory says that the portion of the universe that is observable to us today expanded from a size of 10^{-50} meters (that's 0.00…49-zeroes-here-please…001 meters, which is way, way smaller than an atom) in radius at 10^{-35} seconds after the birth of the universe to almost one whole meter in radius at 10^{-34} seconds. (Just think for a moment

*That's infla-*ton*, like infla-*tion*, which is what the field caused, but spelled wrong so that it matches the spelling of other similar fields, such as the pro-*ton* field.

about how incredibly fast that expansion of space is. It is, for example, much faster than the speed of light. In fact, each time an inflating universe doubles in size, which happens many times, light doesn't even get time to travel from one side of an atom to the other.)

And Guth's theory is even crazier than it seems at first. Guth believes that inflation didn't just happen once. Instead, it is happening continuously, with new universes being born like bubbles in their own tiny nicks of inflationary time, then cooling as their bit of the inflaton field relaxes. And as a universe cools, it expands more gently, inventing its own laws and its own ways of doing things at its own gentle pace—and it is then cut off forever because space outside it keeps on madly inflating, apart from where it forms countless other tiny bubble universes, far, far away.

Guth even believes you could make a new universe in the lab, from a few grams of matter and a special kind of emptiness called a *false vacuum*. Well, maybe you could, but you definitely shouldn't. The huge energy released into our universe would be like 30 of the nuclear bombs dropped on Nagasaki all going off at once. And that's going to hurt, even if you've got your plastic lab glasses and rubber gloves on.

Was it a bug-eyed monster?

The problem with inflation theory is that it is impossible to test. Whichever Big Bang theory you choose (and there are others), they agree that you can't see beyond the Big Bang, or out of our bubble universe. In fact, some would say, it makes little sense to think of what created our universe. The creation is more like an impassable boundary to our universe than an act in it.

But if you're bored with physics, you could come up with your own story. Maybe our universe was created by some bug-eyed monster who'd discovered the same laws as Alan Guth, a slimy bug-eyed monster who just happened to have some false vacuum handy. But remember, if it was, that alien got blown up a long, long time ago, and anyway, there is no possible way for us to know anything about its universe, which may have been very different from ours.

Actually, if Guth is right, and the creation of the universe is basically a free lunch, it seems likely that the vast majority of universes are probably too weird to support anything like life as we understand it. That's because there's only a tiny chance that any universe that coalesces out of the hot, dense post–Big Bang soup will be as cozy for life as ours. So although our universe is vast, violent, and unforgiving, we can also see that if gravity was only slightly less strong, or if there were 5 or 7 or 27 dimensions, or if *dark matter* was less common, then balloons might fall and apples might rise—or, more likely, galaxies and stars could not have formed and there would be no apples, no balloons, and no humans to miss them.

But what is dark matter?

Well, for a start, dark matter isn't dark. It is in fact completely transparent. It's just that space is dark, so we can't see it.

When we look out at the universe and add up all the mass we find, there just isn't enough to make enough gravity to help galaxies form and move like they do. In fact, we now estimate that we can see only 5 percent of the stuff in the universe. The rest is dark.

There must, therefore, be huge clouds of invisible stuff, stuff that light and other forms of electromagnetic radiation pass straight through because it's not made up of protons and neutrons at all, but that supplies the missing gravity to give galaxies the right structure.

It's not just theory. We've seen light from distant galaxies bent by what must be dark matter. But what exactly dark matter is, and how it came to be all over the place, is a mystery. Physicists can't even agree on whether it's cold, or warm, or hot. Worse still, much of the dark stuff in the universe is probably not dark matter: instead, it's dark energy, spread throughout space and, according to general relativity, forcing the expansion of space to happen more quickly than it might. We can measure this increase in the expansion of space. But we don't have a clue about what dark energy is. We know it's dark and we know it's energy and er...that's it.

This is one place where physics is still in the dark ages. Our current best model of the universe—the Standard Model—sheds no light on dark matter, dark energy, and a few other important things, such as gravity. So although we have plenty of theories about why balloons rise and apples fall, at their most basic level the two theories are separate. Apples fall because of gravity, which is explained by relativity. But balloons rise because of temperature and pressure, and that ultimately is caused by quantum physics and the Standard Model.

Why are so many physicists growing a GUT?

Even slim, fit physicists may be working on a Grand Unified Theory (GUT) or a Theory of Everything (TOE): one that will add in what the Standard Model leaves out.

The Standard Model of physics uses the interaction of tiny particles to explain matter, electromagnetism, the strong and weak nuclear forces inside atoms, and how those things affect each other. Remember all those forces we spent so long discussing? Well, there's no such thing—at least on the quantum scale.

First, there are the 12 *fermions*—the particles that make up matter. What happens when these particles meet and interact with light, and how they join together to form atoms, is then explained by 12 force-carrying particles called *bosons,* which fly around at the speed of light, between the fermions, pushing and pulling them around. The bosons include the photon, the particle that carries what we observe as a field of force between things that have electric charge. There's also an elusive 13th boson, the Higgs boson, which gives the other elementary particles their mass.

The problem is that once you try and add in what the Standard Model leaves out, and formulate a GUT, everything gets much more complicated. Some progress has been made, but as yet there is no evidence at all that gravity depends on a new kind of fundamental particle called a graviton—and it seems impossible to find one, other than in a huge particle accelerator such as the Large Hadron Collider built by the European Orginization for Nuclear Research (CERN).

One avenue of research depends on *supersymmetry*—which involves adding in a gaggle of extra particles that no one has ever seen and which creates a whole new set of problems that are possibly answered only by yet another theory, called *string theory*. But it relies on notions like 11-dimensional space and a lot of math that is so complicated and so new that even most physicists can't understand it. And there is no way to test string theory because the effects that it predicts take place at very high energies and over very tiny distances.

There are alternatives to GUTs and TOEs and getting tied up in strings. One was created in the 1990s by Mark Hadley, at Warwick University in England. It's lean and mean and uses Einstein's space-time to explain quantum physics. No one can find much wrong with it, but it's pretty much ignored. The reason? Well, it could be argued that a thousand scientists are working on their GUTs simply because a thousand scientists are working on their GUTs—and because the best way to get funding for your GUT work is for a bunch of other scientists to agree that what you're working on is worth the massive grant your GUT needs.

This doesn't mean that our best GUTs and TOEs are wrong. Maybe we will find ways of checking them indirectly. Or maybe, as the next question shows, our best physics isn't quite as good as we'd like to think.

Can we travel faster than light?

No. Of course not. At least, that's what Einstein argued. So it seems we are stuck in our solar system, forever forbidden by the laws of physics from building a Starship *Enterprise* and seeking out new life and new civilizations.

But actually, in quantum physics there does seem to be something that happens faster than light: communication between what are called *entangled particles*. These entangled particles are pairs of particles emitted when one particle decays (either naturally, or because a physicist smashes it) into two new particles, so that if one has spin of up, the other has spin of down.* But quantum physics also says those particles have no definite spin at all until that spin is measured. And yet, once you do the experiment, and Alice measures the spin of one particle, Bob will find that the spin of the other is opposite, even if Alice and Bob are a long way from each other.

So it seems that, once the spin of one particle is measured, it immediately communicates to its twin what its spin should be. (And when we say immediate here, we mean immediate. Experiments have shown that the communication between entangled particles happens at speeds millions of times faster than the speed of light.)

Physicists tend to argue that actually this experiment does not break special relativity, because nothing in it really moves faster than light. They say that twin particles could not, for example, even be used to communicate information, let alone help something as big as us zip to the other side of the universe through a *Star Trek*–style teleporter.

But that doesn't stop entanglement from being a real problem for current physics. And it doesn't necessarily stop us boldly going and meeting Vulcans, either. Because we still we have one last, best hope for intergalactic travel: a science-fiction shortcut called a wormhole.

*Spin is a strange property of tiny quantum particles. It's complicated and doesn't involve anything actually spinning around.

Can we jump through a wormhole?

Wormholes are space-time tunnels that could, in theory, lead directly to far-off galaxies (or far-off times). By traveling through a wormhole, you could go as far as you want and arrive even before you left. And the good news for budding Stargate SG-1 officers is that the laws of physics, as we understand them, say wormholes aren't pure sci-fi: They could exist. The bad news, though, is that the laws of physics also say that wormholes must be very unstable, and as soon as you try to stuff anything as big you, or your spaceship, or even an atom, through one, it will collapse.

Which leads us to the biggest physicist-stumper of them all...

What is a law of physics?

The idea that there might be laws of nature originally came from thinking about the laws that societies create. The laws of physics were seen as a vast force of cosmic policemen, keeping order among matter and everything else in the universe.

Christianity fired the police force, because it had one powerful God to do all the law making and keeping, and because the universe seemed so well behaved. Newton thought that the simple, elegant, mathematical laws he discovered were thoughts in the mind of a straight-thinking God, and that they were nice proof of just how orderly and rational He was.

Today, the fact that the fundamental laws are small in number (even if the quantum ones are pretty weird) is just part of why few physicists still think we need a god to keep things in order. Instead, the laws have come to be seen as fundamental properties that create the entire universe (and us in it), just like a few simple rules mean water molecules can freeze together in an infinite and beautiful variety of snowflakes.

But the importance of math in physics makes it easy to dodge the question of what the laws of physics are. Lots of physicists like the slogan: "Shut up and calculate!" They plug the numbers in: the acceleration due to gravity; the number of apples in the basket; the size of the balloon; the temperature of the air inside. They make the prediction: balloon to rise to 1.5 miles (2,500 m). They wear that extra sweater. And if they're warm and toasty when they go on their balloon trip, then they like the law.

But the laws of physics aren't only about getting your calculations right. The best laws also explain why the calculations work. For example, in 1915 the German mathematician and physicist Emmy Noether discovered how the conservation laws—which, as we've seen, are some of the most basic and important in all of physics—arise directly from the structure of time and space.

For example, the fact that the laws of physics are the same *at all times* gives us the law of conservation of energy. And the fact that the laws of physics are the same *everywhere* means that momentum must be conserved. And once you know this, and once you understand the shape of space-time, as Einstein did, special and general relativity fall into place. All it takes is knowledge, creativity, and maybe a touch of genius. It's amazing what the human mind can do. And it's even more amazing that we've tested and tested these ideas and they seem exactly right. So maybe that gives us some sort of answer to the question about laws. But it doesn't end the debate.

Noether proved her theorem using math. And theoretical physicists like Einstein routinely come up with new ideas by creating new math, long before these new ideas can be tested in the lab. So, even deeper in physics than laws that explain the laws is the math that explains those basic laws. And the reason why math matches the way the universe works is the deepest mystery of all.

Are there any more questions?

Of course there are. Books full of them. If you ever get the chance to stump a real physicist, you could be talking for hours and hours...

Despite how far we've come, physicists aren't running out of things to do. They are still driven by the lure of discovery: the lure of uncovering a little more of the beauty and strangeness of the world, and of being, for a moment, the first and only person ever to know some new thing, and at the same time, knowing that they alone have found that new thing—and that they have found it purely through the power of their own thought.

Isn't physics fun?

INDEX

L

M

N

O

P

Q

R

METRIC CONVERSION TABLE

TO CHANGE:	INTO:	MULTIPLY BY:
Millimeters	Inches	0.039
Centimeters	Inches	0.394
Meters	Feet	3.28
Meters	Yards	1.09
Meters per second (m/s)	Miles per hour (m.p.h.)	2.25
Kilometers	Miles	0.621
Square centimeters	Square inches	0.155
Square meters	Square feet	10.8
Square meters	Square yards	1.2
Cubic centimeters	Cubic inches	0.061
Cubic meters	Cubic feet	35.3
Cubic meters	Cubic yards	1.31
Liters	Pints	2.11
Liters	Quarts	1.06
Liters	Gallons	0.264
Grams	Ounces	0.035
Kilograms	Pounds	2.2
Metric tons	Tons	1.1